chapter   1

Introduction to Financial Statements

Chapter Overview

Chapter 1 introduces you to a variety of financial accounting topics. You will first learn
why accounting matters. You will also learn about the primary forms of business
organization and the three principal types of business activity. You will then learn
about users of accounting information and how that information is delivered through
the basic financial statements.

Review of Specific Study Objectives

As a result of the recent corporate scandals, the regulators, the investment community,
and the accounting profession recommended changes to business practices, corporate
governance, public oversight, and accountability. The end result of all this is that new
requirements now guide business behaviour as well as accounting and auditing
practices.

It is very clear that reliable accounting information is important. The standards of conduct by which one's actions are judged to be right or wrong, honest or dishonest, fair
or not fair, are **ethics**.

There are three different types of organizations and two different types of interested
users. The types of organizations are:

study objective 1

Explain why
accounting is
important.

study objective 2
Identify the uses and users of accounting.

- A **proprietorship** is a business owned by one person. It is *simple to set up*, and the *owner has control over the business*. Because they are so simple to organize, there are many thousands of proprietorships operating in the business world.

- A **partnership** is a business owned by more than one person. It provides strength in numbers: Each *partner may bring economic resources* or *unique talents or skills* to the combination.

- A **corporation** is a separate legal entity owned by shareholders. *Advantages* are that *shares of ownership are easy to sell* and *the raising of funds is simple*. There are many more proprietorships and partnerships than there are corporations, but corporations produce far more revenue.

The two broad types of users are internal users and external users:
- **Internal users** are the people who work for the business as well as *managers who plan, organize, and run a business*. Accounting information helps answer such questions as, "Does the business have enough resources to build a new manufacturing plant?" Internal reports help provide the required information.

- **External users** work outside of the business and include *investors*, who use accounting information for their share capital decisions; *creditors*, who evaluate the risk of lending to, and the credit-worthiness of, business borrowers; *taxing authorities*, which review compliance with tax laws; *regulatory agencies*, which review compliance with prescribed rules; *customers*; *labour unions*; and *economic planners*.

study objective 3
Explain the three main types of business activity.

- There are **three types of business activity** that the accounting information system tracks: *financing*, *investing*, and *operating*.

- **Financing activities** deal with the ways a business *raises funds for operations*. The **two primary sources of outside funds** are *borrowing money* and *issuing shares*.

- A business may **borrow money** by taking out a loan at a bank or borrow money from other lenders. A **creditor** is a person or entity to whom a business owes money, and a **liability** is a debt or other obligation, which represents creditors' claims on the business. Examples of liabilities are *accounts payable*, resulting from purchases on credit; *notes payable*, resulting from direct borrowing or purchasing on credit; *wages payable*, representing wages owed to employees; and *bonds payable*, sold to investors and usually due several years in the future. A creditor has a legal right to be paid at an agreed-upon time and must be paid before an owner (shareholder) is paid.

- A corporation may also **issue shares** to investors. Share capital is the term that describes the total amount paid into the corporation by shareholders for the shares purchased. Common shares are just one type or class of share that a company can issue. *A shareholder is an owner of the business* and receives payments in the form of dividends. (Please note that there are companies that do *not* pay dividends to shareholders). As noted above, shareholder claims are secondary to creditor claims.

- **Investing activities** involve the purchase of long-lived resources, called **assets**, that a company needs to operate. Examples of assets are property, plant, and equipment, such as land, buildings, and trucks.

Study Guide
to accompany

FINANCIAL ACCOUNTING

TOOLS FOR BUSINESS DECISION-MAKING

Third Canadian Edition

Paul D. Kimmel Ph.D., C.P.A.
University of Wisconsin–Milwaukee
Milwaukee, Wisconsin

Jerry J. Weygandt Ph.D., C.P.A.
Arthur Andersen Alumni Professor of Accounting
University of Wisconsin–Madison
Madison, Wisconsin

Donald E. Kieso Ph.D., C.P.A.
KPMG Emeritus Professor of Accountancy
North Illinois University
DeKalb, Illinois

Barbara Trenholm M.B.A., F.C.A.
University of New Brunswick
Fredericton, New Brunswick

PREPARED BY:

Cecelia M. Fewox
College of Charleston
Charleston, South Carolina

Gerry Dupont BComm, M.B.A.
Carleton University
Ottawa, Ontario

 John Wiley & Sons Canada, Ltd.

National Library of Canada Cataloguing in Publication Data

Dupont, Gerry
    Study guide to accompany Financial accounting : tools for business decision-making, third Canadian edition / Gerry Dupont.

ISBN-13: 978-0-470-83718-4
ISBN-10: 0-470-83718-7

    1. Accounting--Problems, exercises, etc. I. Title.

HF5635.F44 2005 Suppl.   657'.044   C2005-907133-8

Production Credits
Editorial Manager: Karen Staudinger
Publishing Services Director: Karen Bryan
Developmental Editor: Zoë Craig
Marketing Manager: Isabelle Moreau
Editorial Assistant: Sara Vanderwillik
Design: Natalia Burobina
Textbook cover design: Interrobang Graphic Design Inc.
Printing & binding: Tri-Graphic Printing Limited

Printed and bound in Canada
1 2 3 4 5 TRI 10 09 08 07 06

John Wiley & Sons Canada, Ltd.
6045 Freemont Blvd.
Mississauga, Ontario L5R 4J3
Visit our website at: www.wiley.ca

Contents

- **Operating activities** are just that: *operations of the business*. Different businesses have different operations, of course. A paper company produces and sells paper, while a dairy company produces and sells milk. When a company operates, it earns revenues. **Revenues** are increases in economic resources—normally increases in assets but sometimes decreases in liabilities—that result from the operating activities of a business. **Expenses** are the cost of assets consumed, or services used, in the process of generating revenues. If revenues exceed expenses (hopefully!), then a business reports *net earnings*. If expenses exceed revenues, then a business incurs a *net loss*.

- Users of financial information are interested in a company's assets, liabilities, shareholders' equity, revenues, and expenses. This financial **information is provided in the form of financial statements**, which form the backbone of financial accounting. There are *four financial statements*: the *statement of earnings*, the *statement of retained earnings*, the *balance sheet*, and the *cash flow statement*.

study objective 4

Describe the content and purpose of each of the financial statements.

- The **statement of earnings** *reports the success or failure of the company's operations for a period of time*. Only **revenues and expenses** appear on the statement of earnings, along with their difference, either net earnings (revenues exceed expenses) or net loss (expenses exceed revenues). New accounting students often want to put the "Cash" account on the statement of earnings, but this is incorrect because cash is an asset (a resource owned by a business). Only revenues and expenses appear on the statement of earnings.

- The **statement of retained earnings** shows the *amounts and causes of changes in the retained earnings balance during the period*. Net earnings (or if there is a net loss, that amount is deducted) is added to beginning retained earnings, and then dividends are deducted. (Remember that a business will have either net earnings or net loss; it cannot have both at the same time.) *Users of financial statements can find out about management's dividend policy by analyzing this statement.* To summarize, the Retained Earnings account is the total of all the net earnings of the company, all the net losses it has incurred, and all the dividends it has paid. The statement of retained earnings documents this activity.

- The **balance sheet** *reports assets and claims to those assets at a specific point in time*. There are **two types of claims**: *claims of creditors (liabilities)* and *claims of owners (shareholders' equity)*. The balance sheet is an expanded expression of the **basic accounting equation**, which is:

study objective 5

Explain the meaning of assets, liabilities, and shareholders' equity, and state the basic accounting question.

$$\text{Assets} = \text{Liabilities} + \text{Shareholders' Equity}$$

Please note that this is a mathematical equation and must be in balance at all times. It can be used to answer such questions as: If assets total \$100 and liabilities total \$20, what is the total of shareholders' equity? (Answer: \$80. Because \$20 plus something must equal \$100, and that something must be \$80.)

Shareholders' equity consists of **two parts**: *Share capital* (often just one class of shares, common shares, is issued) and *retained earnings*.

- The **cash flow statement** *provides financial information about the cash receipts and cash payments of a business for a specific period of time*. Here, a user will find information about the *financing, investing, and operating activities* of the business.

- Note the **interrelationships between statements**:

    1. Net earnings or net loss from the statement of earnings appears on the statement of retained earnings.

    2. The ending balance of retained earnings is the same number reported on the balance sheet for retained earnings.

    3. The ending balance of cash must be the same, both on the balance sheet and on the cash flow statement.

- Companies usually present **comparative statements**, which are *statements reporting information for more than one period.*

- Please be aware of the following when you **prepare financial statements**:

    1. All statements **must have a heading.** The *company name* appears on the first line, the *name of the document* appears on the second line, and the *date* appears on the third line. With respect to **dates**, the **balance sheet date** is for *one point in time* (June 30, 2006, or December 31, 2006), while the **date on the statement of earnings, the statement of retained earnings, and the cash flow statement** is for *a period of time* ("For the Month ended June 30, 2006" or "For the Year ended December 31, 2006").

    2. The number at the top of a column should have a dollar sign: This indicates that it is the first number in that column. The final number on a statement, such as Net Earnings or Total Assets, should have a dollar sign and be double-underlined. This indicates that it is the "answer." If there is a negative number, such as Net Loss, then it should be presented in parentheses or brackets. These are parts of a type of shorthand used by people who prepare statements and understood by users of statements.

Chapter Self-Test

As you work through the exercises and problems, remember to use the **Decision Toolkit** discussed and used in the text:

1. *Decision Checkpoints*: At this point, you ask a question.

2. *Info Needed for Decision*: You make a choice regarding the information needed to answer the question.

3. *Tool to Use for Decision*: At this point, you review just what the information chosen in step 2 does for the decision-making process.

4. *How to Evaluate Results*: You perform evaluation of information for answering the question.

Note: The notation (SO1) means that the question was drawn from study objective number one.

Multiple Choice

Please circle the correct answer.

1. Which of the following statements is correct? (SO2)
   a. A proprietor has no personal liability for debts of his or her business.
   b. There are far more corporations than there are proprietorships and partnerships.
   c. Revenue produced by corporations is generally greater than that produced by proprietorships and partnerships.
   d. It is very difficult for a corporation to raise capital.

2. Which of the following would not be considered an internal user of accounting data for a particular company? (SO2)
   a. Marketing manager
   b. Receptionist of the employees' labour union
   c. Accounting clerk
   d. Engineering supervisor

3. Which of the following is an example of an external user of accounting information? (SO2)
   a. Marketing manager of the business
   b. President of the labour union
   c. Officer of the corporation
   d. Production supervisor of the business

4. The buying of a delivery truck needed to operate a business is an example of a(n) (SO3)
   a. financing activity.
   b. delivering activity.
   c. operating activity.
   d. investing activity.

5. A business organized as a corporation
   a. is not a separate legal entity in most provinces. (SO2)
   b. requires that shareholders be personally liable for the debts of the business.
   c. is owned by its shareholders.
   d. has tax advantages over a proprietorship or partnership

6. Which of the following groups uses accounting information to determine whether the company's net earnings will result in a share price increase? (SO2)
   a. Investors in common shares
   b. Marketing managers
   c. Creditors
   d. Chief Financial Officer

7. Which of the following activities involves collecting the necessary funds to support the business? (SO3)
   a. Operating
   b. Investing

  c. Financing

  d. Delivering

(SO3)   8. Which activities involve putting the resources of the business into action to generate a profit?

  a. Delivering

  b. Financing

  c. Investing

  d. Operating

(SO3)   9. Which of the following is an investing activity?

  a. Borrowing money from a bank

  b. Earning revenue from the sale of products

  c. Incurring salaries expense

  d. The purchase of a delivery truck

(SO3)   10. A business's earning of revenues is considered to be a(n):

  a. operating activity.

  b. investing activity.

  c. financing activity.

  d. balance sheet activity.

(SO3)   11. Borrowing money from a bank or purchasing goods on credit is considered to be a(n):

  a. operating activity.

  b. investing activity.

  c. financing activity.

  d. balance sheet activity.

(SO4)   12. Which of the following accounts will be found on a statement of earnings?

  a. Revenues, expenses and dividends

  b. Revenues and expenses

  c. Revenues, expenses, and cash

  d. Expenses, dividends, and cash

(SO4)   13. If revenues are $20,000 and expenses are $5,000, then the business:

  a. incurred a net loss of $25,000.

  b. had net earnings of $20,000.

  c. had net earnings of $15,000.

  d. incurred a net loss of $15,000.

(SO4)   14. If beginning retained earnings is $10,000, net loss is $3,000, and dividends are $1,000, then the ending retained earnings shown on the statement of retained earnings is:

  a. $14,000.

  b. $12,000.

  c. $8,000.

  d. $6,000.

15. Which of the following is an appropriate date for a balance sheet?   (SO4)
    a. December 31, 2006
    b. Month ending December 31, 2006
    c. Quarter ending December 31, 2006
    d. Year ending December 31, 2006

16. Which of the following is the correct expression of the basic accounting   (SO4)
    equation?
    a. Liabilities = Assets + Shareholders' Equity
    b. Shareholders' Equity = Assets + Liabilities
    c. Assets = Liabilities + Shareholders' Equity
    d. Assets = Liabilities − Shareholders' Equity

17. Assets total $20,000, common shares total $9,000, and revenues total $6,000.   (SO4)
    What is the dollar amount of liabilities?
    a. $23,000
    b. $17,000
    c. $11,000
    d. $5,000

18. The statement that shows the operating, investing, and financing activities of a   (SO4)
    business is the:
    a. statement of retained earnings.
    b. cash flow statement.
    c. statement of earnings.
    d. balance sheet.

Problems

1. From the appropriate accounts given below, please prepare in good form a balance   (SO5)
    sheet for Jerome Corporation on September 30, 2006:

Common Shares	15,000
Service Revenue	20,000
Note Payable	5,000
Salaries Expense	10,000
Accounts Receivable	7,000
Dividends	2,000
Unearned Revenue	6,000
Retained Earnings	24,000
Supplies	2,000
Insurance Expense	1,500
Prepaid Insurance	3,000
Utilities Expense	4,000
Office Equipment	17,000
Accounts Payable	1,000
Cash	22,000

Jerome Corporation
Balance Sheet
September 30, 2006

2. Use the following accounts and information to prepare, in good form, a statement of earnings, a statement of retained earnings, and a balance sheet for Azro Corporation for the month ended September 30, 2006.

Maintenance Expense	$2,400	Dividends	$1,000
Accounts Receivable	1,400	Insurance Expense	2,200
Office Buildings	60,000	Cash	15,600
Supplies	400	Notes Payable	3,300
Revenues	15,700	Accounts Payable	3,100
Common Shares	52,000	Salaries Expense	10,000
Retained Earnings (beginning)	18,900	Income Tax Expense	400

3. Please refer to the Domtar Inc. and Cascades Inc. financial statements at the end of this workbook for information for answering the following questions. Do not forget to use the **Decision Toolkit** approach for help in the problem-solving.

   a. For Domtar and Cascades, what is the total dollar amount of each of the company's classes of assets in 2004? (SO4)

   b. For Domtar and Cascades, which class of liabilities has the largest total dollar amount in 2004? (SO4)

   c. Were the companies profitable in 2004? What has been the trend for each of the company's net earnings over the three years shown? (SO4)

   d. What was the biggest expense in 2004, for each of the companies? (SO4)

Solutions to Self-Test

(SO5)

Multiple Choice

1. c Proprietors are liable for debts of their businesses, there are more proprietorships and partnerships than there are corporations, and corporations can raise capital through selling of shares and bonds.
2. b The receptionist of the employees' labour union is the only position that **would not** be considered an internal user.

(SO5)

3. b The marketing manager, corporation officer, and production supervisor all work for the business and are therefore internal users.
4. d The buying of a long-lived asset, such as a delivery truck, is a financing activity.
5. c
6. a
7. c

(SO5)

8. d
9. d Borrowing money is a financing activity, and earning revenue and incurring expense are operating activities.
10. a Investing activities deal with the purchase of assets, and financing activities deal with the borrowing of money and selling of shares.

11. c

12. b   Dividends appear on the statement of retained earnings, and cash is an asset on the balance sheet.

13. c $20,000 – $5,000

14. d $10,000 – $3,000 – $1,000

15. a   The balance sheet shows balances on a specific date, not for a period of time.

16. c

17. d   Assets = Liabilities + Shareholders' Equity
Therefore, Assets – Shareholders' Equity = Liabilities
Shareholders' Equity = Common Shares + Retained Earnings. Revenue is part of Retained Earnings, therefore, Shareholders' Equity = Common Shares + Retained Earnings. ($9,000 + $6,000 = $15,000)
Therefore, Liabilities = Assets – Shareholders' Equity ($20,000 – $15,000 = $5,000)

18. b   The statement of retained earnings shows changes in the retained earnings account over the period, the statement of earnings summarizes revenue and expense activity, and the balance sheet shows assets, liabilities, and shareholders' equity items.

Problems

1.

Jerome Corporation
Balance Sheet
September 30, 2006

Assets

Cash		$22,000
Accounts Receivable		7,000
Supplies		2,000
Prepaid Insurance		3,000
Office Equipment		$17,000
Total Assets		$51,000

Liabilities

Notes Payable	$ 5,000	
Accounts Payable	1,000	
Unearned Revenue	6,000	
Total Liabilities		$12,000

Shareholders' Equity

Common Shares	$15,000	
Retained Earnings	24,000	
Total Shareholders' Equity		39,000
Total Liabilities and Shareholders' Equity		$51,000

2.

Azro Corporation
Statement of Earnings
Month Ended September 30, 2006

Revenues		
Revenues		$16,100
Expenses		
Salaries expense	$10,000	
Maintenance expense	2,400	
Insurance expense	2,200	
Total expenses		14,600
Earnings before income taxes		1,500
Income tax expense		400
Net earnings		$ 1,100

Azro Corporation
Statement of Retained Earnings
Month Ended September 30, 2006

Retained earnings, September 1	$18,900
Add: Net earnings	1,100
	20,000
Less: Dividends	8,000
Retained earnings, September 30	$19,000

Azro Corporation
Balance Sheet
September 30, 2006

Assets

Cash		$ 15,600
Accounts receivable		1,400
Supplies		400
Office buildings		60,000
Total assets		$77,400

Liabilities and Shareholders' Equity

Liabilities		
Accounts payable	$ 3,100	
Notes payable	3,300	
Total liabilities		$6,400
Shareholders' Equity		
Common shares	$52,000	
Retained earnings	19,000	71,000
Total liabilities and shareholders' equity		$77,400

3. Please note that all dollars shown on the financial statements and below are stated in millions of Canadian dollars.

a.

	Domtar	Cascades
Current assets	$1,124	$1,116
Property, plant and equipment	4,215	1,700
Goodwill	84	113
Other assets	265	215
Total assets	$5,688	$3,144

b. Long-term debts were in the amounts of $2,026 for Domtar and $1,168 for Cascades.

c. Domtar was not profitable in 2004. It incurred a net loss of $42 in 2004, which compares with a net loss of $193 in 2003 and a net earnings of $141 in 2002. Cascades was profitable in 2004; however, its net earnings have been steadily decreasing from $169 in 2002, to $55 in 2003, to $23 in 2004.

d. Cost of sales was the largest expense for both companies: $4,381 for Domtar and $2,691 for Cascades.

chapter 2

A Further Look at Financial Statements

Chapter Overview

Chapter 2 explains the conceptual framework of accounting, which provides a general guide for financial reporting. You will take a further look at the balance sheet and learn how to evaluate information provided by a company's financial statements.

Review of Specific Study Objectives

Conceptual Framework of Accounting

- The conceptual framework of accounting guides the choice of what to present in financial statements and has four main sections:

  1. The objective of financial reporting
  2. The qualitative characteristics of accounting information
  3. The elements of financial statements
  4. Recognition and measurement criteria (assumptions, principles, and constraints)

- The main objective of **financial reporting** is to provide useful information for decision-making.

Describe the objective of financial reporting and apply the qualitative characteristics of accounting information to the elements of financial statements.

- To be useful, information should have the following **qualitative characteristics**: *understandability, relevance, reliability,* and *comparability.*

- Accounting information is **understandable** if the **average user** has an understanding of accounting concepts and procedures, as well as an understandingand of general business and economic conditions, so that the financial statements can be studied intelligently.

- Accounting information is **relevant** if it **influences a business decision**. If relevant, accounting information provides a *basis for forecasting, confirms or corrects prior expectations,* and is presented on a *timely basis.*

- Accounting information is **reliable** if users **can depend on it**. If reliable, accounting information is *verifiable* (free of error), is a *faithful representation* of what it purports to be, and is *neutral* (does not favour one set of users over another).

- Accounting information is **comparable** when *different companies use the same accounting principles or when one company uses the same accounting principles from year to year.* This does not mean that a company must use the same principles forever after making the initial selection. If it the company makes changes in order to produce more meaningful information, then it must disclose the change in the notes to the financial statements.

- The elements of financial statements include such terms as *assets, liabilities, equity, revenue,* and *expenses*

<table>
<tr><td>

study objective 2

Identify and apply assumptions, principles, and constraints.

</td><td>

- The fourth element of the accounting conceptual framework deals with recognition and measurement criteria which that are needed to help accountants decide when which items should be included in financial statements and how they should be measured. These recognition and measurement criteria are classified as assumptions, principles, and constraints.

</td></tr>
</table>

- Four assumptions guide when to recognize and how to measure events:
  1. the **monetary unit assumption**, which requires that *only those things that can be expressed in money are included in the accounting records.* Customer satisfaction and a loyal, competent workforce are extremely important, but these will do not appear on a financial statement.
  2. the **economic entity assumption**, which states that *every economic entity can be separately identified and accounted for.* If an individual owns a business, that individual must have two sets of records: one for that individual's transactions and one for the business.
  3. **time period assumption**, which states that the *life of a business can be divided into artificial time periods, and that useful reports covering those periods can be prepared for the business.*
  4. the **going concern assumption**, which states that the *business will remain in operation for the foreseeable future.* This principle underlies much of what we do in accounting. If it seems likely that a company will go out of business in the near future, then different assumptions will govern the preparation of the financial statements.

- **Generally accepted accounting principles (GAAP)** are a recognized set of principles used in financial reporting. These principles are established by the Accounting

Standards Board, an independent standard-setting body created by the Canadian Institute of Chartered Accountants (CICA).

- The **principles** are:
  1. the **cost principle**, which dictates that *assets are recorded at their cost*, not only at the time of their acquisition, but also for the entire time that they are held. There is much discussion about the relevance of this principle, but for now, accountants adhere to it for various reasons, one of which is that cost is easy to measure.
  2. the **full disclosure principle**, which requires that *all circumstances and events that would make a difference to the users of the financial statements users should be disclosed*, either in the statements themselves or in the notes and supporting schedules that accompany the statements and are an integral part of them.

Constraints in Accounting

- **Constraints** *permit a company to modify generally accepted accounting principles without jeopardizing the usefulness of the reported information.* **The two constraints are cost-benefit and materiality.**
  1. The **cost-benefit** constraint ensures that the value of the information exceeds the cost of providing it.
  2. An item is **material** if it *influences the decision of an investor or creditor.* It is important to note that what is material for one company may be immaterial for another. Assume that companies A and B each have a $1,000 error in the financial statements. Company A's net earnings are $10,000, while company B's net earnings are $100,000. The $1,000 error most likely will be material for A because it is 10 percent of net earnings, while it most likely will be immaterial for B because it is only 1 percent of net earnings.

The Classified Balance Sheet

- The **balance sheet** of a company presents a *snapshot of its financial position at a point in time.* A **classified balance sheet** breaks the statement components into several classifications, usually having *four asset categories, two liability categories, and the two shareholders' equity categories.*

study objective 3

Identify the sections of a classified balance sheet.

- The following are the **four common asset categories**:
  1. **Current assets** are those *expected to be converted into cash or used in the business within a relatively short period of time, usually within one year. Current assets are listed in the order in which they are expected to be converted into cash* and include **cash, short-term investments, receivables, inventories, and prepaid expenses.**
  2. **Long-term investments** are *investments in shares and bonds of other corporations that are normally held for many years.*
  3. **Property, plant, and equipment** are *assets with physical substance that have relatively long useful lives and are used in the operations of the business.* Examples include **land, buildings, equipment,** and **furniture.** These long-lived assets, except land, have estimated useful lives over which they are expected to generate revenues. Because property, plant, and equipment benefit future periods, their cost is matched to revenues over their estimated useful life through a process called **amortization.** The sum of all past amortization is called **accumulated**

amortization. It is a contra asset which is subtracted from the asset itself. The difference between the cost and accumulated amortization is referred to as the **net book value** of the asset.

4. **Intangible assets** are *assets that have no physical substance*. They are essentially long-lived rights. Examples include **goodwill, patents, copyrights, trademarks, trade names, and licences that give the company exclusive right of use**. Similar to buildings and equipment, intangible assets with estimated useful lives are also amortized over their useful lives. Similar to land, intangible assets with indefinite lives are not amortized.

- The following are the **two common liability categories**:

  1. **Current liabilities** are *obligations that are to be paid within one year*. Examples include **accounts payable, short-term notes payable, salaries payable, interest payable, taxes payable, and current maturities of long-term obligations**. Notes payable are usually listed first, followed by accounts payable and other current liabilities.

  2. **Long-term liabilities** are *expected to be paid after one year from the balance sheet date*. If the balance sheet date is December 31, 2006, and an obligation is due on June 30, 2008, then the obligation is long- term. Examples include **bonds payable, mortgages payable, long-term notes payable, lease liabilities, and pension liabilities**. There is no particular guidance for listing these long-term obligations, and companies simply choose a way of disclosing them that is most useful for to the users of their financial statements.

- **Shareholders' equity** has two components: *share capital and retained earnings*. Share capital consists of shareholders' investments of assets in the business, while retained earnings is just that—earnings retained for use in the business.

Using the Statement of Earnings

study objective 4

Identify and calculate ratios for analyzing a company's profitability.

- Financial statements are used to gauge the strength or weakness of a company. To make the numbers in the statements more useful and meaningful, users conduct **ratio analysis**, a *technique for expressing relationships among selected financial statement data*.

- **Profitability ratios** *measure the earnings or operating success of a company for a given period of time*. Two such ratios are the **earnings per share** and the **price-earnings ratio**.

- The **earnings per share** measures the net earnings for each common share. It is calculated by *dividing net earnings available to the common shareholders by the weighted average number of common shares* issued during the year.

- The **price-earnings ratio** *measures the ratio of the market price of each share to its earnings per share. It is calculated by dividing the market price per share by earnings per share*. The price-earnings ratio reflects the investors' assessment of a company's future earnings.

- Please note that one ratio by itself does n't not convey very much. The ratio must be compared with something—either with the ratios from prior years of the company, the ratios of other companies in the same industry, or the particular industry's averages.

Using the Balance Sheet

- **Liquidity** refers to a *company's ability to pay obligations expected to come due within the next year or operating cycle.*

- One measure of liquidity is **working capital**, which is the *difference between current assets and current liabilities.* It is certainly preferable to have a positive number (current assets exceed current liabilities) because this indicates that a company has a good likelihood of being able to pay its liabilities. If current assets are $300 and current liabilities are $100, then working capital is $200.

> **study objective 5**
>
> Identify and calculate ratios for analyzing a company's liquidity and solvency.

- Another measure of liquidity is the **current ratio**, which is calculated by *dividing current assets by current liabilities.* Referring to the numbers just above, dividing $300 by $100 yields a current ratio of 3:1, meaning that the company has $3 of current assets for every $1 of current liabilities. Remember that a ratio by itself does not convey very much information. The current ratio is impacted by the liquidity of the accounts receivable and inventory, which must also be reviewed before evaluating the current ratio. We will look at each of these effects in later chapters.

- **Solvency** deals with a company's *ability to survive over a long period of time, with its ability to pay its long-term obligations and the interest due on them.*

- The **debt to total assets ratio** is one source of information about a company's solvency and *measures the percentage of assets financed by creditors rather than invested by shareholders.* It is calculated by *dividing total debt (both current and long-term) by total assets.* The higher the percentage of debt financing, the greater is the risk that the company may be unable to pay its debts as they mature. If total debt is $3 million and total assets are $5 million, then the ratio is 60%, percent, meaning that of every dollar invested in company assets, creditors have provided $0.60. A creditor does not like to see a high debt to total assets ratio for a company.

Using the Cash Flow Statement

- The cash flow statement reports the cash effects of a company's operating activities, investing activities, and financing activities. Cash provided by operating activities is often adjusted to take into account that accompany must invest in new assets to maintain its current level of operations. In addition, companies must also keep paying dividends to satisfy investors. The result is known as **free cash flow**, which is a solvency-based measure. It is calculated by *subtracting the sum of net capital expenditures and dividends paid from cash provided by operating activities.* It indicates the cash available for paying dividends or expanding operations.

Chapter Self-Test

As you work through the exercises and problems, remember to use the **Decision Toolkit** discussed and used in the text:

1. *Decision Checkpoints*: At this point, you ask a question.
2. *Info Needed for Decision*: You make a choice regarding the information needed to answer the question.
3. *Tool to Use for Decision*: At this point, you review just what the information chosen in step two does for the decision-making process.

4. *How to Evaluate Results*: You conduct an evaluation of information for answering the question.

Note: The notation (SO1) means that the question was drawn from study objective number one.

Multiple Choice

Please circle the correct answer.

(SO1)   1. If accounting information has relevance, it is useful in making predictions about:
a. future government audits.
b. new accounting principles.
c. foreign currency exchange rates.
d. the future events of a company.

(SO1)   2. Accounting information should be neutral in order to enhance:
a. reliability.
b. materiality.
c. comparability.
d. relevance.

(SO1)   3. Accounting information is _____ if it would make a difference in a business decision.
a. reliable
b. relevant
c. comparable
d. understandable

(SO1)   4. _____ results when different companies use the same accounting principles.
a. Relevance
b. Understandability
c. Comparability
d. Reliability

(SO1)   5. The Accounting Standards Board, which is an independent standard-setting body in Canada, was created by the:
a. federal government.
b. Canadian Institute of Chartered Accountants.
c. Ontario Securities Commission.
d. Accounting Principles Board.

(SO1)   6. Accounting rules having substantial authoritative support and recognized as a general guide for financial reporting purposes are called:
a. general accounting principles.
b. generally accepted auditing principles.
c. generally accepted accounting standards.
d. generally accepted accounting principles.

7. Which of the following assumptions states that every business must be   (SO2)
    separately identified and accounted for?
    a.   Monetary unit assumption
    b.   Economic entity assumption
    c.   Time period assumption
    d.   Going concern assumption

8. Which of the following assumes that a business will remain in operation for the   (SO2)
    foreseeable future?
    a.   Monetary unit assumption
    b.   Economic entity assumption
    c.   Time period assumption
    d.   Going concern assumption

9. Which of the following requires that all circumstances and events, that would   (SO2)
    make a difference to financial statement users, should be disclosed?
    a.   Full disclosure principle
    b.   Economic entity assumption
    c.   Time period assumption
    d.   Cost principle

10. The _____ _____ assumption states that the life of a business can be   (SO2)
    divided into artificial time periods and that useful reports covering those
    periods can be prepared for the business.
    a.   monetary unit
    b.   going concern
    c.   time period
    d.   economic entity

11. An item is _____ if it is likely to influence the decision of an investor or   (SO2)
    creditor.
    a.   consistent
    b.   reliable
    c.   conservative
    d.   material

12. The constraint that says "Make sure the information is worth it," is: (SO2)
    a.   cost-benefit.
    b.   materiality.
    c.   relevance.
    d.   reliability.

13. Which of the following statements report the ending balance of the retained   (SO3)
    earnings account?
    a.   Statement of retained earnings and balance sheet
    b.   Statement of retained earnings only
    c.   Balance sheet only
    d.   Cash flow statement

(SO3)   14. Which of the following is considered a current asset on a classified balance sheet?
    a.   Short-term investments
    b.   Land
    c.   Building
    d.   Patent

(SO3)   15. Which of the following is classified as property, plant, or equipment on a balance sheet?
    a.   Supplies
    b.   Investment in Intel Corporation shares
    c.   Land
    d.   Copyright

(SO3)   16. Current liabilities are $10,000, long-term liabilities are $20,000, common shares is are $50,000, and retained earnings totals $70,000. Total shareholders' equity is:
    a. $150,000.
    b. $140,000.
    c. $120,000.
    d. $ 70,000.

(SO4)   17. Net earnings available to common shareholders are $90,000, and the weighted average number of common shares during the year are 50,000. The earnings per share are:
    a. $2.00.
    b. $1.80.
    c. $1.50.
    d. $1.60.

(SO4)   18. Net earnings available to common shareholders are $140,000, and the weighted average number of common shares during the year are 80,000. The market price of each common share is $8.75. The price-earnings ratio is:
    a.   5 times.
    b.   4 times.
    c.   4.375 times.
    d.   4,775 times.

(SO5)   19. The ability to pay obligations that are expected to become due within the next year is called:
    a.   working capital.
    b.   profitability.
    c.   solvency.
    d.   liquidity.

(SO5)   20. Current assets are $60,000, total assets are $180,000, current liabilities are $30,000, and total liabilities are $50,000. The current ratio is:
    a.   2:1.
    b.   1.2:1.

c.   0.5:1.

d.   0.33:1.

21. Which ratio measures the percentage of assets financed by creditors rather than   (SO5)
by shareholders?

   a.   Current ratio

   b.   Debt to total assets ratio

   c.   Free cash flow ratio

   d.   Price-earnings ratio

22. Which of the following statements provides information about the operating,   (SO5)
investing, and financing activities of a company?

   a.   Cash flow statement

   b.   Balance sheet

   c.   Statement of earnings

   d.   Statement of retained earnings

23. Free cash flow: (SO5)

   a.   Is is a liquidity-based measure.

   b.   Is is calculated by using information shown on the balance sheet.

   c.   Measures a company's ability to pay its short-term debts.

   d.   Helps helps investors assess how much money a company has to pay
dividends.

Problems

1.   The following presents December 31, 2006, year-end balances for the Variety   (SO3)
Corporation:

Cash	$ 5,900
Accounts payable	3,300
Accumulated amortization-equipment	13,500
Prepaid insurance	1,400
Common shares	9,000
Accounts receivable	13,600
Retained earnings	49,300
Equipment	63,000
Inventory	14,400
Long-term note payable	20,000

(SO5)

Prepare a classified balance sheet.

2.   Consider the following data from Meadows Corporation: (SO4, 5)

	2006	2005
Current assets	$61,000	$50,000
Total assets	108,000	85,000
Current liabilities	47,000	39,000
Total liabilities	80,000	62,000
Net sales	200,000	180,000
Net earnings available to common shareholders	30,000	20,000

Market price per common share	9.00	6.40
Weighted average number of common shares	30,000	25,000

Calculate the following and explain what the results mean:

(SO5)	a.	Working capital for 2006 and 2005.
(SO5)	b.	Current ratio for 2006 and 2005.
(SO5)	c.	Debt to total assets for 2006 and 2005.
(SO4)	d.	Earnings per share for 2006 and 2005.
(SO4)	e.	Price-earnings ratio for 2006 and 2005.

Please refer to the Domtar and Cascades financial statements at the end of this workbook for information for answering the following questions. Do not forget to use the **Decision Toolkit** approach for help in the problem solving.

a. The balance sheet for Domtar shows property, plant, and equipment of $4,215 million at the end of 2004. What does this amount represent? What are the components of this amount?

b. Can Cascades meet its near-term obligations in 2004 and 2003? Please comment on the trend that you see.

(SO3)   c. Examine the statement of retained earnings for Domtar. Which figure is shown on both the statement of retained earnings and the balance sheet for 2004? What does that figure represent?

(SO5)   d. Calculate the debt to total assets ratio for both companies for 2004.

Solutions to Self-Test

Multiple Choice

1. d
2. a
3. b Reliability means that information can be depended on, comparability results when different companies use the same accounting principles, and understandable means that the average user is able to study the information.
4. c
5. b The federal government has given the statutory right to set accounting standards to the Canadian Institute of Chartered Accountants.
6. d
7. b The monetary unit assumption requires that only those things which that can be expressed in money are included in the accounting records; the time period assumption states that the life of a business can be divided into artificial time periods; and the going concern assumption assumes that a business will remain in operation for the foreseeable future.
8. d
9. a The economic entity assumption states that every business must be separately identified and accounted for; the time period assumption states that

the life of a business can be divided into artificial time periods; and the cost principle dictates that assets are recorded at their cost.

10. c

11. d   An item is material when it is likely to influence the decision of an investor or creditor.

12. a   The cost-benefit constraint ensures that the value of the information exceeds the cost of providing it.

13. a   The statement of retained earnings reports the ending balance of the retained earnings account. So, too, does the balance sheet, in its shareholders' equity section.

14. a   Land, Building, and Patent are all long-term assets.

15. c   Supplies is a current asset, investment is a non current asset, and copyright is an intangible asset.

16. c $50,000 + $70,000 = $120,000.

17. b $900,000 ÷ 50,000 common shares.

18. a   Earnings per share = $140,000 ÷ 80,000 common shares = $1.75
Price-earnings ratio = $8.75 ÷ $1.75 = 5 times

19. d   Working capital is the difference between current assets and current liabilities. Profitability refers to the operating success of a company during a period. Solvency is the ability of a company to pay interest as it comes due and to repay the face value of the debt at maturity.

20. a $60,000 ÷ $30,000 = 2 to 1

21. b

22. a   The balance sheet reports assets, liabilities, and Shareholders' equity items. The statement of earnings reports revenues and expenses. The statement of retained earnings reports changes in the retained earnings account.

23. d

Problems

1.

Variety Corporation
Balance Sheet
December 31, 2006

Current assets

Cash	$ 5,900	
Accounts receivable	13,600	
Inventory	14,400	
Prepaid insurance	1,400	
Total current assets		$35,300

Property, plant, and equipment

Equipment	$63,000	
Less: Accumulated amortization	13,500	
Total property, plant, and equipment		49,500
Total assets		$84,800

Current liabilities

Accounts payable	$3,300	
Wages payable	3,200	
Total current liabilities		$6,500

Long-term liabilities

Notes payable		20,000
Total liabilities		$26,500

Shareholders' equity

Common shares	$9,000		
Retained earnings	49,300		
Total shareholders' equity		58,300	
Total liabilities and shareholders' equity			$84,800

2.

a.   Current Assets – Current Liabilities = Working Capital
2006: $61,000 – $47,000 = $14,000
2005: $50,000 – $39,000 = $11,000
Working capital is a measure of liquidity. Since this company's working capital is positive, there is a greater likelihood that it will pay its liabilities.

b.   Current Assets ÷ Current Liabilities = Current Ratio
2006: $61,000 ÷ $47,000 = 1.30 : 1
2005: $50,000 ÷ $39,000 = 1.28 : 1
The current ratio is another measure of liquidity. In 2006, the company had $1.30 of current assets for every dollar of current liabilities. In 2005, it had $1.28 of current assets for every dollar of current liabilities.

c.   Total Debt ÷ Total Assets = Debt to Total Assets
2006: $80,000 ÷ $108,000 = 74%
2005: $62,000 ÷ $85,000 = 73%
This ratio measures the percentage of assets financed by creditors rather than by shareholders. In 2006, $0.74 of every dollar invested in assets was provided by creditors. In 2005, $0.73 of every dollar was provided by creditors. The higher the percentage of debt financing, the riskier the company.

d.   Net Earnings Available to Common Shareholders ÷ Weighted Average Number of Common Shares = Earnings per Share
2006: $30,000 ÷ 30,000 = $1.00
2005: $20,000 ÷ 25,000 = $0.80
This ratio is a measure of profitability. It measures the amount of net earnings for each common share. It provides a useful perspective for determining the return for the investment provided by the common shareholder.

e.   Market Price per Share ÷ Earnings per Share = Price-Earnings Ratio
2006: $9.00 ÷ $1.00 = 9 times
2005: $6.40 ÷ $0.80 = 8 times
This ratio reflects the investors' assessment of a company's future earnings. The ratio will be higher if the investor thinks that the company's current earnings level will persist or increase in the future.

3. (all dollars in millions)

a. It represents the net book value of all property, plant, and equipment. Note 11 to the financial statements shows the components as follows: machinery and equipment, buildings, timber limits and land, and assets under construction. For each of these components, the original cost, accumulated amortization, and net carrying value are provided. Net carrying value means the same thing as net book value). The total net carrying value of $5,387, shown in Note 11, is the amount that is shown on the balance sheet.

b. Yes, working capital (current assets less current liabilities) is $1,116 – $614 = $502 in 2004 and $1,022 – $514 = $508 in 2003. The trend shows that working capital has decreased slightly from 2003 to 2004.
Furthermore, the current ratio also showed a small decrease in 2004 as follows: For year 2004, it was $1,116 ÷ $614 = 1.82 : 1, and for 2003 it was $1,022 ÷ $514 = 1.99 : 1.

c. The amount is $412 and represents all past net earnings amounts (revenues less expenses) less all past dividend amounts.

d.

Ratio	Domtar	Cascades
Debt to total assets	($716 + $2,026 + $557 + $343) ÷ $5,688 = 64.0%	($614 + $1,168 + $303) ÷ $3,144 = 66.3%

chapter 3

The Accounting Information System

Chapter Overview

Chapter 3 shows you how to analyze transactions and their effect on the accounting equation. You will learn about accounts, debits, and credits and how to perform the basic steps in the recording process: journalizing, posting transactions to the ledger, and preparing a trial balance.

Review of Specific Study Objectives

Accounting Transactions

- *The system of collecting and processing transaction data and communicating financial information to decision-makers* is known as the **accounting information system**.

- An accounting information system begins with determining what relevant transaction data should be collected and processed.

- An **accounting transaction** *occurs when assets, liabilities, or shareholders' equity items change as a result of some economic event.*

study objective 1

Analyze the effects of transactions on the accounting equation.

Analyzing Transactions

The accounting equation is stated as follows:

$$Assets = Liabilities + Shareholders' Equity$$

- Transactions will affect the components of the accounting equation in various ways, and it is important to remember that the **accounting equation** must **always be in balance** after a transaction is recorded. Remember, it is a mathematical equation. For example, if an individual asset is increased, there must be a corresponding decrease in another asset, increase in a specific liability, or increase in shareholders' equity.

- You should also remember the following with respect to specific parts of the accounting equation:

  1. If a company receives cash for work to be performed in the future, then it should not record revenue. It records an increase in cash on the left side of the equation and an increase in *liabilities* on the right side of the equation. It owes performance of that work in the future.

  2. Revenues increase shareholders' equity.

  3. Expenses decrease shareholders' equity.

  4. Some events in the life of a corporation are not transactions and are not to be recorded. The hiring of an employee and the beginning of an employees' strike are two such events.

study objective 2

Define debits and credits and explain how they are used to record transactions.

- **An accounting information system uses accounts** that are *individual accounting records of increases and decreases in a specific asset, liability, or shareholders' equity item.*

- The simplest form of an account is the **T account**, so named because of its shape. T accounts have *account titles, a left side (called the debit side)*, and a *right side (called the credit side).*

- **Debit (abbreviated DR) means left, while credit (abbreviated CR) means right.** These terms simply denote position. They do not mean good or bad, increase or decrease. The *important thing is to know what a debit does to a particular account and what a credit does to that same account.*

- **To debit an account** means to *enter an amount on the left side of the account.* **To credit an account** means to *enter an amount on the right side of the account.* If an account has $300 on the debit side and $100 on the credit side, then that account has a $200 overall debit balance. If an account has $500 on the credit side and $200 on the debit side, then that account has a $300 overall credit balance. **Debits are always added together, and credits are always added together, but a debit and a credit are subtracted one from the other.**

- The **dollar amount of the debits and the dollar amount of the credits must be equal in each transaction.** This provides the *basis of the double-entry accounting system.* Double-entry simply means that each accounting transaction has two parts.

- The following is a summary of the **debit/credit procedures for the accounts that you know** ("+" means increase, while "−" means decrease):

	Debit	Credit		Debit	Credit
Assets	+	-	Liabilities	-	+
Dividends	+	-	Shareholders' Equity	-	+
Expenses	+	-	Revenues	-	+

- Remember that **shareholders' equity has two components: common shares and retained earnings.** *Both follow the procedures indicated for "Shareholders' Equity" above.*

- **Retained earnings** can be further divided into three components: revenues and expenses that determine net earnings and dividends. **Dividends and expenses both reduce shareholders' equity**; therefore, they follow procedures opposite from those followed by equity. **Common shares, retained earnings, and revenues all increase shareholders' equity.**

- Since assets are on the left side of the accounting equation and liabilities and shareholders' equity are on the right side, the procedures for assets are opposite from the procedures for liabilities and equity items.

- The **normal balance** is the balance expected to be in an account. Please note that the normal balance is *found on the side that increases a particular account*. Dividends are increased by debits, and the normal balance is a debit. Revenues are increased by credits, and the normal balance is a credit. Occasionally, an account may have a balance other than its normal balance. As your text points out, the Cash account will have a credit balance when the cash account is overdrawn at the bank.

- The **recording process begins with a source document.**

- Each **transaction is analyzed and entered in a journal.** Then, the **journal information is transferred to** the appropriate accounts in **the ledger.**

study objective 3

Identify the basic steps in the recording process.

- A **journal** is a *place where a transaction is initially recorded before it is transferred to the accounts.* It may be in the form of paper or it may be a file on a computer. **Transactions are entered in chronological order.**

- **Journalizing** is the *process of entering transaction data in the journal.* A **complete journal entry** consists of the following:

  1. The *date* of the transaction.
  2. The *accounts and amounts* to be debited and credited.
  3. An *explanation* of the transaction.

- A typical journal entry has the following format:

```
May 12   Supplies                          500
               Cash                                     500
          (Purchased supplies for cash)
```

Please note that the **credit account title is indented**. This decreases the possibility of switching the debit and credit amounts. It also makes it easy to see that the Cash account is credited without having to have eyes glance right to see in which column the Cash amount is residing. It is tiring to have your eyes continually scan back and forth across a page.

- The **ledger** is the *entire group of accounts maintained by a company*. It keeps all the information about changes in specific account balances, in one place. A **general ledger** contains all the *assets, liabilities, and shareholders' equity accounts*.

- As is true for the journal, a general ledger may be in the form of paper or may be an electronic file on a computer.

- The **chart of accounts** is a *listing of all the ledger accounts used in the business*.

- **Posting** is the *procedure of transferring journal entries to ledger accounts*. Posting accumulates the effects of journalized transactions in the individual accounts.

- To **illustrate posting**, consider the entry above in which Supplies was debited and Cash was credited for $500 on May 12. In the ledger account Supplies, the date is recorded, and $500 is written in the debit column. In the ledger account Cash, the date is again recorded, and $500 is written in the credit column.

study objective 4

Prepare a trial balance.

- A **trial balance** is a *list of general ledger accounts and their balances at a given time*. A trial balance is usually prepared at the end of an accounting period. Accounts are listed in their ledger order with the balances listed in the appropriate column, debit or credit. The **dollar amount of the debits must equal the dollar amount of the credits**; otherwise, there is an error that must be corrected. The **primary purpose** of a trial balance is to *prove the mathematical equality of debits and credits in the ledger. It also helps uncover errors in journalizing and posting and is useful in the preparation of financial statements*.

- It is, of course, preferable that **a trial balance have equal debits and credits, but mistakes can still be present**. If a *journal entry has not been posted*, then an error has occurred, but the trial balance will be in balance. If a *journal entry is posted twice*, then the same is true. If a *journal entry is recorded as $500 instead of $5,000 on both the debit and the credit sides*, then an error has occurred, but, once again, the trial balance will be in balance. If a $200 *debit is posted to Cash instead of to another asset*, then an error is present, but the trial balance will be in balance.

Chapter Self-Test

As you work through the exercises and problems, remember to use the **Decision Toolkit** discussed and used in the text:
1. *Decision Checkpoints*: At this point, you ask a question.
2. *Info Needed for Decision*: You make a choice regarding the information needed to answer the question.
3. *Tool to Use for Decision*: At this point, you review just what the information chosen in step 2 does for the decision-making process.
4. *How to Evaluate Results*: You conduct an evaluation of information for answering the question.

Note: The notation (SO1) means that the question was drawn from study objective number one.

Multiple Choice

Please circle the correct answer.

1. If a company receives cash from a customer before performing services for the customer, then: (SO1)
    a. assets increase, and liabilities decrease.
    b. assets increase, and shareholders' equity increases.
    c. assets decrease, and liabilities increase.
    d. assets increase, and liabilities increase.

2. If a company performs services for a customer and receives cash for the services, then: (SO1)
    a. assets increase, and liabilities decrease.
    b. assets increase, and shareholders' equity increases.
    c. assets decrease, and liabilities increase.
    d. assets increase, and liabilities increase.

3. When collection is made on an accounts receivable balance, then: (SO1)
    a. total assets will remain the same.
    b. total assets will decrease.
    c. total assets will increase.
    d. shareholders' equity will increase.

4. Which of the following items has no effect on retained earnings?   (SO1)
    a. Expense
    b. Dividends
    c. Land purchase
    d. Revenue

5. A payment of a portion of accounts payable will: (SO1)
    a. not affect total assets.
    b. increase liabilities.
    c. not affect shareholders' equity.
    d. decrease net earnings.

6. An accountant has debited an asset account for $1,000 and credited a liability account for $400. What can be done to complete the recording of the transaction?   (SO2)
    a. Credit a different asset account for $400.
    b. Debit a shareholders' equity account for $400.
    c. Debit another asset account for $600.
    d. Credit a different asset account for $600.

7. An account will have a credit balance if the: (SO2)
    a. credits exceed the debits.
    b. first transaction entered was a credit.
    c. debits exceed the credits.
    d. last transaction entered was a credit.

(SO2)   8. An account has $600 on the debit side and $400 on the credit side. The overall balance in the account is a:
    a.   debit of $200.
    b.   credit of $200.
    c.   debit of $600.
    d.   credit of $400.

(SO2)   9. Which of the following statements is correct?
    a.   A debit decreases an asset account.
    b.   A credit decreases a liability account.
    c.   A credit increases shareholders' equity.
    d.   A credit decreases a revenue account.

(SO2)   10. Which of the following statements is incorrect?
    a.   A debit increases the Dividends account.
    b.   A debit increases an expense account.
    c.   A credit increases a revenue account.
    d.   A credit increases the Dividends account.

(SO3)   11. Which of the following is the correct sequence of events?
    a.   Analyze a transaction; record it in the ledger; record it in the journal.
    b.   Analyze a transaction; record it in the journal; record it in the ledger.
    c.   Record a transaction in the journal; analyze the transaction; record it in the ledger.
    d.   None of the above is the correct sequence.

(SO3)   12. Transactions are initially recorded in chronological order in a _____ before they are transferred to the accounts.
    a.   journal
    b.   register
    c.   ledger
    d.   T account

(SO3)   13. If a corporation borrows money and issues a three-month note in exchange, then the journal entry requires a:
    a.   debit to Notes Payable and a credit to Cash.
    b.   debit to Notes Payable and a credit to Unearned Revenue.
    c.   debit to Cash and a credit to Notes Payable.
    d.   debit to Cash and a credit to Unearned Revenue.

(SO3)   14. If a company pays its employees their weekly salaries, then the journal entry requires a:
    a.   debit to Unearned Revenue and a credit to Cash.
    b.   debit to Retained Earnings and a credit to Cash.
    c.   debit to Cash and a credit to Salaries Expense.
    d.   debit to Salaries Expense and a credit to Cash.

(SO3)   (SO3) 15. A general ledger of a company contains:
    a.   only asset and liability accounts.

b.   all the asset, liability, and shareholders' equity accounts.

c.   only shareholders' equity accounts.

d.   only asset and shareholders' equity accounts.

16. The entire group of accounts maintained by a company is referred to collectively   (SO3)
    as the:

    a.   ledger.

    b.   journal.

    c.   register.

    d.   T accounts.

17. If a corporate accountant wanted to know the balance in the company's Cash   (SO3)
    account, then she would look in:

    a.   the journal.

    b.   the ledger.

    c.   both the journal and the ledger.

    d.   neither the journal nor the ledger.

18.   When an accountant posts, he is transferring amounts from: (SO3)

    a.   the ledger to the journal.

    b.   T accounts to the ledger.

    c.   the journal to the ledger.

    d.   the ledger to T accounts.

19. If an account is debited in the journal entry, then: (SO3)

    a.   that account will be debited in the ledger.

    b.   that account will be credited in the ledger.

    c.   that account will be both debited and credited in the ledger.

    d.   none of the above is correct.

20. Which of the following is the correct sequence of events?   (SO3)

    a.   Prepare a trial balance; journalize; post.

    b.   Journalize; post; prepare a trial balance.

    c.   Post; journalize; prepare a trial balance.

    d.   Prepare a trial balance; post; journalize.

21. The primary purpose of a trial balance is to: (SO4)

    a.   get a total of all accounts with a debit balance.

    b.   get a total of all accounts with a credit balance.

    c.   prove the mathematical equality of debits and credits after posting.

    d.   get a list of all accounts used by a company.

22. Which of the following errors, each considered individually, would cause the   (SO4)
    trial balance to be out of balance?

    a.   A payment of $75 to a creditor was posted as a debit to accounts payable
         and a debit of $75 to cash.

    b.   Cash received from a customer on account was posted as a debit of $350
         to cash and as a credit of $350 to revenue.

    c.   A payment of $59 for supplies was posted as a debit of $95 to supplies and a credit of $95 to cash.

    d.   A transaction was not posted.

(SO4)   23. If the totals of a trial balance are not equal, it could be due to:

    a.   a failure to record a transaction or to post a transaction.

    b.   recording the same erroneous amount for both the debit and the credit parts of a transaction.

    c.   an error in calculating the account balances.

    d.   recording the transaction more than once.

Problems

(SO3) 1.   Journalize the following business transactions in general journal form. Identify each transaction by letter. You may omit explanations for the transactions.

    a.   Shareholders invest $40,000 in cash to start an interior decorating business.

    b.   Purchased office equipment for $5,500, paying $2,000 in cash, and signed a 30-day, $3,500 note payable.

    c.   Purchased $350 of office supplies on credit.

    d.   Billed $3,000 to clients for services provided during the past month.

    e.   Paid $750 in cash for the current month's rent.

    f.   Paid $225 cash on account for office supplies purchased in transaction 3.

    g.   Received a bill for $500 for advertising for the current month.

    h.   Paid $2,300 cash for office salaries.

    i.   Paid $1,000 cash dividends to shareholders.

    j.   Received a cheque for $2,000 from a client in payment on account for amount owed in transaction d.

(SO4) 2.   The following is an alphabetical listing of accounts for Davis Corporation. Please prepare a trial balance on September 30, 2006, assuming that all accounts have their normal balance. List the accounts in their proper order.

Accounts payable	$ 4,000
Advertising expense	5,000
Cash	35,000
Common shares	20,000
Dividends	2,000
Equipment	15,000
Prepaid insurance	3,000
Rent expense	6,000
Retained earnings	30,000
Salaries expense	8,000
Service revenue	15,000
Unearned revenue	5,000

Davis Corporation
Trial Balance
September 30, 2006

(SO3)   3.   For each of the following accounts, indicate whether the account is an Asset, Liability, or Shareholders' Equity account and whether the account normally possesses a debit (DR) or credit (CR) balance.

	Type of Account: Asset, Liability, or Shareholders' Equity	Normal Balance: Debit or Credit
a. Cash		
b. Accounts payable		
c. Unearned revenue		
d. Land		
e. Service revenue		
f. Accounts receivable		
g. Rent expense		
h. Common shares		
i. Loan payable		
j. Dividends		
k. Prepaid rent		
l. Notes payable		

4.   Please refer to the Domtar and Cascades financial statements at the end of this workbook for information for answering the following questions. Do not forget to use the **Decision Toolkit** approach for help in the problem solving.

(SO2)   a.   Did the companies pay dividends in 2004? What were the amounts for each company, and where do you find this information?   (SO2)

(SO3)   b.   What were the total assets, liabilities, and shareholders' equity for Domtar in 2004?   (SO3)

Solutions to Self-Test

Multiple Choice

1. d   Cash (an asset) increases, and Unearned Revenue (a liability) increases.
2. b   Cash (an asset) increases, and Equity increases because one of its components, Revenue, increases.
3. a   Cash (an asset) increases, and accounts receivable (an asset) decreases; therefore, total assets remain the same.
4. c   Land is an asset.
5. c   The asset is decreased, the liability is decreased, and shareholders' equity is not affected.
6. d   An example would be:

Dr Office Supplies	$1,000	
Cr Accounts payable		$400
Cr Cash		$600

7. a

8. a $600 DR – $400 CR = $200 DR

9. c   A debit increases an asset, a credit increases a liability, and a credit increases a revenue account.

10. d   A debit increases the Dividends account.

11. b

12. a   The ledger is a collection of accounts, and a T account is a form of account.

13. c   The company receives an asset (Cash is increased by the debit), and its liabilities increase (Notes Payable is increased by the credit).

14. d   Expenses increase with the debit, and cash decreases with the credit to Cash.

15. b

16. a   The journal is the book of original entry, and T accounts are simply a form of account.

17. b   The easiest place to find the information is the ledger. She could find it in the journal, but she would have to add and subtract all the entries to Cash, which would be very time-consuming.

18. c

19. a   Whatever is done to an account in the journal entry is done to that account in the ledger.

20. b

21. c   While the trial balance may give a list of all accounts (an account with a zero balance may not be listed) and certainly lists debit and credit balances, these are not the primary purpose of the document.

22. a   Two debits will cause the trial balance to be out of balance.

23. c

Problems

1.

a.	Cash	40,000	
	Common Shares		40,000
b.	Office Equipment	5,500	
	Cash		2,500
	Notes Payable		3,500
c.	Office Supplies	350	
	Accounts Payable		350
d.	Accounts Receivable	3,000	
	Decorating Revenue		3,000
e.	Rent Expense	750	
	Cash		750
f.	Accounts Payable	225	
	Cash		225

g. Advertising Expense   500
      Accounts Payable   500

h. Office Salaries Expense   2,300
      Cash   2,300

i. Dividends   1,000
      Cash   1,000

j. Cash   2,000
      Accounts Receivable   2,000

2.

Davis Corporation
Trial Balance
September 30, 2006

	Debit	Credit
Cash	$35,000	
Prepaid insurance	3,000	
Equipment	15,000	
Accounts payable		$ 4,000
Unearned revenue		5,000
Common shares		20,000
Retained earnings		30,000
Dividends	2,000	
Service revenue		15,000
Advertising expense	5,000	
Salaries expense	8,000	
Rent expense	6,000	
	$74,000	$74,000

3.

	Type of Account: Asset, Liability, or Shareholders' Equity	Normal Balance: Debit or Credit
a. Cash	Asset	Debit
b. Accounts payable	Liability	Credit
c. Unearned revenue	Liability	Credit
d. Land	Asset	Debit
e. Service revenue	Shareholders' Equity	Credit
f. Accounts receivable	Asset	Debit
g. Rent expense	Shareholders' Equity	Debit
h. Common shares	Shareholders' Equity	Credit
i. Loan payable	Liability	Credit
j. Dividends	Shareholders' Equity	Debit
k. Prepaid rent	Asset	Debit
l. Notes payable	Liability	Credit

4.
    a.   Both companies paid dividends in 2004.
         Domtar paid dividends of $54 million to its common shareholders and
         dividends of $1 million to its preferred shareholders. Cascades paid divi-
         dends of $13 million to its common shareholders. The information was
         found in the Consolidated Statement of Retained Earnings.
    b.   Total assets were $3,144; total liabilities were $2,085; and total shareholder-
         s'equity was $1,059. The total liabilities and total shareholders' equity total
         $3,144, which equals total assets.

chapter 4

Accrual Accounting Concepts

Chapter Overview

In Chapter 4, you will learn about two generally accepted accounting principles: the revenue recognition principle and the matching principle. The chapter will explain what adjusting journal entries are, why adjustments are needed, and how to prepare them. You will learn how to prepare an adjusted trial balance and closing journal entries, as well as the different steps in the accounting cycle.

Review of Specific Study Objectives

Timing Issues

- **Accounting divides the economic life of a business into artificial time periods**, such as a month, a quarter, or a year. Some business transactions affect more than one accounting period, and it is necessary to consider a transaction's impact on the affected periods.

study objective 1

Explain the revenue recognition principle and the matching principle.

- The **revenue recognition principle** states that *revenue must be recognized in the accounting period in which it is earned*. (To "recognize" means to record in a journal entry.) For a service firm, revenue is earned *at the time that the service is performed*, which may or may not be the time at which cash is received. A company may perform services for a client and receive in return the client's promise to pay the firm in the future.

- The **matching principle** states that *(efforts) expenses must be matched with (accomplishments) revenues.* This means the following: If a company performs services and, thus, earns revenue in a given accounting period, then any expenses that helped the company earn the revenue must be recorded in that same accounting period. The **critical issue** is *determining when the expense makes its contribution to revenue.* The principle is easy to state but sometimes difficult to implement.

- **Accrual basis accounting**, resulting from application of the revenue recognition and matching principles, means that *transactions that change a company's financial statements are recorded in the periods in which the events occur,* rather than in the periods in which the company receives or pays cash.

- With **cash basis accounting**, *revenue is recorded only when cash is received, and an expense is recorded only when cash is paid.* Because of its potential for violating the revenue recognition and matching principles, the *cash basis of accounting does not satisfy generally accepted accounting principles.*

study objective 2

Prepare adjusting entries for prepayments.

- **Adjusting entries** are *needed to ensure that the revenue recognition and matching principles are followed.* Before adjusting entries are recorded, some accounts may have incorrect balances because some events are not journalized daily. Some events are not journalized during the accounting period because these costs expire with the passage of time, and some items may simply be unrecorded for a variety of reasons.

- **Adjusting entries** are *required every time financial statements are prepared.* Sometimes, students will comment that adjusting entries are simply "cooking the books," but the opposite is actually true. Because of the reasons noted above, some accounts may have incorrect balances, and adjusting entries will correct them.

- There are **two broad groups of adjusting entries: prepayments and accruals. Prepayments** include *prepaid expenses* (expenses paid in cash and recorded as assets before they are used) and *unearned revenues* (cash received and recorded as liabilities before revenue is earned). **Accruals** include *accrued revenues* (revenues earned but not yet received in cash or recorded) and *accrued expenses* (expenses incurred but not yet paid in cash or recorded).

- There are **two important items** to note before we look at the specifics of adjusting entries:
  1. The *adjusting entries* that you will learn will *always involve one statement of earnings account and one balance sheet account.* Please note that this does *not* say that the statement of earnings account is always increased and the balance sheet account is always decreased, or vice versa. The usefulness of this fact lies in the following: If you prepare an adjusting entry and know that the debit to an expense (a statement of earnings account) is correct, then the credit must be to a balance sheet account.
  2. The account *Cash is never used in an adjusting entry.* If cash is involved, then the event is simply a transaction, not an adjustment to the accounts.

- **Prepaid expenses** (or prepayments) are *payments of expenses that will benefit more than one accounting period.* They are initially recorded as assets and expire either with the passage of time or through use. An adjusting entry for a prepaid expense *results in an increase (debit) to an expense account and a decrease (credit) to an asset account.* A good general rule to remember is that *as an asset is used up or consumed, its cost becomes an expense.*

- **Supplies** are one example of a prepaid expense. A company purchases $800 of supplies at the beginning of the accounting period. At the end of the period, a physical count shows that only $200 of supplies are left. Therefore, $600 of supplies were used up. The asset account Supplies still has the $800 balance and, if that number is recorded on the balance sheet, then the statement will not be telling the truth. An accountant may not record $200, the correct number, on the balance sheet if the ledger account for Supplies shows an amount of $800. So, an adjusting entry to adjust the Supplies account by $600 ($800 − $200) is required:

Supplies Expense	600	
Supplies		600
(To show supplies used)		

- After the entry is recorded and posted, the Supplies account will show the correct balance, $200 ($800 − $600), and that number will then correctly be shown on the balance sheet. **If the entry had not been made,** *expenses would have been understated, net earnings would have been overstated, and assets and shareholders' equity would have each been overstated by $600.*

- **Insurance** and **rent** are two more examples of a prepaid expense. A company pays six months' rent, $2,400, at the beginning of March and wants to prepare financial statements at the end of March. The asset account Prepaid Rent shows a balance of $2,400, but this is no longer correct because the company has used up one month's rent. The balance sheet should show Prepaid Rent of $2,000, but the amount of $2,000 should not be recorded in the adjusting entry if the ledger account for Prepaid Rent shows a balance of $2,400. Again, an adjusting entry is required in the amount of $400 ($2,400 − $2,000) to adjust the Prepaid Rent account to its correct balance:

Rent Expense	400	
Prepaid Rent		400
(To record expired rent)		

  After the entry is recorded and posted, the Prepaid Rent account will show the correct balance, $2,000 ($2,400 − $400), and that number will then correctly be shown on the balance sheet. **If the entry had not been made,** *expenses would have been low, net earnings would have been high, and assets and shareholders' equity would have been high by $400.*

- The adjusting entry for **amortization** is another example of a prepayment. Long-lived assets, such as vehicles, equipment, and buildings, are recorded at cost. Their acquisition is basically a long-term prepayment for services. As the *useful life* of those long-lived assets with limited useful lines progresses, part of the cost should be recorded as an expense. **Amortization** is the *process of allocating the cost of an asset to expense over its useful life in a rational and systematic manner.* It is important to remember that **amortization is an allocation concept, not a valuation concept**. It does not attempt to reflect the actual change in the value of the asset.

A common practice for calculating amortization expense is to divide the cost of the asset by its estimated useful life. This is known as the straight-line method of amortization. Assume that a vehicle costs $18,000 and has an estimated useful life of five years. The amortization on that vehicle is $3,600 per year, or $300 per month. The following entry records one month of amortization:

Amortization Expense	300	
Accumulated Amortization – Vehicle		300
(To record monthly amortization)		

- **Accumulated Amortization** is a *contra asset account,* offset against, or subtracted from, the Vehicle account on the balance sheet. Its normal balance is a credit. The use of this account allows the user to see the original cost of the asset as well as the total cost that has expired to date. The balance sheet presentation of this vehicle after adjustment is:

Vehicle	$18,000
Less: Accumulated amortization - Vehicle	300
Net book value	$17,700

The $17,700 is the **net book value** or book value of the asset. *Book value is calculated by subtracting the accumulated amortization from the cost of the asset.*

As was true with Supplies and Prepaid Rent, **failure to record this adjusting entry** for amortization would have meant that *expenses would have been understated, net earnings would have been overstated, and assets and shareholders' equity would have each been overstated by $300.*

- **Unearned revenues** occur when *cash is received before revenue is earned.* Magazine subscriptions and rent are two examples. Unearned revenues are the *opposite of prepaid expenses*—an unearned revenue on one company's books is a prepaid expense on another company's books. If my company pays your company $6,000 toward six months' rent in advance, then my company will have Prepaid Rent of $6,000, while your company will have Unearned Rent of $6,000. After one month has elapsed, your company must write the following adjusting entry to show that it has earned one month's rent revenue, or $1,000 ($6,000 ÷ 6):

Unearned Rent	1,000	
Rent Revenue		1,000
(To record revenue earned)		

Please note that the entry involves a *decrease (debit) to the liability account and an increase (credit) to the revenue account.* **If the entry is not recorded**, then *revenues, net earnings, and shareholders' equity will be understated by $1,000, while liabilities will be overstated by $1,000.* Most liabilities are discharged by the payment of money. Note that **an unearned revenue, a liability, is discharged by the performance of a service.**

- Adjusting entries for **accruals** are required in order to *record revenues earned and expenses incurred in the current accounting period that have not been recognized through daily entries and, thus, are not yet reflected in the accounts.* Accruals occur in the form of **accrued revenues** and **accrued expenses**.

study objective 3

Prepare adjusting entries for accruals.

- The adjusting entry for accruals will **increase both the balance sheet and the statement of earnings account.**

- **Accrued revenues** are *revenues earned but not yet received in cash or recorded on the financial statement's date.* Examples are interest, rent, and services. They may accrue with the passage of time or may result from services performed, but they may be neither billed nor collected. The adjusting entry for an accrued revenue will always involve an **increase in a receivable (debit) and an increase in a revenue (credit).** A company has earned $300 in interest revenue but has not been paid that amount in cash. If financial statements are to be prepared, then an adjusting entry to recognize that revenue is required:

Interest Receivable	300	
Interest Revenue		300
(To record interest revenue)		

If this entry is not made, then *assets and shareholders' equity on the balance sheet, as well as revenues and net earnings on the statement of earnings, will be understated.* When the company receives that interest in cash, it will record a debit to Cash and a credit to Interest Receivable, not to Interest Revenue.

- **Accrued expenses** are *expenses incurred but not yet paid or recorded on the statement date.* Examples include interest, rent, taxes, and salaries. The company, which owes the $300 of interest in the above example has an accrued expense of $300. The adjusting entry for an accrued expense will always involve **an increase (debit) to an expense account and an increase (credit) to a liability account.**

Assume that a company borrows $12,000 at 6 percent interest for six months on November 1. The principal and all the interest are due on May 1. If financial statements are prepared on December 31, then the company must journalize an adjusting entry for the interest owed but not yet paid. *Interest is calculated by multiplying the face value of the note by the rate by the time.* In our example, $12,000 x .06 x 2/12, or $120, the entry is:

Interest Expense	120	
Interest Payable		120
(To record accrued interest)		

- It is **important to note** that the *account Notes Payable is not used in the entry.* Notes Payable was credited when the money was borrowed and will be debited when the note principal of $12,000 is repaid. **If this adjusting entry is not made**, then *liabilities and interest expense will be understated, and net earnings and shareholders' equity will be overstated.*

Regarding **accrued income taxes**, for accounting purposes, corporate income taxes must be accrued on the basis of the current period's earnings. Corporations pay corporate income taxes in monthly instalments. The payment is based on the income tax that was actually payable in the prior year. If there was no prior year or if there was no tax payable in the prior year, then no income tax instalments are required. However, the tax liability must still be accrued if there are earnings in the current year. In that case, an adjusting entry would be required to record the estimate of corporate taxes owed on the earnings as follows (assume that the amount is $500):

Income Tax Expense	500	
Income Tax Payable		500
(To record income tax expense)		

study objective 4

Describe the nature and purpose of the adjusted trial balance.

- A **trial balance is prepared after many journal entries have been journalized and posted**. Just as a trial balance was prepared after journalizing and posting regular transactions, so is an **adjusted trial balance** prepared after adjusting entries have been journalized and posted. The *purpose of an adjusted trial balance is to prove the equality of debits and credits in the general ledger.*

- Since all account balances have been brought up to date, the *adjusted trial balance can be used in the preparation of financial statements*. The **statement of earnings** is prepared from the revenue and expense accounts. The **statement of retained earnings** is derived from the retained earnings account, the dividends account, and the net earnings (or net loss) shown on the statement of earnings. The **balance sheet** is then prepared from the asset and liability accounts and the ending retained earnings as reported in the statement of retained earnings.

- **Temporary accounts** relate to only a given accounting period and *include revenues, expenses, and dividends*. **Permanent accounts** have balances that carry forward into future accounting periods and include *assets, liabilities, and shareholders' equity*—the balance sheet accounts.

- At the end of the accounting period, **temporary account balances are closed, or zeroed out**. Their balances are transferred to the permanent shareholders' equity account, Retained Earnings. **Closing entries** *transfer net earnings or net loss and dividends to Retained Earnings.* Revenues and expenses are closed to another temporary account, Income Summary, and the resulting net earnings or net loss are then transferred to Retained Earnings.

- **Closing entries accomplish two things.** They *update the retained earnings account, and they zero out the balance in the temporary accounts,* making them ready to accumulate data in the next accounting period.

- **After closing entries have been journalized and posted, a post-closing trial balance is prepared.** Once again, the purpose is to prove the equality of debits and credits in the ledger. It also helps show all temporary accounts have been closed. If, for example, the accountant prepares a post-closing trial balance and finds a balance of $5,000 in Salaries Expense, then she will know that a temporary account was improperly excluded when closing entries were prepared. *Only permanent accounts should appear on the post-closing trial balance.*

- The following are the steps in the **accounting cycle**:
  1. Analyze business transactions.
  2. Journalize the transactions.
  3. Post to general ledger accounts.

4. Prepare a trial balance.
5. Journalize and post adjusting entries.
6. Prepare an adjusted trial balance.
7. Prepare financial statements.
8. Journalize and post closing entries.
9. Prepare a post-closing trial balance.

● These steps are repeated in each accounting period.

Chapter Self-Test

As you work through the exercises and problems, remember to use the **Decision Toolkit** discussed and used in the text:
1. *Decision Checkpoints:* At this point, you ask a question.
2. *Info Needed for Decision:* You make a choice regarding the information needed to answer the question.
3. *Tool to Use for Decision:* At this point, you review just what the information chosen in step 2 does for the decision-making process.
4. *How to Evaluate Results:* You conduct an evaluation of information for answering the question.

Note: The notation (SO1) means that the question was drawn from study objective number one.

Multiple Choice

Please circle the correct answer.

(SO1)

1. The generally accepted accounting principle that dictates that revenue be recognized in the accounting period in which it is earned is the:
   a. time period principle.
   b. matching principle.
   c. revenue recognition principle.
   d. accrued revenues principle.

(SO1)

2. In 2006, the Abbott Corporation performs work for a customer and bills the customer $10,000; it also pays expenses of $3,000. The customer pays Abbott in 2007. If Abbott uses the cash basis of accounting, then Abbott will report:
   a. revenue of $10,000 in 2006.
   b. revenue of $10,000 in 2007.
   c. expenses of $3,000 in 2007.
   d. net earnings of $7,000 in 2006.

(SO1)

3. In 2006, the Abbott Corporation performs work for a customer and bills the customer $10,000; it also pays expenses of $3,000. The customer pays Abbott in 2007. If Abbott uses the accrual basis of accounting, then Abbott will report:
   a. revenue of $10,000 in 2006.
   b. revenue of $10,000 in 2007.

    c.   expenses of $3,000 in 2007.

    d.   net earnings of $7,000 in 2007.

(SO1)   4.   Adjusting journal entries must be prepared:

    a.   at the end of every calendar year.

    b.   at the end of every month.

    c.   when the accountant has time to write them.

    d.   whenever financial statements are to be prepared.

(SO1)   5.   The generally accepted accounting principle that dictates that efforts be matched with accomplishments is the:

    a.   accrued expenses principle.

    b.   matching principle.

    c.   revenue recognition principle.

    d.   time period principle.

(SO2)   6.   A company has the following results for the year ended December 31, 2006:

Revenues	$160,000
Amortization Expense	50,000
Rent Expense	10,000
Wages Expense	25,000
Advertising Expense	30,000
Dividends	10,000
Utilities Expense	15,000

The corporate income tax rate is 40 percent, and no instalment payments were made during 2006. The corporate income taxes for 2006 will be paid on March 31, 2007. What adjusting entry, if any, is required on December 31, 2006, with respect to corporate income tax?

a.	Income Tax Expense	8,000	
	Income Tax Payable		8,000
b.	Income Tax Expense	12,000	
	Income Tax Payable		12,000
c.	Income Tax Payable	8,000	
	Income Tax Expense		8,000
d.	No entry is required.		

(SO2)   7.   Cash received and recorded as a liability before revenue is earned is called:

    a.   an accrued revenue.

    b.   an unearned revenue.

    c.   an unrecorded revenue.

    d.   none of the above is correct.

(SO2)   8.   On October 1, a company paid $6,000 for a one-year insurance policy, debiting Prepaid Insurance and crediting Cash. The adjusting entry on December 31 will require a:

    a.   debit to Insurance Expense for $1,500.

    b.   debit to Insurance Expense for $4,500.

c.   credit to Prepaid Insurance for $4,500.

d.   credit to Cash for $1,500.

9. At the beginning of an accounting period, a company purchased $800 of sup-   (SO2)
plies, debiting Supplies and crediting Cash. At the end of the accounting period,
a physical count of supplies showed that only $100 of supplies were still on
hand. The adjusting entry will require a:

   a.   credit to Supplies Expense for $700.

   b.   debit to Supplies Expense for $100.

   c.   debit to Supplies for $700.

   d.   credit to Supplies for $700.

10. Little Corporation received $5,000 from a customer for whom it is to perform   (SO2)
work in the future, debiting Cash and crediting Unearned Revenue. At the end
of the accounting period, Little has earned $2,000 of the revenue. The adjusting
entry will require a:

   a.   debit to Cash for $2,000.

   b.   debit to Service Revenue for $2,000.

   c.   credit to Service Revenue for $2,000.

   d.   credit to Service Revenue for $3,000.

11. At the end of its accounting period, Pooky Corporation has not billed a cus-   (SO3)
tomer for $400 rent. The adjusting entry will require a:

   a.   debit to Cash for $400.

   b.   credit to Accounts Receivable for $400.

   c.   credit to Unearned Revenue for $400.

   d.   credit to Rent Revenue for $400.

12. If the adjusting entry for an accrued expense is not written, then: (SO3)

   a.   liabilities and interest expense will be understated.

   b.   liabilities and interest expense will be overstated.

   c.   net earnings will be understated.

   d.   liabilities and shareholders' equity will be overstated.

13. Buddy Corporation pays its employees $1,000 per five-day week. The last day of   (SO3)
the month falls on a Thursday, and financial statements will be prepared that
day. The adjusting entry for salaries will require a:

   a.   debit to Salaries Payable for $200.

   b.   credit to Salaries Expense for $200.

   c.   debit to Salaries Expense for $200.

   d.   debit to Salaries Expense for $800.

14. Failure to prepare an adjusting entry at the end of the period to record an   (SO3)
accrued expense would cause:

   a.   net earnings to be understated.

   b.   an overstatement of assets and an overstatement of liabilities.

   c.   an understatement of expenses and an understatement of liabilities.

   d.   an overstatement of expenses and an overstatement of liabilities.

(SO3)   15. Failure to prepare an adjusting entry at the end of a period to record an accrued revenue would cause:
- a.   net earnings to be overstated.
- b.   an understatement of assets and an understatement of revenues.
- c.   an understatement of revenues and an understatement of liabilities.
- d.   an understatement of revenues and an overstatement of liabilities

(SO4)   16. Which of the statements below is not true?
- a.   An adjusted trial balance should show ledger account balances.
- b.   An adjusted trial balance can be used to prepare financial statements.
- c.   An adjusted trial balance proves the mathematical equality of debits and credits in the ledger.
- d.   An adjusted trial balance is prepared before all transactions have been journalized.

(SO4)   17. Financial statements can be prepared directly from the:
- a.   trial balance.
- b.   adjusted trial balance.
- c.   post-closing trial balance.
- d.   reversing trial balance.

(SO4)   18. Which of the following is a temporary account?
- a.   The dividends account
- b.   An asset account
- c.   A liability account
- d.   A shareholders' equity account

(SO4)   19. Which of the following is true?
- a.   Only permanent accounts are closed.
- b.   Both permanent and temporary accounts are closed.
- c.   Neither permanent nor temporary accounts are closed.
- d.   Only temporary accounts are closed.

(SO4)   20. Which of the following correctly describes the closing process?
- a.   Net earnings or net loss is transferred to the Cash account.
- b.   Net earnings or net loss is transferred to Retained Earnings.
- c.   Permanent accounts become ready to accumulate data in the next accounting period.
- d.   Each revenue and each expense account is closed individually to Retained Earnings.

(SO4)   21. Which is the correct order of steps in the accounting cycle?
- a.   Post transactions, journalize transactions, prepare a trial balance, prepare financial statements.
- b.   Journalize and post transactions, journalize and post closing entries, journalize and post adjusting entries.
- c.   Journalize and post transactions, journalize and post adjusting entries, journalize and post closing entries.
- d.   Prepare financial statements, prepare adjusting entries, prepare closing entries, prepare a post-closing trial balance.

Problems

1.   (SO2, 3)

a.   Prepare adjusting entries for the following situations for Cassie Corporation, as
        of June 30:

    i   The Supplies account shows a balance of $1,500, but a physical count on
                June 30 shows only $300 worth of supplies.

    ii   The corporation purchased a one-year insurance policy for $3,600 on May
                1, debiting Prepaid Insurance.

    iii   On June 1, the corporation received $1,200 from another corporation,
                which is renting a small building from Cassie for six months. Cassie credit-
                ed Unearned Rent Revenue.

    iv   Cassie's accountant discovered that Cassie had performed services for a
                client totalling $900 but has not yet billed the client or recorded the trans-
                action.

    v   Cassie pays employees $2,000 per five-day work week, and June 30 falls on
                a Wednesday.

    vi   The corporation owns a van that cost $18,000 and has a useful life of six
                years. The corporation purchased the van in early April this year.

b.   What type of an account is the account that you credited in (vi) above? Please
        show the balance sheet presentation for the van after you have recorded the
        amortization entry.

Date		Debit	Credit

(SO2, 3)   2.   The Upshaw Park Corporation prepares monthly financial statements. Presented below is a statement of earnings for the month of June:

Upshaw Park Corporation
Statement of Earnings
Month Ended June 30

Revenues		
Admission revenues		$30,000
Expenses		
Salary expense	$4,000	
Advertising expense	700	
Insurance expense	4,200	
Amortization expense	2,200	
Total expenses		11,100
Earnings before income tax		18,900
Income tax expense		0
Net earnings		$18,900

Additional Data: When the statement of earnings was prepared, the company accountant neglected to take into consideration the following information:

a.   An electricity bill for $1,500 was received on the last day of the month for electricity used in the month of June.

b.   An advance payment of $1,000 was received in June for a park rental space to be used in July. That amount was included in the admission revenues for June.

c.   Supplies on hand at the beginning of the month were $2,000. The corporation purchased additional supplies during the month for $1,500 in cash and $1,100 of supplies were on hand at June 30.

d.   The corporation purchased a new truck, with an estimated useful life of eight years, at the beginning of the month for $38,400 cash. That amount was not included in the amortization expense for June.

e.   Salaries owed to employees at the end of the month total $4,400. The salaries will be paid on July 3.

f.   Income tax expense not yet paid is estimated to be at the rate of 40 percent of net earnings before income taxes.

Prepare a corrected statement of earnings.

(SO2, 3)   3.   Please refer to the Domtar and Cascades financial statements at the end of this workbook for information for answering the following questions. Do not forget to use the **Decision Toolkit** approach for help in the problem solving.

a.   Using Domtar's consolidated balance sheet, identify items that may result in adjusting entries for prepayments.

b.   Using Cascades' consolidated statements of earnings and consolidated balance sheets, identify accounts that may be involved in adjusting entries for accruals.

Multiple Choice

1. c   The time period assumption says that the economic life of a business can be divided into artificial time periods, the matching principle dictates that expenses be matched with revenues, and the accrued revenues principle is a nonexistent principle.

2. b   Revenue cannot be reported in 2006 because Abbott did not receive cash. It paid the expenses in 2006 and must report them in that year. Since it recorded no revenue in 2006, it had a net loss of $3,000 (the expenses it paid) in 2006.

3. a   It reports revenue in the year when the work is performed (2006, not 2007). Expenses are reported in 2006, when incurred, and net earnings of $7,000 is reported in 2006, not 2007.

4. d

5. b   "Accrued expenses principle" is a nonexistent term. The revenue recognition principle states that revenue must be recognized when it is earned, and the time period assumption says that the economic life of a business can be divided into artificial time periods.

6. b   Earnings before income taxes = $30,000. So, income tax expense = $30,000 x 40% = 12,000. Remember that Dividends is not an expense and, therefore, does not enter into the calculation of earnings before (or after) income taxes.

7. b   An accrued revenue arises when money is owed to a company, not when it owes money. "Unrecorded revenue" is an accounting term, but it is not appropriate in this instance.

8. a   The journal entry is:

Insurance Expense	1,500	
Prepaid Insurance		1,500

9. d   The journal entry is:

Supplies Expense	700	
Supplies		700

10. c   The journal entry is:

Unearned Revenue	2,000	
Service Revenue		2,000

11. d   The journal entry is:

Accounts Receivable	400	
Rent Revenue		400

12. a   The journal entry debits an expense and credits a liability, thereby increasing both accounts. If an expense is not recorded, then net earnings will be overstated (as will shareholders' equity) and, if a liability is not recorded, then liabilities will be understated.

13. d   The journal entry is:

Salaries Expense	800	
Salaries Payable		800

14. c

15. b

16. d   The adjusted trial balance is prepared after all adjusting entries have been journalized and posted. It shows the balance of all accounts at the end of the accounting period. The purpose of the adjusted trial balance is to

prove the equality of total debits and total credits of the accounts in the general ledger after adjustments have been made.

17. b   The trial balance does not have the adjustments updates, the post-closing trial balance has no temporary accounts, and there is no such thing as a reversing trial balance.

18. a   The other three types of accounts are all permanent accounts.

19. d   Permanent accounts are not closed.

20. b   Net earnings and loss are not transferred to the Cash account, permanent accounts are not closed, and revenue and expense accounts are closed first to Income Summary (which is itself closed to Retained Earnings).

21. c

Problems

1. a.

i.	Supplies Expense	1,200	
	Supplies		1,200
	(To record supplies used)		
ii.	Insurance Expense	600	
	Prepaid Insurance		600
	(To record insurance expired)		
	$3,600 ÷ 12 months = $300 per month x 2 months		
iii.	Unearned Rent Revenue	200	
	Rent Revenue		200
	(To record rent earned)		
	$1,200 ÷ 6 months = $200 per month		
iv.	Accounts Receivable	900	
	Service Revenue		900
	(To record revenue earned)		
v.	Salaries Expense	1,200	
	Salaries Payable		1,200
	(To record accrued salaries)		
	$2,000 ÷ 5 days = $400 per day x 3 days		
vi.	Amortization Expense		750
	Accumulated Amortization—Van	750	
	(To record amortization)		
	$18,000 ÷ 6 years = $3,000 per year x 3/12		

b. Accumulated Amortization is a contra asset account, which is offset against, or subtracted from, the asset account. The advantage of this presentation is that the user sees both the original cost of the asset and the total cost that has expired to date.

Van	$18,000
Less: Accumulated amortization Van	750
Net book value	$17,250

The $17,250 is the book value of the asset and has no relationship to the fair market value (what a willing buyer would pay a willing seller) of the asset. Remember that amortization is an allocation concept, not a valuation concept.

2.

Upshaw Park Corporation
Statement of Earnings
Month Ended June 30

Revenues		
Admission revenues ($30,000 − $1,000)		$29,000
Expenses		
Salary expense ($4,000 + $4,400)	$8,400	
Advertising expense	700	
Insurance expense	4,200	
Amortization expense ($2,200 + $400)	2,600	
Electricity expense ($0 + $1,500)	1,500	
Supplies expense ($0 + $2,400)	2,400	
Total expenses		19,800
Earnings before income tax		9,200
Income tax expense ($9,200 x 40%)		3,680
Net earnings	$5,520	

(*Note*: Amortization on new truck is $38,400 ÷ 8 years=$4,800 ÷ 12 months = $400)

3. a. Examples of prepayments found on Domtar's balance sheet would include prepaid expenses and property, plant, and equipment. Expenses such as insurance expense and property tax expense, likely included in the selling, general, and administrative expense category shown on the statement of earnings, would result in an adjusting entry for their prepaid portions. Amortization expense, related to the long-term prepayment for property, plant, and equipment, is reported on the earnings statement.

b. Examples of accruals found on Cascades' balance sheet include accounts receivable and accounts payable and accrued liabilities. Accounts receivable would be used to record sales invoices for sales made but not yet collected. Accounts payable and accrued liabilities would include accruals for some of the selling and administrative expenses, such as salaries and utilities. In addition, some of the interest expense reported on the statement of earnings would likely have resulted from accruing the interest incurred on the long-term debt reported on the balance sheet.

chapter 5

Merchandising Operations

Chapter Overview

Chapter 5 discusses the differences between service companies and merchandising companies. You will learn about the two types of inventory systems used by merchandisers and how to record purchases and sales of inventory using the perpetual inventory system. You will take a close look at a merchandising company's financial statements, particularly the statement of earnings, and at factors affecting a firm's profitability.

Review of Specific Study Objectives

- The **primary source** of revenue for a merchandising company is the *sale of merchandise*, called sales revenue. **Expenses** are divided into **two categories**: *cost of goods sold* (the total cost of merchandise sold during the period) and *operating expenses.* Net earnings is determined as follows:

	Sales revenue
−	Cost of goods sold
=	Gross profit
−	Operating expenses
	Earnings before income tax
−	Income tax expense
=	Net earnings (loss)

- The **operating cycle of a merchandising company** is *longer than that of a service company* because of the purchase and sale of merchandise inventory.

- There are **two systems of inventory** available to a merchandising company: the *perpetual inventory system* and the *periodic inventory system*.

- With a **perpetual system**, *detailed records of the cost of each inventory purchase and sale are maintained*. These records show at all times the inventory that should be on hand for every item. *Cost of goods sold is determined each time a sale occurs*. The use of calculator systems, bar codes, and optical scanners makes such a system practicable.

- With a **periodic system**, *detailed records are not kept throughout the period. Cost of goods sold is determined only at the end of the accounting period* when a physical count of goods is taken. The calculation is as follows:

	Beginning inventory
+	Cost of goods purchased
=	Cost of goods available for sale
–	Ending inventory
=	Cost of goods sold

- A **perpetual system** provides *better inventory control*. Goods can be counted at any time to see whether they exist, and shortages can be investigated immediately. The quantity of inventory can be managed so that neither too much, nor too little, is on hand at a given time.

study objective 2

Explain the recording of purchases under a perpetual inventory system.

- **Purchases**, either for cash or on account (credit), are normally *recorded when the goods are received from the seller*. A business document (a cancelled cheque or a cash register receipt for a cash purchase, or a purchase invoice for a credit purchase) will provide written evidence of the purchase.

- A **purchase is recorded by a debit to Merchandise Inventory and a credit to Cash or Accounts Payable.** *The Merchandise Inventory account is used for purchases of goods that will be resold only.* If the company buys another type of asset (such as equipment), then the debit will be to the individual asset account (e.g., Equipment).

- The sales/purchase invoice should indicate whether the seller or buyer must pay the cost of transporting the goods to the buyer's place of business. Freight terms generally say who pays the freight and who is responsible for the risk of damage to the merchandise during transit. Terms are often expresses as **FOB shipping point** or **FOB destination**. FOB means "free on board.".

- **FOB shipping point** means that the goods are delivered to the point of shipping (normally the seller's place of business) by the seller. The buyer pays the freight costs to get the goods from the point of shipping to the destination (normally the buyer's place of business.) In this situation, the shipping is considered to be *part of the cost of purchasing the inventory*. **The cost of the shipping is recorded by a debit to Merchandise Inventory and a credit to Cash or Accounts Payable.**

- **FOB destination** means that the goods are delivered by the seller to their destination. The seller pays the freight to get the goods to their destination.

- **Purchased goods might be unsuitable** because they are damaged or defective, are of inferior quality, or do not meet the purchaser's specifications. *A purchase return* occurs when goods are returned to the seller. A purchase allowance occurs when the purchaser keeps the merchandise but is granted an allowance (deduction) by the seller. **A purchase return or allowance is recorded by debiting Cash or Accounts Payable and crediting Merchandise Inventory.**

- The terms of a purchase may include a **quantity discount** for a bulk purchase. Quantity discounts are not recorded or accounted for separately. The net amount of the invoice is simply recorded as the purchase cost. On the other hand, a purchase **discount** may be offered to the buyer of merchandise to induce early payment for the goods. Purchase discounts are noted on the invoice through *credit terms*. For example, credit terms of 1/10, n/30 means that the purchaser will receive a one percent cash discount on the invoice price (net of any purchase returns or allowances) if the invoice is paid within 10 days; otherwise, the net amount is due in 30 days. Assume that on May 1, a buyer purchased $5,000 of merchandise on account with terms of 2/10, n/30. If the invoice is paid by May 11, then the following entry is required:

Accounts Payable	5,000	
Cash		4,900
Merchandise Inventory		100
(To record payment within the discount period)		

  If the buyer pays after May 11, then the entry will be:

Accounts Payable	5,000	
Cash		5,000
(To record payment – no discount)		

- It is usually very advantageous **for the buyer to take all cash discounts**. Passing up a 2/10, n/30 discount is the equivalent of paying an annual interest rate of 36.5 percent (2% x 365 ÷ 20)! Some companies even borrow money at 8 to 12 percent to take the discount because that is cheaper than paying 36.5 percent.

- **Sales revenues are recorded when earned**, in accordance with the revenue recognition principle. As is true for purchases, sales may be for cash or on account (credit) and should be supported by a business document (a cash register tape for cash sales and a sales invoice for credit sales).

- **Two entries are made for each sale** in the perpetual inventory system. One records the sale, the other records the *cost of merchandise sold*. If goods costing $200 are sold for cash of $400, then the following entries are required:

Cash	400	
Sales		400
(To record a cash sale)		

Cost of Goods Sold	200	
Merchandise Inventory		200
(To record the cost of merchandise sold)		

study objective 3

Explain the recording of sales under a perpetual inventory system.

If the goods had been sold on account, then the only thing that would have changed in either entry is that the debit in the first entry would have been to Accounts Receivable instead of Cash.

- The **Sales account is used only for sales of merchandise inventory**. If an asset is sold, then the credit is to the asset account. *A company may choose to have several Sales accounts*, each one dedicated to a type of product. This *helps to give management information needed to manage its inventory*. Such a company will report only one Sales figure on the statement of earnings. To report many sales accounts would lengthen the statement of earnings and perhaps give too much detail on operating results to competitors. There are many users of a company's financial statements, and one such group of users is a company's competition.

- As discussed earlier, **freight** terms on the sales invoice—FOB destination or FOB shipping point—indicate who is responsible for shipping costs. If the term is FOB destination, the seller assumes responsibility for getting the goods to their destination. Freight costs incurred by the seller on the outgoing merchandise are an *operating expense*. These costs are debited to *Freight Out or Delivery Expense* and a credited to *Cash or Accounts Payable*.

- If **sold goods are returned to the company**, then *two entries are required*. Assume that the goods sold above are all returned in good working order to the company. The required entries are:

Sales Returns and Allowances	400	
Cash		400
(To record return of goods)		
Merchandise Inventory	200	
Cost of Goods Sold		200
(To record cost of goods returned		

- **Sales Returns and Allowances** is a *contra revenue account* to Sales. If the debit had been to Sales, then the return would have been buried in that account. Management needs to monitor the amount of returned goods so that it may correct an unsatisfactory situation. The goods the company is selling may be of poor quality or defective, and management will have to deal with the supplier of the goods. If the company itself is making mistakes in delivery or shipment of goods, then management will have to deal with this internal problem.

- Like a purchase discount, **the seller may offer the buyer a cash discount to induce early payment of the balance due**. Using the previous example, on May 1, a buyer purchased $5,000 of merchandise on account with terms of 2/10, n/30. If the buyer pays by May 11, then the selling company records the following entry:

Cash	4,900	
Sales Discounts	100	
Accounts Receivable		5,000
(To record collection within the discount period)		

If the buyer pays after May 11, then the entry is:

Cash   5,000
    Accounts Receivable   5,000
(To record collection - no discount allowed)

Sales Discounts is another *contra revenue account* to Sales.

- The following provides a summary of the revenue and contra revenue accounts used in merchandising companies:

Account Name	Account Type	Normal Balance
Sales	Revenue	Credit
Sales Returns and Allowances	Contra Revenue	Debit
Sales Discounts	Contra Revenue	Debit

- A **single-step statement of earnings** works in the following way: *all revenues are totalled, all expenses are totalled*, and *expenses are then subtracted from revenues* to determine earnings or net loss before income tax. (The subtraction gives the name "single-step" to this statement of earnings.) Income tax expense is normally separated and shown separately, making it a modified single-step statement of earnings. This form is simple and easy to read and understand.

study objective 4

Distinguish between a single-step and a multiple-step statement of earnings.

- A **multiple-step statement of earnings** breaks net earnings (or loss) into several components that financial statement users find useful.

1. *Gross sales revenues are shown.* **Any sales returns and allowances and sales discounts are deducted from gross sales**; the resulting *difference is called net sales.*

2. *Net sales, less cost of goods sold*, yields **gross profit or gross margin**. This is merchandising profit, the difference between what the company paid for its inventory and what it received when it sold the inventory. Gross profit should be large enough to cover operating expenses and leave something for net earnings.

3. *Gross profit, less operating expenses*, yields **earnings from operations**. Sometimes, operating expenses are subdivided into selling expenses (associated with making sales) and administrative expenses (related to the general operation of the company). The former include advertising expense and shipping expense, and the latter include such expenses such as those related to human resources management and accounting.

4. Non-operating activities consist of other revenues and expenses that are unrelated to the company's main operations. These items are presented in the statement of earnings right after "earnings from operations."

5. *Earnings from operations, less non-operating activities*, yields **net earnings (or loss)** before income tax. Non-operating activities are revenues, expenses, gains, and losses unrelated to a company's main operations. Examples include interest revenue, dividend revenue, interest expense, and gains or losses on the sale of machinery.

- **Earnings from operating activities** are considered *sustainable and long-term*, while those from **non-operating activities** are considered *non-recurring and short-term*. It is obviously important for a company to derive the bulk of its income from its main line of operations and not from peripheral activities, such as the sale of factories and equipment.

To recap, if there are no non-operating activities:

Sales revenue
– Cost of goods sold
= Gross profit
– Operating expenses
= Earnings before income tax
– Income tax expense
= Net earnings (loss)

If there are non-operating activities, then the statement appears as follows:

Sales revenue
– Cost of goods sold
= Gross profit
– Operating expenses
= Earnings from operations
+ Other revenues
– Other expenses
Earnings before income tax
– Income tax expense
= Net earnings (loss)

study objective 5
Calculate the gross profit margin and profit margin.

- A **company's gross profit may be expressed as a percentage**: The *gross profit margin is calculated by dividing gross profit by net sales.* The gross profit margin is closely monitored. A decline in the margin may result from selling items with lower markup, from having to lower selling prices due to increased competition, or from having to pay higher prices for merchandise without being able to pass those higher costs on to customers.

- The **profit margin** *measures the percentage of each dollar of sales that results in net earnings.* It is calculated by dividing *net earnings by net sales* for the period. High High-volume stores usually have low profit margins, while low low-volume stores have high profit margins.

study objective 6
Explain the recording of purchases and sales under a periodic inventory system (Appendix 5A).

- A **periodic inventory system differs from a perpetual inventory system in various ways**, one of which is the time at which cost of goods sold is calculated. With a **periodic system**, *cost of goods sold is calculated only at the end of an accounting period,* while with a **perpetual system**, *cost of goods sold is calculated each time inventory is sold.*

- With a **periodic system**, *a physical count of inventory is taken at the end of the accounting* period to determine the cost of merchandise on hand. This figure is then used to calculate the cost of goods sold during the period. **Purchases of inventory are recorded in a Purchases account**, not in Merchandise Inventory, and there are *separate accounts for purchase returns and allowances, purchase discounts, and freight costs on purchases.*

- Consider the following data. On April 4, Orion Corporation purchased $5,000 of inventory on account with credit terms of 2/10, n/30. It paid shipping costs of $200 on April 5 and, on April 7, it returned $500 of merchandise. It paid the amount due on April 13. The journal entries for these transactions are as follows:

April	4	Purchases	5,000	
		Accounts Payable		5,000
	5	Freight In	200	
		Cash		200
	7	Accounts Payable	500	
		Purchase Returns and Allowances		500
	13	Accounts Payable	4,500	
		Purchase Discounts		90
		Cash		4,410

Please note the following:

a. **Purchases** is a *temporary expense account* with a *normal debit balance* that is reported on the statement of earnings.
b. **Purchase Returns and Allowances and Purchase Discounts** are *temporary accounts with a normal credit balance.*
c. Discounts do not apply to freight in charges. **Freight in is part of the cost of goods purchased** and is a temporary account with a normal debit balance.

- **Sales of merchandise are recorded in the same way as they are recorded in a perpetual system.** Sales has a normal credit balance, while the contra revenue accounts, —Sales Returns and Allowances and Sales Discounts, —have normal debit balances.   (SO1)

- Under a periodic inventory system, the cost of goods sold is **calculated**. The following provides an example of the calculation:

Cost of goods sold:			
Inventory, January 1			$30,000
Purchases		$90,000	
Less: Purchase returns and allowances	$15,000		
Purchase discounts	5,000	20,000	
Net purchases		70,000	
Add: Freight in		10,000	
Cost of goods purchased			80,000
Cost of goods available for sale			110,000
Inventory, December 31			70,000
Cost of goods sold			$40,000

Chapter Self-Test

As you work through the exercises and problems, remember to use the **Decision Toolkit** discussed and used in the text:

1. *Decision Checkpoints*: At this point, you ask a question.
2. *Info Needed for Decision*: You make a choice regarding the information needed to answer the question.
3. *Tool to Use for Decision*: At this point, you review just what the information chosen in step two does for the decision-making process.
4. *How to Evaluate Results*: You conduct an evaluation of information for answering the question.

Note: The notation (SO1) means that the question was drawn from study objective number one. All questions marked with an asterisk (*) relate to material in Appendix 5A.

Multiple Choice

Please circle the correct answer.

(SO1)   1. The operating cycle of a merchandising company is ordinarily
_____ that of a service firm.
    a.   the same as
    b.   shorter than
    c.   longer than
    d.   four times as long as

(SO1)   2. Which of the following statements is correct?
    a.   A periodic inventory system gives better control over inventories than does a perpetual inventory system does.
    b.   A perpetual inventory system gives better control over inventories than does a periodic inventory system does.
    c.   A periodic inventory system calculates cost of goods sold each time a sale occurs.
    d.   A perpetual inventory system calculates cost of goods sold only at the end of the accounting period.

(SO2)   3. Poobah Corporation, which uses a perpetual inventory system, purchased $3,000 of merchandise on account on June 4. What entry is required on June 8, when it returned $500 of the merchandise to the seller?

a.	Accounts Payable	500	
	Merchandise Inventory		500
b.	Merchandise Inventory	500	
	Accounts Payable		500
c.	Accounts Payable	500	
	Purchases Returns		500
d.	Cash	500	
	Merchandise Inventory		500

4. Cassie Corporation, which uses a perpetual inventory system, purchased $2,000   (SO2)
   of merchandise on account on July 5. Credit terms were 2/10, n/30. It returned
   $400 of the merchandise on July 9. When the company pays its bill on July 11,
   the journal entry will require a:
   a.   debit to Accounts Payable for $2,000.
   b.   debit to Accounts Payable for $1,600.
   c.   credit to Cash for $1,600.
   d.   debit to Merchandise Inventory for $32.

5. Cosmos Corporation, which uses a perpetual inventory system, purchased   (SO2)
   $2,000 of merchandise on account on July 5. Credit terms were 2/10, n/30. It
   returned $400 of the merchandise on July 9. When the company pays its bill on
   July 21, the journal entry will require a:
   a.   debit to Accounts Payable for $2,000.
   b.   credit to Accounts Payable for $1,600.
   c.   credit to Cash for $1,600.
   d.   debit to Cash for $1,600.

6. Elizabeth Company uses a perpetual inventory system and purchased merchan-   (SO2)
   dise on November 30 for which it must pay the shipping charges. When the
   company pays the shipping charges of $200, the journal entry will require a
   debit to:
   a.   Delivery Expense for $200.
   b.   Cash for $200.
   c.   Freight in In for $200.
   d.   Merchandise Inventory for $200.

7. Which of the following statements is correct?   (SO3)
   a.   A company that uses a perpetual inventory system needs only one journal
        entry when it sells merchandise.
   b.   A company that uses a perpetual inventory system needs two journal
        entries when it sells merchandise.
   c.   A company that uses a perpetual inventory system debits Merchandise
        Inventory and credits Cost of Goods Sold when it sells merchandise.
   d.   None of the above is correct.

8. Cynthia Corporation, which uses a perpetual inventory system, received $500 of   (SO3)
   returned merchandise, which it had sold a week earlier. When it records the
   return, the journal entries will require a:
   a.   debit to Sales Returns and Allowances.
   b.   debit to Cost of Goods Sold.
   c.   debit to Accounts Receivable.
   d.   credit to Merchandise Inventory.

9. Sales Returns and Allowances and Sales Discounts are: (SO3)
   a.   revenue accounts.
   b.   expense accounts.
   c.   contra revenue accounts.
   d.   contra expense accounts.

(SO3)   10. A company that uses a perpetual inventory system sold $400 of merchandise on July 23 with credit terms of 1/10, n/30. The purchaser paid the amount due on July 30. Which journal entry will the selling company record on July 30?

a.	Cash	400	
	Accounts Receivable		400
b.	Cash	400	
	Sales Discounts		4
	Accounts Receivable		396
c.	Accounts Receivable	400	
	Sales Discounts		4
	Cash		396
d.	Cash	396	
	Sales Discounts	4	
	Accounts Receivable		400

(SO4)   11. Sales revenues are $10,000, sales returns and allowances are $500, and sales discounts are $1,000. What is the dollar amount of net sales?
   a. $11,500
   b. $10,500
   c. $10,000
   d. $8,500

(SO4)   12. Gross profit is $50,000, operating expenses are $15,000, and net sales total $75,000. What is the cost of goods sold?
   a. $10,000
   b. $25,000
   c. $35,000
   d. $80,000

(SO4)   13. Gross profit is $50,000, operating expenses are $15,000, and net sales total $75,000. What are the net earnings?
   a. $10,000
   b. $25,000
   c. $35,000
   d. $80,000

(SO4)   14. Net earnings are $15,000, operating expenses are $20,000, and net sales total $75,000. What is the gross profit?
   a. $60,000
   b. $40,000
   c. $35,000
   d. $15,000

(SO4)   15. Net earnings are $15,000, operating expenses are $20,000, and net sales total $75,000. What is the cost of goods sold?
   a. $60,000
   b. $40,000
   c. $35,000
   d. $15,000

16. Which of the following is *not* true about a multiple-step statement of earnings? (SO4)
    a. Operating expenses are often classified as selling and administrative expenses.
    b. There may be a section for non-operating activities.
    c. There may be a section for operating assets.
    d. There is a section for cost of goods sold.

17. Net earnings are $15,000, operating expenses are $20,000, and net Sales sales (SO5) total $75,000. What is the gross profit margin?
    a. 20%
    b. 27%
    c. 47%
    d. 75%

18. After gross profit is calculated, operating expenses are deducted to determine: (SO5)
    a. gross margin.
    b. net earnings.
    c. cost of goods sold.
    d. profit margin.

19. A decline in a company's gross profit could be caused by all of the following, (SO5) except
    a. selling products with a lower markup.
    b. clearance of discontinued inventory.
    c. paying lower prices to its suppliers.
    d. increased competition resulting in a lower selling price.

*20. Frank Corporation has the following account balances: (SO6)

Purchases	$28,000
Sales Returns and Allowances	4,000
Purchase Discounts	2,500
Freight in	1,875
Freight out	2,500

The cost of goods purchased for the period is:
    a. $30,500.
    b. $27,375.
    c. $29,875.
    d. $25,875.

*21. The Wales Corporation has a beginning merchandise inventory of $15,000. (SO6) During the period, purchases were $70,000; purchase returns, $2,000; and freight in $5,000. A physical count of inventory at the end of the period revealed that $10,000 was still on hand. The cost of goods available for sale was:
    a. $82,000.
    b. $78,000.
    c. $88,000.
    d. $92,000.

(SO6)   *22. The calculation of the cost of goods sold under the periodic system is:
   a. Beginning Inventory + Ending Inventory – Purchases.
   b. Beginning Inventory + Ending Inventory + Purchases.
   c. Beginning Inventory + Purchases – Ending Inventory.
   d. Ending Inventory + Purchases – Beginning Inventory.

(SO6)   *23. Under a periodic inventory system, acquisition of merchandise is debited to the:
   a. merchandise inventory account.
   b. cost of goods sold account.
   c. purchases account.
   d. accounts payable account.

Problems

(SO4)   1. From the appropriate accounts below, prepare a multiple-step statement of earnings for Buff Corporation for the year ended January 31, 2006.

Cash	$13,000
Rental revenue	5,000
Interest revenue	1,000
Utilities expense	15,000
Cost of goods sold	24,000
Insurance expense	2,000
Accounts receivable	12,000
Sales returns and allowances	4,000
Advertising expense	7,000
Merchandise inventory	35,000
Amortization expense	8,000
Sales revenues	98,000
Freight out	3,000
Loss on sale of equipment	1,500
Sales discounts	5,000
Salaries expense	23,000
Rent expense	10,000
Interest expense	2,000
Income tax expense	7,800

Buff Corporation
Statement of Earnings
Year Ended January 31, 2006

2. Hiller Corporation is a merchandising company, and the following accounting transactions occurred during the month of January.

Jan. 5 Purchased goods costing $10,000. The goods were shipped free on board shipping point with terms of 2/10, n/30.
Jan. 7 Hiller paid freight costs of $100 on the January 5 purchase
Jan. 10 Hiller returned $2,000 of the goods purchased on January 5 to its supplier. (Ignore freight on this return.)

Jan. 12 Hiller sold $2,000 of merchandise to Ms. Jones with terms 2/10, n/30 and FOB destination. The cost of the goods sold was $1,600.

Jan. 14 Hiller paid the amount due to its supplier.

Jan. 16 Hiller paid $50 in freight costs on the goods sold and shipped them to Ms. Jones.

Jan. 20 Ms. Jones returned $100 of goods sold on January 12. The returned goods cost $80 and were put back on Hiller's store shelf for resale, as they were in good condition. (Ignore freight on this return.)

Jan. 21 Ms. Jones paid her account in full.

Jan. 25 Hiller purchased $500 of general office supplies on account.

Required:

a. Journalize the above transactions for Hiller Corporation using the perpetual inventory system. (SO3, 4)

*b. Journalize the above transactions for Hiller Corporation using the periodic inventory system. (SO6)

3. The Willis Merchandising Corporation employs the periodic inventory system and prepares monthly financial statements. All accounts have been adjusted except for merchandise inventory. A physical count of merchandise inventory on September 30, 2006 indicates that $3,300 was on hand. A partial listing of account balances follows:

Accounts receivable	$ 5,000
Cash	9,000
Accounts payable	7,000
Merchandise inventory, September 1	2,500
Freight in	1,000
Purchase returns and allowances	900
Sales discounts	700
Purchases	26,000
Sales	49,000

Required:

Prepare a statement of earnings through gross profit for Willis Merchandising Corporation for the month ended September 30, 2006. (SO6)

4. Please refer to the Domtar and Cascades financial statements for information for answering the following questions. Do not forget to use the **Decision Toolkit** approach for help in the problem solving.

a. Compare the gross profit and gross profit margin for both companies for 2004. (SO4,5)

b. What are the operating expenses and earnings from operations for each company for 2004? (SO4)

c. What is the profit margin for both companies for 2004? (SO5)

d. The industry ratios were as follows for 2004: (SO5)

Gross profit margin: 27.7%
Net profit margin: 3.9%

Compare the profitability of Domtar and Cascades to with each other and to with the industry for 2004.

Solutions to Self-Test

Multiple Choice

1. c

2. b   Periodic systems do n't not show the quantity of goods that should be on hand, making control more difficult. Cost of goods sold is calculated each time a sale occurs under the perpetual system.

3. a   Since the sale was on account, the return entry requires a decrease in the liability, and Accounts Payable is debited. Since the company uses a perpetual system, all merchandise dollar amounts are recorded in the Merchandise Inventory account. A decrease due to the returned merchandise requires a credit to Merchandise Inventory. Purchases Returns would have been used if the company had used a periodic system.

4. b   The journal entry is:

Accounts Payable	1,600	
Merchandise Inventory		32
Cash		1,568

5. c   The journal entry is:

Accounts Payable	1,600	
Cash		1,600

6. d   The journal entry is:

Merchandise Inventory	200	
Cash		200

7. b   A perpetual inventory system requires two entries when merchandise is sold. One of the entries is a debit to Cost of Goods Sold, and the other entry is a credit to Merchandise Inventory.

8. a   The journal entries are:

Sales Returns and Allowances	500	
Accounts Receivable		500
Merchandise Inventory	500	
Cost of Goods Sold		500

9. c   While these accounts have a normal debit balance, they are not expenses, nor are they revenue accounts. They are subtracted from a revenue account, making them contra revenue accounts.

10. d   The entry requires a debit to Cash, but not for $400, since the purchaser receives a $4 discount. Accounts Receivable must be credited for $400, the full amount owed. The $4 difference between the amount owed and the amount of cash received is the debit to Sales Discounts.

11. d $10,000 – $500 – $1,000

12. b $75,000 – $50,000

13. c $50,000 – $15,000

14. c $15,000 + $20,000

15. b $15,000 + $20,000 = $35,000 of gross profit; $75,000 – $35,000 = $40,000

16. c

17. c $15,000 + $20,000 = $35,000 of gross profit; $35,000 ÷ $75,000 = 47% (rounded)

18. b
19. c
20. b $28,000 – $2,500 + 1,875 = $27,375
21. c $15,000 + $70,000 - $2,000 + $5,000 = $88,000
22. c
23. c

Problems

1.

Buff Corporation
Statement of Earnings
Year Ended January 31, 2006

Sales revenues		
Sales		$118,000
Less: Sales returns and allowances	$ 4,000	
Sales discounts	5,000	9,000
Net sales		109,000
Cost of goods sold		24,000
Gross profit		85,000
Operating expenses		
Salaries expense	$ 23,000	
Utilities expense	15,000	
Rent expense	10,000	
Amortization expense	8,000	
Advertising expense	7,000	
Freight out	3,000	
Insurance expense	2,000	
Total operating expenses		68,000
Earnings from operations		17,000
Other revenues		
Rental revenue	$5,000	
Interest revenue	1,000	
Total non-operating revenues	6,000	
Other expenses		
Interest expense	$2,000	
Loss on sale of equipment	1,500	
Total non-operating expenses	3,500	
Net non-operating revenue		2,500
Earnings before income tax		19,500
Income tax expense		7,800
Net earnings		$11,700

Perpetual Inventory System

2.

a. Jan. 5   Merchandise Inventory   10,000
             Accounts Payable   10,000
             (To record purchase of goods, with terms 2/10, n/30, FOB shipping point)

      7   Merchandise Inventory   100
             Cash   100
             (To record freight on purchases)
             [The terms of FOB shipping point means Hiller, the buyer, is responsible for picking up the goods from the supplier's warehouse or shipping point.]

     10   Accounts Payable   2,000
             Merchandise Inventory   2,000
             (To record return of goods to supplier)

     12   Accounts Receivable   2,000
             Sales   2,000
             (To record sales with terms 2/10, n/30 and FOB destination)

        Cost of Goods Sold   1,600
             Merchandise Inventory   1,600
             (To record cost of merchandise sold)

     14   Accounts Payable   8,000
             Merchandise Inventory   160
             Cash   7,840
             (To record payment, net of purchase return within the discount period)
             Discount = ($10,000 − $2,000) x .02 = $160
             [Discount does not apply to freight.]

     16   Freight Out   50
             Cash   50
             (To record freight on sales)
             [FOB destination means that it is Hiller's responsibility to pay the freight.]

     20   Sales Returns and Allowances   100
             Accounts Receivable   100
             (To record return of goods by Ms. Jones)

        Merchandise Inventory   80
             Cost of Goods Sold   80
             (To record the cost of merchandise return)

21	Cash	1,862	
	Sales Discounts	38	
	Accounts Receivable		1,900

(To record collection of account within the discount period)
Discount = (2,000 – 100) x .02 = 38

| 25 | Office Supplies (or expense) | 500 | |
| | Accounts Payable | | 500 |

(To record purchase of office supplies)
[Note that the amount is not debited to merchandise inventory because these are not goods for resale.]

Periodic Inventory System

b. Jan. 5   Purchases   10,000
               Accounts Payable   10,000

(To record purchase of goods with terms 2/10, n/30, FOB shipping point)

Jan. 7   Freight In   100
             Cash   100

(To record freight on purchases)
[The terms of FOB shipping point means Hiller, the buyer, is responsible for picking up the goods from the supplier's warehouse or shipping point.]

Jan. 10 Accounts Payable   2,000
             Purchase Returns and Allowances   2,000

(To record return of goods to supplier)

Jan. 12 Accounts Receivable   2,000
             Sales   2,000

(To record sales with terms 2/10, n/30 and FOB destination)

Jan. 14 Accounts Payable   8,000
             Purchase Discounts   160
             Cash   7,840

(To record payment, net of purchase return within the discount period
Discount = ($10,000 - $2,000) x .02 = $160
[Discount does not apply to freight.]

Jan. 16 Freight Out   50
             Cash   50

(To record freight on sales)
[FOB destination means that it is Hiller's responsibility to pay the freight.]

Jan. 20 Sales Returns and Allowances   100
                    Accounts Receivable   100
              (To record return of goods by Ms. Jones)

Jan. 21 Cash   1,862
                    Sales Discounts   38
                    Accounts Receivable   1,900
              (To record collection of account within the discount period)
              Discount = ($2,000 - $100) x .02 = $38

Jan. 25 Office Supplies (or expense)   500
                    Accounts Payable   500
              (To record purchase of office supplies)
              [Note that the amount is not debited to purchases because these are
              not goods for resale.]

3.

Willis Merchandising Corporation
Statement of Earnings
Month Ended September 30, 2006

Sales revenues
   Sales $49,000
   Less: Sales discounts   700
   Net sales   2,500

Cost of goods sold
   Merchandise inventory, September 1 $ 2,500
   Purchases $26,000
   Less: Purchase returns and allowances   900
   Net purchases   25,100
   Add: Freight in   1,000
   Cost of goods purchased   26,100
   Cost of goods available for sale   28,600
   Merchandise inventory, September 30   3,300
      Cost of goods sold   25,300
Gross profit   23,000

4.
a.

	Domtar ($millions)	Cascades ($millions)
Net sales	$5,115	$3,254
Cost of sales	4,381	2,691
Gross profit	$ 734	$ 563
Gross profit margin	$ 734 / $5,115 = 14.3%	$563 / $3,254 = 17.3%

b.   Each of the companies uses slightly different terminology that has the same
      meaning as earnings from operations, as follows:

	Domtar ($millions)	Cascades ($millions)
Gross profit (from above)	$734	$563
Less operating expenses:		
Domtar: ($306+$368+$48 – $37) =	685	
Cascades: ($313+$18 – $6+$159) =		484
Operating profit	$ 49	
Operating income		$ 79

c.   (all dollars in millions)

$$\text{Profit margin} = \frac{\text{Net earnings}}{\text{Net sales}} \quad \frac{\$(42)}{\$5{,}115} = (0.8)\% \qquad \frac{\$23}{\$3{,}254} = 0.7\%$$

The gross profit margin for both companies is lower than the industry average of 27.67
percent; however, Cascades' profit margin of 0.7 percent is higher than both Domtar's
net loss of 0.8 percent but lower than the industry average of 3.9 percent.

chapter 6

Reporting and Analyzing Inventory

Chapter Overview

Chapter 6 explains the methods used to calculate the cost of goods sold during the period and the cost of inventory on hand at the end of the period. You will learn about the various ways to assign costs to inventory and about cost flow assumptions and the effect of using those cost flow assumptions on financial statements. You will see the effects of inventory errors on the statement of earnings and the balance sheet. Finally, methods to report and analyze inventory will be discussed.

Review of Specific Study Objectives

- All companies need to determine inventory quantities at the end of the accounting period, regardless of whether a company uses **a periodic inventory system or a perpetual inventory system.**

study objective 1

Describe the steps in determining inventory quantities.

- If a **perpetual** inventory system is used, a company takes a physical inventory at the end of the year for two purposes:
  1. to check the accuracy of their perpetual inventory records, and
  2. to determine the amount of inventory lost due to shrinkage or theft.

- If a **periodic** inventory system is used, a company takes a physical inventory at the end of the year for two different purposes:

1. to determine the inventory on hand at the balance sheet date, and
2. to determine the cost of goods sold for the period.

- Taking a **physical inventory** count involves actually counting, weighing, or measuring each kind of inventory on hand. To minimize errors, a company should ensure that it has a good system if of internal control in place. **Internal control** consists of policies and procedures to optimize resources, prevent and detect errors, safeguard assets, and enhance the accuracy and reliability of accounting records. Some internal control measures include the following:
  1. The counting should be done by employees who do not have responsibility for the custody or recordkeeping of the inventory.
  2. Each counter should establish the validity of each inventory item: this means checking that if the items actually exists, how many there are of them are there, and what condition they are in.

- Before the counting process begins, the **ownership** of the goods must be determined. The terms of sale determines ownership as follows:
  1. When terms are **free on board (FOB) shipping point**, ownership of the goods passes to the buyer when the public carrier accepts the goods from the seller.
  2. When terms are **FOB destination**, ownership of the goods remains with the seller until the goods reach the buyer.

- In some lines of businesses, it is customary to hold goods belonging to other parties and sell them, for a fee, without ever taking ownership of the goods. These are called **consigned goods**. These goods must be included in the inventory count of the other party and not the dealer. For example, Charlie takes goods that he wishes to sell to Barb's Barb's place of business. Barb agrees to try to sell them for Charlie, for a commission, of course. Charlie is at all times the owner of the goods until they sellare sold. Even though the goods are physically at Barb's place of business, Barb never has title to the goods. So, at the time of the physical count of the inventory, Charlie must remember to *count those consigned goods as part of the inventory*.

<table>
<tr><td>

study objective 2

Apply the inventory cost flow assumptions under a periodic inventory system.

</td><td>

- After the quantity of units of inventory has been determined, unit costs are applied to those quantities to determine the **total cost of goods sold and cost of ending inventory**. The cost of goods sold and of ending inventory will differ depending on which cost flow assumption is selected.

</td></tr>
</table>

- The first method that can be used to determine cost of goods sold and ending inventory is *specific identification*, which requires that records be kept of the original cost of each individual inventory item. This method is most practical to use when a company sells a limited number of items, such as cars or antiques, that have high unit cost and can easily be traced from purchase through to sale. Today, with bar coding, it is theoretically possible to use specific identification with nearly any type of product. However, The the reality is, however, that this method is rarely used.

- Because specific identification is often impractical, there are three **cost flow assumptions**:
  1. First-in, first-out (FIFO)
  2. Average
  3. Last-in, first-out (LIFO)

These three cost flow assumptions can be used in both the periodic and perpetual inventory systems.

- **First-in, first-out** assumes that the *earliest ("first") goods purchased are the first sold*. FIFO parallels the actual physical flow of goods. With few exceptions, retailers want to sell the oldest inventory first because of shelf life or style issues. *Ending inventory consists of the most recent purchases.*

- **Average cost** removes the effects of rising or falling prices. An *average unit cost is calculated by dividing the cost of goods available for sale by the total units available for sale.* That unit cost is then applied to the units in the ending inventory and the units sold. It is a *weighted average cost* that is calculated.

- **Last-in, first-out** assumes that the *most recent ("last") goods purchased are the first sold*. This is usually opposite from the physical flow of goods, but there is no accounting requirement that the cost flow assumption approximate the physical flow of goods. *Ending inventory consists of the oldest purchases.*

- Using the following data, let's let us calculate the ending inventory and cost of goods sold under each of the cost flow assumptions using a periodic inventory system. Under a periodic system, the different dates of each of the sales is ignored. Instead, at the end of the period, an assumption is made that the entire pool of cost is available for allocation between cost of goods sold and ending inventory.

Date	Units	Unit Cost	Total Cost
Feb. 1	300	$4	$ 1,200
Mar. 9	400	5	2,000
May 8	600	6	3,600
June 3	500	7	3,500
	1,800		$10,300

A physical count shows that there are 550 units in ending inventory. The February 1 units are the beginning inventory, and $10,300 is the cost of goods available for sale. Please note that this is a time of rising prices.

To allocate the costs, the first step involves the calculation of the ending inventory, and the second step involves the calculation of cost of goods sold.

FIFO:

There are 1,250 units that were sold;, therefore, there are 550 units remaining in ending inventory. (1,800 units – 1,250 units).

The ending inventory consists of the most recent purchases (remember, in *FIFO*, the first goods in are the first goods out, and so what is left in ending inventory is the last goods to be received). To get to 550, begin counting with the June 3 purchase.

June 3	500	x	$7	=	$3,500
May 8	50	x	6	=	300
	550				$3,800

The cost of goods sold is calculated by subtracting the ending inventory from the cost of goods available for sale. If you subtract what is still on hand from the total goods available for sale, the difference must be the amount sold. The cost of goods sold calculation is as follows:

Cost of goods available for sale	$10,300
Less: Ending inventory	3,800
Cost of goods sold	$ 6,500

Average cost:

To calculate an average unit cost, divide cost of goods available for sale of $10,300 by the total units available for sale, 1,800. The average unit cost is $5.722. Please note, too, that the company never paid $5.722 for any units purchased: This is simply a weighted average unit cost.

This unit cost is applied to ending inventory as follows:

Ending inventory: 550   x $5.722   = $3,147

The cost of goods sold calculation is as follows:

Cost of goods available for sale	$10,300
Less: Ending inventory	3,147
Cost of goods sold	$ 7,153

LIFO:

The ending inventory consists of the oldest purchases (remember, in LIFO, the last goods in are assumed to be the first goods out, and so what is left in ending inventory are the oldest goods received).To get to 550, begin counting with the February 1 beginning inventory.

Feb. 1	300	x	$4	=	$1,200
Mar. 9	250	x	5	=	1,250
	550				$2,450

Cost of goods available for sale	$10,300
Less: Ending inventory	2,450
Cost of goods sold	$ 7,850

Summarizing these results:

	FIFO	Average Cost	LIFO
Cost of goods sold	$6,500	$7,153	$7,850
Ending inventory	3,800	3,147	2,450
Cost of goods available for sale	$10,300	$10,300	$10,300

Please note that the results of average cost are between those of FIFO and LIFO. Average cost removes the effects of rising, or falling, prices.

- Companies can use the specific identification method or any of the three cost flow methods - all are acceptable, and *a company may use more than one cost flow assumption at the same time*. It may have two classes of inventories and may use average cost for one and FIFO for the other.

- You can see the **statement of earnings effects** of the three cost flow assumptions with the above summarization. Remember that the example shows a period of **rising prices**.

  FIFO: Lowest cost of goods sold, highest net earnings.

  Average cost: In the middle for both items.

  LIFO: Highest cost of goods sold, lowest net earnings.

  Overall, LIFO provides the best statement of earnings valuation. It matches current costs with current revenues, since, under LIFO, the cost of goods sold is assumed to be the cost of the most recently acquired goods.

- The **balance sheet effects** of the three cost flow assumptions can also be seen with the summarization. Remember that *results would have been opposite had this been a period of falling prices*.

  FIFO: Highest inventory valuation (because most recent purchases are in the ending inventory).

  Average cost: In the middle.

  LIFO: Lowest inventory valuation (because oldest purchases are in ending inventory). LIFO can produce a severe understatement of inventory if inventories contain items purchased in one or more prior accounting periods.

- Overall, FIFO provides the best balance sheet valuation. It reports the cost of ending inventory at the current cost, which is relevant to users, since the inventory must be replaced once sold.

- **Inventory errors affect the determination of cost of goods sold and net earnings in two periods** because the ending inventory of one period becomes the beginning inventory of the next period.

- An **error in beginning inventory** will have a *reverse effect on net earnings of the same accounting period* (if beginning inventory is understated, then net earnings will be overstated). An **error in ending inventory** will have the same *effect on net earnings of the same accounting period* (if ending inventory is understated, then net earnings will be understated, too).

- An **error in ending inventory of the current period** will have *a reverse effect on net earnings of the next accounting period*. Even though there is an error, **total net earnings will be correct over the two periods because the errors offset each other**.

- An **error in beginning inventory** *does not result in a corresponding error in the ending inventory for that same period*.

- On the **balance sheet**, if *ending inventory is overstated, then both assets and shareholders' equity will be overstated. If ending inventory is understated, then both assets and shareholders' equity will be understated.*

study objective 3

Explain the financial statement effects of each of the inventory cost flow assumptions and inventory errors.

study objective 4

Demonstrate the presentation and analysis of inventory.

- **At times, companies have in inventory items for which they paid one price but for which they would currently pay a lower price if they were to purchase those same inventory items.**

- This situation **requires a departure from the cost principle**, and the inventory will be *valued at the lower of cost and market (LCM)*. Market is not defined under GAAP, but the most commonly used definition in Canada is net realizable value.

- **LCM is an example of the accounting concept of conservatism**, which means that *the best choice among accounting alternatives is the method that is least likely to over-state assets and net earnings*. (Conservatism does not mean that items should be intentionally understated.)

- The classification of inventory depends on whether a company is a merchandiser or a manufacturer. A **merchandising company** has only one inventory account, called Merchandise Inventory. A **manufacturing company** has three inventory accounts: Finished Goods, consisting of goods completed and awaiting sale; Work in Process, consisting of goods partially completed; and Raw Materials, consisting of materials waiting to be placed into production.

- **Managing inventory levels** so that neither too much nor too little is on hand can be complex and but is critical to a company's success.

- The **inventory turnover ratio** can help in managing inventory levels. It is *calculated by dividing cost of goods sold by average inventory*. (Average inventory is calculated by adding together the beginning and the ending inventories of a period and dividing the sum by two.) If a company's cost of goods sold is $50,000 and its average inventory is $16,000, then its inventory turnover ratio is 3.13 (rounded). This means that the company sells its entire inventory about three times every accounting period.

- **Days in inventory** is *calculated by dividing the inventory turnover into 365*. Using the same example above, $365 \div 3.13 = 116.6$ days. This means that it takes the company about 116 days to sell its inventory.

- **Both the inventory turnover and days in inventory ratios must be compared with something to be meaningful.** They may be compared with the same company's numbers from prior periods or with the numbers of other companies in the same industry.

study objective 5

Apply the inventory cost flow assumptions under a perpetual inventory system (Appendix 6A).

- The **cost flow assumptions that you've you have learned to use with a periodic system of inventory can also be applied to a perpetual system.**

- For **FIFO** and **LIFO**, it is *important to keep each purchase of inventory in a separate layer*. Consider the following data:

Purchases
Oct. 10   100 units @ $2
Nov. 11   200 units @ $3
Dec. 15   300 units @ $4

If 400 units are finally sold on December 20, **FIFO** yields the following:

	Purchases			Cost of Goods Sold			Balance		
Date	Units	Cost	Total	Units	Cost	Total	Units	Cost	Total
Oct. 10	100	$2	$ 200				100	$2	$ 200
} Nov. 11	200	3	600				100	2	
							200	3	800
Dec. 15	300	4	1,200				100	2	
}							200	3	2,000
							300	4	
20				100	$2				
}				200	3	$1,200			
				100	4		200	4	800

Please note that FIFO always yields the same results, regardless of whether a periodic or a perpetual inventory system is used. The same is not true for LIFO.

- The **average cost flow assumption** when applied to a perpetual inventory system is called the *moving average cost flow assumption*. **A new average cost is calculated after each purchase.** When the 400 units are sold, *moving average* yields the following:

	Purchases			Cost of Goods Sold			Balance		
Date	Units	Cost	Total	Units	Cost	Total	Units	Cost	Total
Oct. 10	100	$2	$ 200				100	$2.00	$ 200
Nov. 11	200	3	600				300	2.67	800
Dec. 15	300	4	1,200				600	3.33	2,000
20				400	$3.33	$1,333[1]	200	3.33	667[1]

[1]Adjusted for the effects of rounding.

- When the 400 units are sold, **LIFO** yields the following:

	Purchases			Cost of Goods Sold			Balance		
Date	Units	Cost	Total	Units	Cost	Total	Units	Cost	Total
Oct. 10	100	$2	$ 200				100	$2	$ 200
Nov. 11	200	3	600				100	2	
}							200	3	800
Dec. 15	300	4	1,200				100	2	
}							200	3	2,000
							300	4	
20				300	$4		100	2	
}				100	3	$1,500	100	3	500

Whereas FIFO always yields the same results, regardless of whether a periodic or a perpetual inventory system is used, the same is not true for LIFO.

Chapter Self-Test

As you work through the exercises and problems, remember to use the **Decision Toolkit** discussed and used in the text:

1. *Decision Checkpoints*: At this point, you ask a question.
2. *Info Needed for Decision*: You make a choice regarding the information needed to answer the question.
3. *Tool to Use for Decision*: At this point, you review just what the information chosen in step two does for the decision-making process.
4. *How to Evaluate Results*: You conduct an evaluation of information for answering the question.

Note: The notation (SO1) means that the question was drawn from study objective number one. All questions marked with an asterisk (*) relate to material in Appendix 6A.

Multiple Choice

Please circle the correct answer.

(SO1)   1. The taking of a physical inventory count in a perpetual inventory system is done for the following reasons:
   a.   to check the accuracy of the perpetual records and to determine the inventory lost due to employee theft.
   b.   to determine the inventory lost due to employee theft and to determine the cost of goods sold.
   c.   to determine the inventory on hand and cost of goods sold.
   d.   to determine the inventory on hand and to check the accuracy of the perpetual records.

(SO1)   2. Goods held on consignment are:
   a.   never owned by the consignee.
   b.   included in the consignee's ending inventory.
   c.   kept for sale on the premises of the consignor.
   d.   included as part of no one's ending inventory.

(SO1)   3. If goods are shipped FOB destination, then which of the following parties includes in its inventory the goods while they are in transit?
   a.   shipping company
   b.   buyer
   c.   seller
   d.   both the buyer and the seller include the goods in their inventory

(SO1)   4. Ceil gives goods on consignment to Jerry who agrees to try to sell them for a 25 percent commission. At the end of the accounting period, which of the following parties includes in its inventory the consigned goods?
   a.   Ceil
   b.   Jerry
   c.   Both Ceil and Jerry
   d.   Neither Ceil nor Jerry

5. Which of the following inventory cost flow assumptions often parallels the physical flow of goods?   (SO2)
    a. LIFO
    b. FIFO
    c. Average cost
    d. Specific identification

Please use the following data for #6, 7, and 8, where a periodic inventory system is used:

Date	Units	Unit Cost	Total Cost
Feb. 5	200	$2	$ 400
Mar. 6	500	4	2,000
Apr. 9	400	6	2,400
June 7	300	7	2,100
	1,400		$6,900

On June 30, there are 350 units in ending inventory.

6. What is the cost of the ending inventory using FIFO?   (SO2)
    a. $1,000
    b. $1,726
    c. $2,400
    d. $5,177

7. What is the cost of goods sold using average cost?   (SO2)
    a. $1,000
    b. $1,726
    c. $2,400
    d. $5,177

8. What is the cost of ending inventory using LIFO?   (SO2)
    a. $1,000
    b. $1,726
    c. $2,400
    d. $5,177

9. In a period of rising prices, which of the following cost flow assumptions will give the highest ending inventory?   (SO3)
    a. Specific identification
    b. Average cost
    c. LIFO
    d. FIFO

10. In a period of falling prices, which of the following cost flow assumptions will give the highest net earnings?   (SO3)
    a. Specific identification
    b. Average cost
    c. LIFO
    d. FIFO

(SO3)   11. Which inventory cost flow assumption generally results in costs allocated to ending inventory that will approximate their current cost?
a.   LIFO
b.   FIFO
c.   Average cost
d.   Whichever cost flow assumption that produces the highest ending inventory figure

(SO3)   12. Two companies report the same cost of goods available for sale but each employs a different inventory cost flow assumption. If the price of goods has increased during the period:
a.   LIFO will have the highest ending inventory.
b.   average cost will have the highest ending inventory.
c.   FIFO will have the highest ending inventory.
d.   the ending inventory will be the same regardless of the inventory cost flow assumption used.

(SO3)   13. Which inventory cost flow assumption provides the best statement of earnings valuation?
a.   FIFO
b.   LIFO
c.   Average cost
d.   All are equal.

(SO4)   14. Using lower of cost and market is an example of the accounting concept of:
a.   revenue recognition.
b.   conservatism.
c.   matching.
d.   full disclosure.

(SO4)   15. Net sales are $80,000, cost of goods sold is $30,000, and average inventory is $20,000. The inventory turnover is:
a.   4.00 times.
b.   2.67 times.
c.   1.50 times.
d.   0.25 times.

(SO4)   16. If the beginning inventory is overstated, then the current year's:
a.   cost of goods sold is overstated.
b.   cost of goods sold is understated.
c.   ending inventory is overstated.
d.   ending inventory is understated.

(SO4)   17. A company reports net earnings of $50,000 in 2006 and $75,000 in 2007. Later, it was discovered that two errors were made: the ending inventory in 2006 was understated by $10,000, and the ending inventory in 2007 was overstated by $5,000. The corrected net earnings are:
a.   2006: $60,000; 2007: $60,000
b.   2006: $60,000; 2007: $80,000

c.   2006: $40,000; 2007: $80,000

d.   2006: $40,000; 2007: $60,000

18. On January 1, a company had an inventory of $14,000. On December 31 of the same year, the company had an inventory of $18,000. Sales for the year were $400,000, and the gross profit margin was 30%. percent. What is the company's inventory turnover for the year?   (SO4)

a.   7.5 times.

b.   20.0 times.

c.   17.5 times.

d.   15.6 times.

19. Using the information in #18 above, calculate the number of days of inventory that the company has.   (SO4)

a.   18.25 days

b.   20.86 days

c.   23.46 days

d.   48.67 days

*20. The results under _____ in a perpetual inventory system are the same as in a periodic inventory system.   (SO5)

a.   average cost

b.   FIFO

c.   LIFO

d.   None of these.

*21. In a perpetual inventory system, the cost of the earliest goods on hand prior to each sale is charged to cost of goods sold under: (SO5)

a.   LIFO.

b.   average cost.

c.   FIFO.

d.   specific identification.

Problems

1.   Jensen Corporation has just completed a physical inventory count at year end, December 31, 2006. Only the items on the shelves, in storage, and in the receiving area were counted and costed, using the FIFO cost flow assumption. The ending inventory amounted to $88,000. During the audit, the following additional information was discovered: (SO1)

a.   Some office supplies in the amount of $400 were included in the inventory count. These supplies will be used in the office and will not be available for sale.

b.   On December 27, 2006, Jensen shipped goods to a customer. The goods costing $900 were sold for $1,200. The goods were shipped FOB destination and were received by the customer on January 3, 2007. Because the goods were not on the shelves, Jensen excluded them from the physical inventory count.

c.   Jensen, on On the date of the inventory, Jensen received notice from a supplier that goods ordered earlier, at a cost of $3,500, had been delivered to the transportation company on December 28, 2006; the terms were FOB shipping point. Because the shipment had not arrived on December 31, 2006, it was excluded from the physical inventory.

d. On December 31, 2006, there were goods in transit to customers, with terms FOB shipping point, amounting to $750 (expected delivery on January 8, 2007). Because the goods had been shipped, they were excluded from the physical inventory count.

e. On December 31, 2006, Jensen shipped $1,200 worth of goods to a customer, FOB destination on January 5, 2007. Because the goods were not on hand, they were not included in the physical inventory count.

f. Jensen, as the consignee, had goods on consignment that cost $3,700. Because these goods were on hand as of December 31, 2006, they were included in the physical inventory count.

Required:

Analyze the above information and calculate a corrected amount for the ending inventory. Explain the basis for your treatment of each item.

2.   A company, in its first year of operations, has the following inventory transactions for the year:

Date	Units Purchased	Unit Cost	Units Sold
Jan. 5	500	$ 5.00	
Feb. 10	800	6.75	
Mar. 6			1,000
June 15	700	7.00	
July 16			400
Aug. 12	500	8.00	
Sep.11	300	10.00	
Oct. 25			500
Nov. 25	200	12.00	
Dec. 20			500

(SO2)   a. Assume a periodic inventory system with a FIFO cost flow assumption. What is the cost of goods sold for the year?

(SO2)   b. Assume a periodic inventory system with a LIFO cost flow assumption. What is the cost of goods sold for the year?

(SO2)   c. Assume a periodic inventory system with the average cost flow assumption. What is the cost of goods sold for the year?

(SO5)   *d. Assume a perpetual inventory system with an average cost flow assumption. What is the cost of goods sold for the March 6 sale?

(SO5)   *e. Assume a perpetual inventory system with a FIFO cost flow assumption. What is the cost of goods sold for the March 6 sale?

3. A company has the following statement of earnings:

	2006	2007
Sales	$50,000	$70,000
Cost of goods sold	30,000	45,000
Gross profit	20,000	25,000
Operating expenses	14,000	15,000
Net earnings	$ 6,000	$10,000

After the preparation of the above statements, it was discovered that the ending inventory on December 31, 2006, was understated by $3,000. The value of the ending inventory on December 31, 2007, was correct. The company uses a periodic inventory system, and the average inventory, before the understatement was discovered, was $8,000 for 2006 and $10,000 for 2007.

a. Recalculate the statement of earnings to reflect the correct inventory amount.   (SO4 in Chapter 6)

b. Calculate the effect of the inventory correction on the gross profit margin. [This is a good integration question from both chapters.]   (SO5 in Chapter 5)

c. Calculate the effect of the inventory correction on the profit margin.   (SO5 in Chapter 5)

d. Calculate the effect of the inventory correction on the inventory turnover.   (SO4 in Chapter 6)

e. Calculate the effect of the inventory correction on the days in inventory ratio.   (SO4 in Chapter 6)

4. Please refer to the Domtar and Cascades financial statements for information for answering the following questions. Do n't not forget to use the **Decision Toolkit** approach for help in the problem solving.   (SO5)

a. What cost flow assumption does Cascades use for its Raw Materials and Supplies inventories?   (SO2)

b. How does Domtar value its Raw Materials and Operating and Maintenance Supplies inventories?   (SO2)

c. For both Domtar and Cascades, calculate the inventory turnover and days in inventory for 2004.   (SO4)

d. The industry ratios were as follows for 2004:   (SO4)
   Inventory turnover: 6.5
   Days in inventory: 55
   Compare the performance of Domtar and Cascades according to how they have managed their inventories in 2004.

Solutions to Self-Test

Multiple Choice

1. a
2. a
3. c   When goods are shipped FOB destination, the seller retains title to the goods until they reach the buyer's place of business. Since the seller has title, he pays the shipping costs.
4. a   Consigned goods are always the property of the person who has put them out on consignment. They are Ceil's; Jerry never has title to the goods.
5. b   LIFO is opposite the physical flow of the goods, and average cost and specific identification do not parallel the physical flow.
6. c

June 7	300	x	$7	=	$2,100
Apr. 9	50	x	6	=	300
	350				$2,400 ending inventory

7. d $6,900 ÷ 1,400 = $4.93 (rounded)/unit x 1,050 units
8. a

Feb. 5	200	x	$2	=	$ 400
Mar. 6	150	x	4	=	600
	350				$1,000 ending inventory

9. d   LIFO gives the lowest ending inventory, and average cost results will be between those of FIFO and LIFO.
10. c   The assumption with the lowest cost of goods sold will yield the highest net earnings. This cost flow assumption is LIFO.
11. b
12. c
13. b
14. b   Revenue recognition says that revenue is recognized when it is earned, matching dictates that expenses be matched with revenues, and full disclosure says that circumstances and events that make a difference to financial statement users should be disclosed.
15. c $30,000 ÷ $20,000 = 1.5
16. a   An error in beginning inventory does not have an effect on ending inventory of the same year.
17. a   2006: $50,000 + $10,000 = $60,000
2007: $75,000 − $10,000 − $5,000 = $60,000
18. c   The percentage for cost of goods sold = 100% − 30% = 70%
Cost of goods sold = 70% x $400,000 = $280,000
$$\text{Inventory turnover} = \frac{\text{Cost of goods sold}}{\text{Average inventory}}$$
$$= \frac{\$280,000}{(\$14,000 + \$18,888) \div 2} = 17.5 \text{ times}$$
19. b   365 ÷ 17.5 = 21 days
20. b
21. c

Problems

1.

		$88,000	Unadjusted ending inventory amount
a.		-400	The office supplies are not for sale and are to be excluded from ending inventory.
b.		+900	Goods should be included as Jensen owns them until they are received by the customer on January 3rd.
c.		+3,500	Goods belong to Jensen. Title passed when supplier delivered the goods to the transportation company.
d.		0	Because the goods were shipped FOB shipping point, Jensen no longer has title to these goods. The items were properly excluded from ending inventory.
e.		+1,200	Goods were shipped FOB destination. Jensen retains title until the customer receives them.
f.		-3,700	These goods are owned by the consignor, not the consignee, and should not be included in Jensen's inventory.
		$89,500	Corrected ending inventory amount

2. a.   Under a periodic inventory system, the individual sales dates are ignored. Instead, at the end of the period, we assume that the entire pool of cost of goods available for sale is allocated between cost of goods sold and ending inventory. The calculation of the cost of goods available for sale is shown in the following table:

Date	Units Purchased	Unit Cost	Total Cost
Jan. 5	500	$ 5.00	$ 2,500
Feb. 10	800	6.75	5,400
June 15	700	7.00	4,900
Aug. 12	500	8.00	4,000
Sep.11	300	10.00	3,000
Nov. 25	200	12.00	2,400
Total goods available for sale	3,000		$22,200

The total sales are 1,000 + 400 + 500 + 500 = 2,400 units.

The ending inventory is: 3,000 – 2,400 units = 600 units.

The ending inventory, under FIFO, consists of the most recent purchases as follows:

Nov. 25	200	X	$12	=	$2,400
Sep. 11	300	X	10	=	3,000
Aug. 12	100	X	8	=	800
	600				$6,200

The cost of goods sold is calculated by subtracting the ending inventory from the cost of goods available for sale as follows:

Cost of goods available for sale	$22,200
Less: Ending inventory	6,200
Cost of goods sold	$16,000

b. The ending inventory, under LIFO, consists of the oldest purchases as follows:

Jan. 5	500	x	$5	=	$2,500
Feb. 10	100	x	6.75	=	675
	600				$3,175

The cost of goods sold is calculated by subtracting the ending inventory from the cost of goods available for sale as follows:

Cost of goods available for sale	$22,200
Less: Ending inventory	3,175
Cost of goods sold	$19,025

c. The ending inventory, under average cost, consists of the number of units in ending inventory times the weighted average unit cost of the units purchased, as follows:

Weighted average unit cost is: $\dfrac{\$22,200}{3,000 \text{ units}}$ = $7.40 per unit

Ending inventory is: 600 units x $7.40 = $4,440

The cost of goods sold is calculated by subtracting the ending inventory from the cost of goods available for sale as follows:

Cost of goods available for sale	$22,200
Less: Ending inventory	4,440
Cost of goods sold	$17,760

*d.

	Purchases			Cost of Goods Sold			Balance		
Date	Units	Costs	Total	Units	Costs	Total	Units	Costs	Total
Jan. 5	500	$ 5.00	$2,500				500	$5.00	$ 2,500
Feb. 10	800	6.75	5,400				1,300	6.08	7,900
Mar. 6				1,000	$6.08	$6,077	300	6.08	1,823
June 15	700	7.00	4,900				1,000	6.72	6,723
July 16				400	6.72	2,689	600	6.72	4,034
Aug. 12	500	8.00	4,000				1,100	7.03	8,034
Sep. 11	300	10.00	3,000				1,400	7.88	11,034
Oct. 25				500	7.88	3,941	900	7.88	7,093
Nov. 25	200	12.00	2,400				1,100	8.63	9,493
Dec. 20				500	8.63	4,315	600	8.63	5,178

Note: The above numbers have been rounded to two decimal points where required.

The cost of goods sold, under the perpetual average cost flow assumption, is shown in the above table each time a sale is made. Total cost of goods sold is $17,022 ($6,077 + $2,689 + $3,941 + $4,315).

*e. Under a perpetual inventory system, the cost of goods sold is calculated each time a sale is made. The cost of goods sold, under FIFO for the 1,000 units sold on March 6 is:

Jan. 5:	500	units	x	$5.00	=	$2,500
Feb. 10:	500	units	x	6.75	=	3,375
	1,000					$5,875

3. a.   In a periodic inventory system, the cost of goods sold is calculated as follows:

Beginning Inventory
+ Purchases (of merchandise inventory for resale)
= Cost of goods available for sale

– Ending Inventory
= Cost of goods sold

Therefore, if ending inventory is understated by $3,000 in 2006, then cost of goods sold is overstated in 2006 because of the inverse relationship between cost of goods sold and ending inventory. Furthermore, the beginning inventory for 2007 will also be understated in 2007 because the ending inventory in 2006 is carried forward to 2007. As a result, the cost of goods sold for 2007 is understated by $3,000. The following statement of earnings reflects the inventory correction:

	2006	2007
Sales	$50,000	$70,000
Cost of goods sold	27,000	48,000
Gross profit	23,000	22,000
Operating expenses	14,000	15,000
Net earnings	$9,000	$ 7,000

b.   Gross profit margin = Gross profit ÷ Net sales

	2006	2007
Before inventory correction:		
$20,000 ÷ $50,000	40%	
$25,000 ÷ $70,000		35.7%
After inventory correction:		
$23,000 ÷ $50,000	46%	
$22,000 ÷ $70,000		31.4%

c.   Profit margin = Net earnings ÷ Net sales

	2006	2007
Before inventory correction:		
$6,000 ÷ $50,000	12%	
$10,000 ÷ $70,000		14.37%
After inventory correction:		
$9,000 ÷ $50,000	18%	
$7,000 ÷ $70,000		10.0%

d.   Inventory turnover = Cost of goods sold ÷ Average inventory

	2006	2007
Before inventory correction:		
$30,000 ÷ $8,000	3.75 times	
$45,000 ÷ $10,000		4.5 times
After inventory correction:		
$27,000 ÷ $9,500*	2.8 times	
$48,000 ÷ $11,500**		4.2 times

*   If ending inventory increases by $3,000 (because it was understated), then the increase in average inventory is $3,000 ÷ 2 = $1,500 ($8,000 + $1,500 = $9,500).

**   An ending inventory increase of $3,000 in 2006 carries over to 2007. Therefore, the increase in average inventory for 2007 is also $3,000 ÷ 2 = $1,500 ($10,000 + $1,500 = $11,500).

e.   Days in inventory = 365 ÷ Inventory turnover

	2006	2007
Before inventory correction:		
365 ÷ 3.75	97.3 days	
365 ÷ 4.5		81.1 days
After inventory correction:		
365 ÷ 2.8	130.4 days	
365 ÷ 4.2		86.9 days

4. a.   In the Accounting policies (note 1) under "Inventories," Cascades states that average cost is used for Raw Materials and FIFO is used for Supplies.

b.   In the Accounting policies (note 1) under "Inventories," Domtar states that its Raw Materials and Operating and Maintenance Supplies inventories are valued at the lower of average cost and replacement cost.

Domtar: Average inventory = ($723 million + $670 million)÷2 = $696.50 million
Inventory turnover = cost of goods sold ÷ average inventory
$4,381 million ÷ $696.50 million = 6.29 times
Days in inventory = 365 ÷ inventory turnover
365 ÷ 6.29 = 58.03 days
Cascades: Average inventory = ($559 million + $501 million) ÷ 2 = $530 million
Inventory turnover = cost of goods sold ÷ average inventory
$2,691 million ÷ $530 million = 5.08 times
Days in inventory = 365 ÷ inventory turnover
365 ÷ 5.08 = 71.85 days

c.   Domtar's inventory ratios are slightly below the industry averages of 6.5 times for the inventory turnover and 55 days in inventory. Cascades ratios are below the industry averages and means that Cascades had a more difficult time in managing its inventory levels as compared to with Domtar.

chapter 7

Internal Control and Cash

Chapter Overview

Chapter 7 discusses the essential features of an internal control system and describes how these controls apply to cash receipts and disbursements. You will learn about the limitations as well as the strengths of internal control. You will learn how to prepare a bank reconciliation and how to report cash on the balance sheet. Finally, you will learn the basic principles of cash management and tools for help in managing and monitoring cash.

Review of Specific Study Objectives

- **Internal control** consists of all the related *methods and measures adopted within a business to*:
    1. **optimize the use of resources** to reduce inefficiencies and waste.
    2. **prevent and detect errors and irregularities** in the accounting process.
    3. **safeguard assets** from theft, robbery, and unauthorized use.
    4. **maintain reliable control systems** to enhance the accuracy and reliability of accounting records.

> study objective 1
>
> Identify the principles of internal control.

- There are **six principles of internal control**:
    1. *Establishment of responsibility*. Control is most effective when only one person is responsible for a given task. This area includes authorization and approval of transactions.

2. *Segregation of duties.*
    a. The responsibility for related activities should be assigned to different individuals. This should decrease the potential for errors and irregularities. Related purchasing activities include ordering merchandise, receiving goods, and paying (or authorizing payment) for merchandise. Related sales activities include making a sale, shipping (or delivering) the goods, and billing the customer.
    b. The responsibility for accounting for an asset should be separate from the responsibility for physical custody of that asset. For example, the accountant, as a record keeper, should not have physical custody of the asset or access to it.

3. *Documentation procedures.* Wherever possible, **documents should be prenumbered, and all documents should be accounted for** (this includes voided documents). Source documents should be forwarded promptly to the accounting department to ensure accurate and timely recording of a transaction.

4. *Physical controls.* Their use is essential. Physical controls include mechanical and electronic controls to safeguard assets and enhance the accuracy and reliability of the accounting records.

5. *Independent verification.* This principle involves the **review, comparison, and reconciliation of data prepared by employees** internally or externally. Three measures are recommended to obtain maximum benefit from independent *internal* verification:
    a. Verification should be made periodically or on a surprise basis.
    b. The verification should be done by an employee who is independent of the personnel responsible for the information.
    c. Discrepancies and exceptions should be reported to a management level that can take appropriate corrective action.

    In large companies, independent internal verification is often assigned to **internal auditors** who are employees of the company, and who evaluate the effectiveness of the company's system of internal control. Independent *external* verification involves external auditors who are independent of the company.

6. *Other controls.* These include **bonding of employees who handle cash, rotating employees' duties, and requiring employees to take vacations.** The former involves acquiring insurance protection against misappropriation of assets by dishonest employees. The latter two help to deter employees from attempting theft because the employees know that they cannot permanently conceal their theft.

- **Internal controls** generally *provide reasonable assurance that assets are safeguarded and that the accounting records are accurate and reliable.* In constructing the system, a company tries to have the best system at the lower cost. It attempts to have the benefits of the system outweigh the costs. There are, however, **limitations of any internal control system.** One involves the *human element* - a dishonest or incompetent employee can render the system ineffective, and two or more employees may collude to circumvent the system. (Performing a thorough background check when considering hiring a person is crucial.) The *size of the company* is also a factor. A large company has the resources, both human and financial, to put into place a sophisticated system of internal control. A small company may be very limited in both areas and must do the best it can with what it has. *Computer systems* provide unique internal control problems. In many instances, computerization has shifted the responsibility for internal control to programmers and end-users. It is especially important to maintain effective control over authorization, documentation, and access in computerized systems.

- **Cash** consists of *coins, currency (paper money), cheques, money orders, and money on hand or on deposit in a bank or similar depository.* If a bank will accept an item at face value for deposit, then it is cash. Debit card transactions and bank credit card receipts, such as VISA and MasterCard, are considered as cash, but nonbank credit card receipts are not. Because cash is readily convertible into other assets, easily concealed and transported, and highly desired, internal control over cash is absolutely necessary. **Cash** does not include postdated cheques, staledated (more than six months old) cheques, or returned cheques (due to insufficient funds). Postage stamps or IOUs from employees also are not cash.

study objective 2

Apply internal control to cash receipts and disbursements.

- A company must have effective **internal control over cash receipts**. Based on company sizes, different companies may apply them differently, all six internal control principles are important:
  1. *Establishment of responsibility.* Only designated personnel should be authorized to handle cash receipts.
  2. *Segregation of duties.* Custody of, and record-keeping for, cash should be separated.
  3. *Documentation procedures.* A company must use remittance devices, cash register tapes, and deposit slips.
  4. *Physical controls.* A company must store cash in secure areas, limit access to storage areas, and use cash registers.
  5. *Independent verification.* Supervisors should count receipts daily, and the treasurer should compare total receipts to bank deposits daily.
  6. *Other controls.* Cash-handling personnel should be bonded and required to take vacations, and all cash should be deposited on a daily basis.

- **A major internal control over cash disbursements** is to *make payments by cheque.* Again, all six internal control principles apply:
  1. *Establishment of responsibility.* Only authorized personnel should sign cheques.
  2. *Segregation of duties.* Again, custody and record-keeping should be separated. Those who make payments should not record the transactions.
  3. *Documentation procedures.* Cheques should be prenumbered and used in sequence, and they should be issued only if an invoice has been approved.
  4. *Physical controls.* Blank cheques should be secured, and cheque amounts should be printed electronically.
  5. *Independent verification.* Cheques and invoices should be compared, and a monthly bank reconciliation should be prepared.
  6. *Other controls.* Invoices should be stamped "Paid."

- The **use of a bank can increase good internal control over cash**. A company may *use a bank as a depository and clearinghouse for cheques received and written.* Use of a bank *minimizes the amount of currency that must be kept on hand, and a double record of all transactions is kept.*

study objective 3

Prepare a bank reconciliation.

- A **company receives monthly bank statements** and must reconcile the ending balance on the statement with the ending balance in the general ledger account "Cash." The two numbers are often not the same because of *time lags (the bank has recorded something that the company has not, or vice versa) and errors made by either the bank or the company.*

- It is **customary to reconcile the balance per books and balance per bank to their adjusted (correct or true) cash balances.** The reconciliation should be prepared by someone who has no other responsibilities for cash.

- The following are **adjustments made to the column called "Balance per bank statement":**
  1. *Deposits in transit* (deposits that the company has recorded but the bank has not) are always *added* to the balance per bank column.
  2. *Outstanding cheques* (cheques recorded by the company that have not yet been paid by the bank) are always subtracted from the balance per bank column.
  3. *Errors* may either be added to or *subtracted* from the column depending on the nature of the error.

- The following are **adjustments made to the column called "Balance per books":**
  1. NSF *cheques* (bounced cheques) are *subtracted* from the balance per books column.
  2. *Bank service charges are subtracted* from the balance per books column.
  3. *Interest received* is *added* to the balance per books column.
  4. Errors may either be added to or subtracted from the column depending on the nature of the error.

- The **key question to ask when preparing a bank reconciliation** is: *"Who knows about the transaction and has already recorded it, and who does not yet know about it?"* For example, with respect to bank service charges, the bank knows about them and has already subtracted them from the company account, reflecting this on the bank statement, but the company does not know the exact amount of the charges until it receives the statement.

- After the bank reconciliation has been prepared, **each reconciling item in the balance per books column must be recorded by the company in a journal entry.** (Bank personnel record any adjustments in the balance per bank statement column.) It is important to note that an *NSF cheque is debited to Accounts Receivable,* signalling the intention of the company to try to collect on the bounced cheque. *After the entries are journalized and posted, the balance in the Cash account should equal the total shown on the bank reconciliation.*

study objective 4

Explain the reporting of cash.

- **Cash is reported on the balance sheet and the cash flow statement.** When presented on the balance sheet, cash on hand and cash in banks is combined and reported simply as **Cash.** *Cash is listed first in the current assets section because it is the most liquid of assets.* The sources and uses of cash are shown on the cash flow statement and reconciled to the ending cash balance reported on the balance sheet.

- Companies often label the first current asset **"Cash and cash equivalents."** A **cash equivalent** is a *short-term, highly liquid investment that is readily convertible to cash and so near its maturity that its market value is relatively insensitive to changes in interest rates.* Examples include treasury bills, commercial paper, and money market funds.

- If **cash is restricted for a special purpose**, then it should be *reported separately as "restricted cash."* If it is to be used within the next year, then it is reported as a current asset; if it is to be used at a time beyond one year, then it is reported as a non-current asset.

- In making loans to depositors, banks commonly require borrowers to maintain minimum cash balances. These minimum balances, called **compensating balances**, provide the bank with support for the loans. They are a form of restriction on the use of cash. A compensating balance should be reported as a noncurrent asset and disclosed in the notes to the financial statements.

- A **company's objective in the management of cash** is to *have sufficient cash to meet payments as they come due but to minimize the amount of non–revenue-generating cash on hand.* Many companies have employees whose sole job responsibility is to manage cash.

study objective 5

Identify ways to manage and monitor cash.

- **Management of cash is the job of a company's controller and is critical to a company's success.** There are **five principles of cash management**:
  1. *Increase the speed of collection on receivables.* A company wants to receive cash as speedily as possible so that it can have the use of this money.
  2. *Keep inventory levels low.* There are many so-called "carrying costs" of inventory that a company wants to minimize as much as possible.
  3. *Delay payment of liabilities.* A company wants to pay its bills on time but not too early. It certainly wants to take advantage of all cash discounts offered.
  4. *Plan the timing of major expenditures.* A company tries to make major expenditures when it has excess cash, usually during its off-season.
  5. *Invest idle cash.* Cash that does not earn a return does a company little good. Invested cash should be highly liquid (easy to sell) and risk-free (there is no concern that the party will default on its promise to pay principal and interest).

- A **cash budget is an important tool in effective cash management**. It helps a company plan its cash needs by showing its anticipated cash flows. The cash budget *has three sections: cash receipts, cash disbursements,* and *financing.*

- The **cash receipts section** shows all anticipated cash receipts from cash sales and collections of accounts receivable, from interest and dividends, and from proceeds from planned sales of investments, property, plant and equipment, and the company's share capital.

- The **cash disbursements section** shows expected payments for the purchases of merchandise, operating expenses, income taxes, dividends, investments, and property, plant, and equipment.

- The **financing section** shows expected borrowings and the repayment of borrowed funds plus interest.

- The **accuracy of the cash budget** *depends on the accuracy of the assumptions made by the company.* Any significant error in the budget will affect all subsequent cash budgets because the ending balance on one budget is the beginning balance on the next budget.

Chapter Self-Test

As you work through the exercises and problems, remember to use the **Decision Toolkit** discussed and used in the text:

1. *Decision Checkpoints*: At this point, you ask a question.
2. *Info Needed for Decision*: You make a choice regarding the information needed to answer the question.
3. *Tool to Use for Decision*: At this point, you review just what the information chosen in step 2 does for the decision-making process.
4. *How to Evaluate Results:* You conduct an evaluation of information for answering the question.

Note: The notation (SO1) means that the question was drawn from study objective number one.

Multiple Choice

Please circle the correct answer.

(SO1)   1.   Which of the following statements is correct?
   a.   Control is most effective when two or three people are given responsibility for the same task.
   b.   The person who has custody of assets should not perform the record-keeping for the assets.
   c.   The person who has custody of assets should also perform the record-keeping for the assets.
   d.   It is a waste of company resources to have an employee perform independent internal verification.

(SO1)   2.   Which of the following statements is incorrect?
   a.   Related purchasing activities should be assigned to different individuals.
   b.   Safeguarding of assets is enhanced by the use of physical controls.
   c.   Independent internal verification should be done by an employee independent of the personnel responsible for the information.
   d.   The use of prenumbered documents is not an important internal control principle.

(SO1)   3.   The custodian of a company asset should:
   a.   have access to the accounting records for that asset.
   b.   be someone outside the company.
   c.   not have access to the accounting records for that asset.
   d.   be an accountant.

(SO1)   4.   Each of the following is a feature of internal control, *except*
   a.   documentation of procedures.
   b.   ensuring employees take their vacation.
   c.   establishing a good cash management policy.
   d.   recording of all transactions.

5. Having one person responsible for the related activities of making a sale,   (SO1)
   shipping goods to a customer, and billing the customer
      a.   is a good example of ensuring that transactions are recorded properly.
      b.   decreases the potential for errors and fraud.
      c.   is an example of good internal control.
      d.   increases the potential for errors and fraud.

6. An employee authorized to sign cheques should *not*   (SO2)
      a.   record cash deposits.
      b.   receive company mail.
      c.   record cash disbursement transactions.
      d.   sales transactions.

7. Which of the following is not considered cash?   (SO2)
      a.   Coins
      b.   Money orders
      c.   Short-term investment in another company's shares
      d.   Chequing account

8. A company has the following items: cash on hand, $1,000; cash in a   (SO2)
   chequing account, $3,000; cash in a savings account, $5,000; postage stamps,
   $50; and treasury bills, $10,000. How much should the company report as cash
   and cash equivalents on the balance sheet?
      a. $ 9,000
      b. $ 9,050
      c. $19,000
      d. $19,050

9. Effective internal control over cash disbursements includes: (SO2)
      a.   the use of prenumbered cheques.
      b.   the storage of blank cheques in a secure place.
      c.   the separation of authorization of cheques and the actual writing of the
          cheques.
      d.   All of the above are part of effective internal control over cash
          disbursements.

10. Internal controls for cash include all of the following, except: (SO2)
      a.   all major disbursements should be made by serially numbered cheques.
      b.   bank accounts should be reconciled monthly.
      c.   the function of receiving cash should be separated from the function of
          disbursing cash.
      d.   only one person should handle cash receipts and cash disbursements so as
          to centralize the record keeping and limit access to cash.

11. Fiddler Corporation gathered the following information in preparing its June   (SO3)
   bank reconciliation:

Cash balance per books, June 30	$3,500
Deposits-in-transit	150
Electronic deposit	850
Bank charge for cheque printing	20
Outstanding cheques	2,000
NSF cheque	170

The adjusted cash balance per books on July 30 is:
a. $4,160
b. $4,010
c. $2,310
d. $2,460

(SO3)   12. Which of the following is added to the balance per books side of a bank reconciliation?
a.   An outstanding cheque for $300
b.   An electronic deposit of $500 made by a customer
c.   A deposit in transit of $150
d.   A bank service charge for $50 for cheque printing

(SO3)   13. Cooper Corporation showed a balance in its Cash account of $1,250 when it received its monthly bank statement. It found the following while reconciling items: deposits in transit, $256; outstanding cheques, $375; NSF cheque in the amount of $102; bank service charges of $27; and an electronic funds transfer into the bank account for $850. What is the adjusted cash balance Cooper will show on its bank reconciliation?
a. $1,131
b. $1,852
c. $1,971
d. $1,981

(SO3)   14. Which of the following errors should be added to the balance per bank on a bank reconciliation?
a.   A returned $200 cheque from the bank for insufficient funds
b.   Deposit of $600 incorrectly recorded by the bank as $60
c.   Deposit for $991 incorrectly recorded in the company's books for $919
d.   Cheque for $87 recorded as $78 in company's books

(SO3)   15. Which of the following bank reconciliation items would *not* result in an adjusting entry?
a.   An error made by the company in recording a cheque
b.   Outstanding cheques
c.   Interest revenue earned on a bank account
d.   Collection of a note by the bank

(SO4)   16. Cash equivalents *do not* include:
a.   temporary investments.
b.   short-term notes.

    c.   guaranteed investment certificates.

    d.   investment securities, such as investment in shares of other companies.

17. On which two financial statements is Cash reported?   (SO4)
    a.   Balance sheet and cash flow statement
    b.   Balance sheet and statement of earnings
    c.   Balance sheet and statement of retained earnings
    d.   Statement of earnings and cash flow statement

18. If cash is restricted as to its use and will be used within the next year, then it   (SO4)
    should be:
    a.   included in the Cash and Cash Equivalents line on the balance sheet.
    b.   reported as a current liability on the balance sheet.
    c.   reported as a noncurrent asset on the balance sheet.
    d.   reported as a current asset separate from Cash and Cash Equivalents on
    the balance sheet.

19. Keeping inventory levels low and planning the timing of major expenditures are   (SO5)
    two basic principles of:
    a.   internal control.
    b.   cash management.
    c.   inventory management.
    d.   share capital management.

20. With respect to cash management, most companies try to: (SO5)
    a.   keep as much spare cash on hand as possible in case of emergency.
    b.   keep a lot of cash in a non–interest-bearing chequing account because that
    type of account has the lowest fees.
    c.   invest idle cash, even if only overnight.
    d.   invest idle cash in liquid investments because that is where money earns
    the greatest return.

21. Expected incoming dividends and interest will be listed in the _____   (SO5)
    section of a cash budget.
    a.   cash receipts
    b.   cash disbursements
    c.   cash investments
    d.   financing

22. Expected payments for purchases of merchandise will be listed in the   (SO5)
    _____ section of a cash budget.
    a.   cash receipts
    b.   cash disbursements
    c.   cash investments
    d.   financing

Problems

(SO1)   1.   You have been asked to help the Basil Corporation with its internal control problems. Basil has 12 employees. There have not been any staff rotation between positions for at least six years because management believes that "the training costs of doing this would be too high". The company has a small Stores Department with one person who also works in the accounting department. That individual orders and receives goods and also pays the invoices. There is another person in the Accounting Department who handles all revenues. That individual makes deposits to the bank when "the deposit is large enough to make it worthwhile to go to the bank". That person also opens the mail and holds any cash or cheques in a desk drawer until the deposit is made.

Required:

Identify four weaknesses in internal control and make recommendations to correct the weaknesses.

(SO4)   2.   The following information is available for the J By J Corporation as of June 30, 2006, to assist you in preparing its bank reconciliation.
   a.   Balance per bank, June 30, $2,417.
   b.   Balance per books, June 30, $2,151.
   c.   Outstanding cheques at June 30 totalled $559.
   d.   Deposits in transit at June 30, totalled $802.
   e.   An NSF cheque for $67 that was returned by the bank. The cheque was originally received by the company from a customer who made a payment on account.
   f.   The bank statement showed bank service charges totalling $35.
   g.   An electronic deposit of $760 was made by a customer in payment of her account.
   h.   On June 15, the company issued a cheque for $1,587 to a supplier on account. The cheque, which cleared the bank in June, was incorrectly journalized by the company for $1,578 by the company.
   i.   Included with the cancelled cheques was a cheque issued by the G By G Corporation for $100 that was incorrectly charged to J By J Corporation by the bank.
   j.   A printing charge of $40 for company cheques was recorded on the bank statement.

Required:
   a.   Prepare a bank reconciliation for J By J Corporation as of June 30, 2006, using the above data.

J By J Corporation
Bank Reconciliation
June 30, 2006

b. Prepare any journal entries required by the reconciliation.

Date	Account Titles	Debit	Credit

3.   Please refer to the Domtar and Cascades financial statements for information
     for answering the following questions. Do not forget to use the **Decision Toolkit**
     approach for help in the problem solving.
     a.   What is the name of the first current asset on each company's balance   (SO4)
          sheet? Please explain the two components.
     b.   On a percentage basis, for each company, how much did Cash and Cash   (SO4)
          Equivalents increase or decrease from 2003 to 2004?
     c.   How did Domtar and Cascades use their cash in 2004?   (SO5)

4.   The Major Corporation requires a minimum monthly cash balance of $5,000.   (SO5)
     The beginning cash balance in February is budgeted to be $50,000.
     Additional information has been provided for February and March:

Particulars	Feb.	Mar.
Cash collections from customers	$43,600	$62,800
Sale of short-term investment		90,000
Cash purchases of merchandise inventory	50,000	60,000
Operating expenses (all paid in cash)	40,000	50,000
Equipment purchase	100,000	
Dividend Payment	4,000	4,000

Required:
Prepare a cash budget for the months of February and March.

Solutions to Self-Test

Multiple Choice

1. b   Only one person should have responsibility for a task, and custody and record-keeping should always be separated. Internal verification is a critical function, certainly not a waste of resources.
2. d   The use of prenumbered documents is very important.
3. c
4. c
5. d
6. c
7. c   The short-term investment in another company's stock is not a cash equivalent.
8. c $1,000 + $3,000 + $5,000 +$10,000. Postage stamps are office supplies or are expensed when purchased. Treasury bills are investments [and again often reported as cash equivalents].
9. d
10. d
11. a $3,500 + $850 - $20 - $170 = $4,160
12. b   The outstanding cheque and the deposit in transit are dealt with on the balance per bank side, and the service charge is subtracted from the balance per books side.
13. c $1,250 - $102 - $27 + $850.
14. b   All of the other items would be recorded on the balance per books side.
15. b
16. d
17. a   Cash does not appear on the statement of earnings and the statement of retained earnings.
18. d   To be included in Cash and Cash Equivalents, cash must be unrestricted. It certainly is not a liability and is not noncurrent, since it will be used within the next year.
19. b

20. c   Keeping spare cash on hand or in a non–interest-bearing account is not taking advantage of cash's interest-earning ability. It is unwise to invest in illiquid investments because they cannot be converted into cash when the need arises.

21. a   The cash receipts section lists receipts from the company's principal sources of revenue, and the cash disbursements section deals with payments, not receipts. There is no cash investments section.

22. b

Problems

1.

a. There is no rotation of employees which means that the company is more susceptible to employee fraud. The company should institute a rotation system where a few employees at a time would change jobs. That action would deter employee fraud as it would be more difficult to permanently conceal fraudulent activity.

b. The weakness of having one person do ordering and receiving of goods and paying the invoice involves segregation of duties. These three activities are referred to as "related activities". When one person is responsible for such related activities, the potential for errors and irregularities is increased. To remedy this weakness, separate individuals should do these different jobs. If the company cannot afford the required additional employees, then it should reorganize the jobs to at least remove the invoice paying function from the ordering and receiving function. The invoice paying could be done by the individual that handles the sales and cash handling functions, and perhaps the mail handling function could then be assigned to the stores person.

c. The internal control over cash receipts under "Other Controls" is violated by not depositing cash daily. The weakness is further exacerbated by keeping cash in an unlocked desk drawer. Cash should be deposited daily unless the amount of cash on some days is insignificant. In any event, any cash should be held in a locked safe or locked filing cabinet.

d. The opening of mail with deposits should be done with two people present. That would prevent the possibility of having an employee from keeping the deposit. The supervisor or another person should be present when mail is opened.

2.

a.

J By J Corporation
Bank Reconciliation
June 30, 2006

Balance per bank statement			$2,417
Add: Deposits in transit		802	
Cheque error		100	
	3,319		
Less: Outstanding cheques		559	
Adjusted cash balance per bank			$2,760
Cash balance per books			$2,151
Add: Electronic deposit			760
	2,911		
Less: NSF cheque	$67		
Bank service charges	35		
Cheque recording error ($1,587 - $1,578)	9		
Cheque printing charge	40	151	
Adjusted cash balance per book		$2,760	

b. Journal entries are recorded only for the "cash balance per books" side of the bank reconciliation. Bank personnel record journal entries for the "balance per bank" side.

June 30	Cash	760	
	Accounts Receivable		760
	(To record electronic deposit)		
	Accounts Receivable	67	
	Cash		67
	(To record NSF cheque)		
	Bank Charges Expense ($35 + $40)	75	
	Cash		75
	(To record bank service charges plus cheque printing costs)		
	Accounts Payable	9	
	Cash		9
	(To record cheque error)		

3.

a. The first current asset is cash and cash equivalents. Cash represents all coins, currency, and amounts in bank accounts. Cash equivalents are short-term highly liquid investments.

b. Domtar: The amount has increased by 8.3%. ($52 million - $48 million
    = $4 million ÷ $48 million)
    Cascades: The amount has increased by 11.1%. ($30 million - $27 million
    = $3 million ÷ $27 million)

c. The statements of cash flow indicate that both companies had to obtain cash
    from financing activities to assist in paying for investing activities and to add
    small amounts to their cash and cash equivalents balances. The statements of
    cash flow also show that neither company generated sufficient cash from operat-
    ing activities to pay for their investing activities. A summary follows:

	Domtar ($ millions)	Cascades ($ millions)
Cash flows provided by operating activities	$122	$156
Cash flows used by investing activities	(183)	(244)
Cash flows provided by financing activities	64	93
Net increase in cash and cash equivalents before adjustments	3	5
Translation adjustments	1	(2)
Net increase in cash and cash equivalents	$4	$3

4.

Major Corporation
Cash Budget
February 1 - March 31

Particulars	Feb.	Mar.
Beginning Cash Balance	$ 50,000	$ 5,000
Add: Receipts		
Sale of short term investment	90,000	
Cash collections	43,600	62,800
Total available cash	93,600	157,800
Less: Disbursements		
Purchases of merchandise in cash	50,000	60,000
Operating expenses	40,000	50,000
Equipment purchases	100,000	
Dividends	4,000	4,000
Total disbursements	194,000	114,000
Excess (deficiency) of available cash over disbursements	(100,400)	43,800
Financing		
Borrowing	105,400	
Repayments		38,800
Ending cash Balance	$ 5,000	$ 5,000

Note: $105,400 needs to be borrowed in February to provide a minimum ending cash
balance of $5,000. The Corporation can repay $38,800 and maintain a minimum cash
balance of $5,000.

chapter 8

Reporting and Analyzing Receivables

Chapter Overview

In this chapter, you will learn how to recognize and value accounts receivable, including how to record both estimated and actual bad debts. You will also learn how to recognize and value notes receivable. Finally, you will learn about the issues involved in managing receivables.

Review of Specific Study Objectives

- The term **"receivables" refers to amounts due from individuals and companies.** They are *claims that are expected to be collected in cash*. Receivables are often one of the largest assets for a company and are one of the most liquid assets.

- **Accounts receivable** are *amounts owed by customers on account*, and they result from the sale of goods and services.

- **Notes receivable** represent *claims for which formal instruments of credit are issued as evidence of the debt*. Unlike accounts receivable, notes receivable involve receipt of interest from the debtor. Notes and accounts receivable that result from sales transactions are called *trade receivables*.

study objective 1

Explain how accounts receivable are recognized in the accounts.

- **Other receivables** include *interest receivable, loans to company officers, advances to employees, recoverable sales taxes, and income taxes.* They are classified and reported as separate items in the current or noncurrent assets section of the balance sheet, according to their due dates.

- For a **service organization**, accounts receivable are *recorded when service is provided on account.*

- For a **merchandiser**, accounts receivable are *recorded at the point of sale of merchandise on account.*

- Receivables are **reduced as a result of sales discounts and sales returns.**

- A **subsidiary accounts receivable ledger** is used to help companies, with a large number of customers, to organize and track individual customer balances. The subsidiary accounts receivable ledger keeps track of individual account balances by customer, and the total of these balances agrees with the overall accounts receivable balance contained in the general ledger. Thus, the general ledger contains only one Accounts Receivable account, which acts as a **control account** to the subsidiary ledger.

- **Receivables are reported on the balance sheet as a current asset.**

study objective 2
Account for bad debts.

- The amount of receivables can be problematic. If a credit customer cannot pay his bill, then the credit loss is debited to Bad Debts Expense, a statement of earnings account. If we wait to record Bad Debt Expense until it is known with certainty that a credit customer is unable to pay their his bill, *bad debts expense will show only actual losses.* Because revenues might be recorded in one period while the (bad debts) expense might be recorded in the next period, **waiting until the loss occurs has the potential for violating the matching principle.**

- To avoid this potential mismatch, the **allowance method is used to record estimated uncollectibles.** A feature of this method is that *uncollectible accounts receivable are estimated and matched against sales in the same account period in which the sales occurred.* It also ensures that receivables are stated at their net realizable value, which is the amount that is actually expected to be received.

- The allowance method has three essential features:
  1. **Recording estimated uncollectibles.** Uncollectible accounts receivable are estimated and matched against sales in the accounting period in which sales occur. The adjusting journal entry to record estimated uncollectibles is as follows:

Bad Debts Expense	XXX	
Allowance for Doubtful Accounts		XXX
(To record estimate of uncollectible accounts)		

  Bad Debts Expense is reported on the *statement of earnings as an operating expense.* **Allowance for Doubtful Accounts** is reported on the balance sheet *as a contra asset account.* When it is subtracted from accounts receivable, *the difference represents the net realizable value of the accounts receivable at the statement date.*

The number in this journal entry is purely an estimate. At this point, the company does not know which customer will not pay its bill. Failure to write the entry would violate the matching principle. Recording this entry keeps the matching principle in operation.

While there are several acceptable ways to estimate uncollectible accounts, most companies apply a percentage to the outstanding receivables to determine the allowance for doubtful accounts.

Under the percentage of receivables basis, management establishes a percentage relationship between net amount of receivables and expected losses from uncollectible accounts. This percentage can be applied to total receivables, or to various classifications of receivables. For the latter approach, a schedule is prepared in which customer balances are classified by length of time they have been unpaid. Because of its emphasis on time, this schedule is called an aging schedule, and its completion is called aging of accounts receivable. The longer the period unpaid, the higher is the percentage. Consider the following example. Edison Inc. aged its receivables and calculated that estimated bad debts totalled $2,500. At the time, the Allowance for Doubtful Accounts had a credit balance of $300. The required adjusting entry is:

Bad Debts Expense	2,200	
Allowance for Doubtful Accounts		2,200
(To record estimate of uncollectible accounts)		

The Allowance account must have $2,500 in it after the adjusting entry is written. Since there is already a balance of $300, $2,200 must be added to the account to bring it up to that balance.

If the *Allowance account had had a $400 debit balance* in it before adjustment, then the adjusting entry would have been:

Bad Debts Expense	2,900	
Allowance for Doubtful Accounts		2,900
(To record estimate of uncollectible accounts)		

Remember that the Allowance account must have $2,500 in it after the adjusting entry is written. If there is a debit balance of $400, then the account must be credited for $2,900 in order to have an overall credit balance of $2,500.

2. **Recording the write-off of an uncollectible account.** Actual uncollectibles are written off at the time the specific account is determined to be uncollectible. The journal entry to record the write-off of an uncollectible account is as follows:

Allowance for Doubtful Accounts
    Accounts Receivable
(To write off an uncollectible account)

Bad Debts Expense is not used in this entry because it was used in the adjusting journal entry (in order to match revenues of the period to their related expense). *The number in this entry is an actual, not an estimated, number;* at this point, the company knows which customer is not paying its bill and the exact dollar amount of the bill.

Proper authorization of a write-off is critical. The entry to record a cash collection on an account requires a debit to Cash and a credit to Accounts Receivable. If an employee wished to steal money from customers paying on their accounts and to hide it from the company, then the employee could use the write-off entry. In each case—the cash collection and the write-off—the credit is to Accounts Receivable, thereby closing out that account balance. The write-off entry would allow the employee to steal the cash and to close out the customer's account balance.

Net realizable value is the same after a write-off as it was before a write-off. This is because both accounts receivable and the allowance account are reduced by the same amount.

3. **Recovery of an uncollectible account.** When an account previously written off is subsequently collected, the original write-off is reversed and the collection recorded. Neither the write-off nor the subsequent recovery has an impact on the statement of earnings, and, thus, matching is not distorted. Two journal entries are required to record the recovery of an amount previously written off: The first reinstates the customer's account, and the second records the cash collection.

Accounts Receivable
    Allowance for Doubtful Accounts
(To reverse the write write-off of an account)

Cash
    Accounts Receivable
(To record collection on account)

The first entry is simply a reversal of the original write-off entry. While the net effect of the two entries is a debit to Cash and a credit to the allowance account, it is important to reinstate the receivable and then show its collection for an information trail on the customer.

study objective 3
Explain how notes receivable are recognized and valued in the accounts.

- Credit may also be granted in exchange for a formal credit instrument known as a promissory note. A **promissory note** is a *written promise to pay a specified amount of money on demand or at a definite time.* The **maker** of a note is the *party making the promise to pay*; the **payee** is *the party to whom payment is to be made.*

- **Notes receivable give the holder a stronger legal claim** to assets than do accounts receivable; both types of receivables can readily be sold to another party. The majority of notes arise from lending transactions.

- The **formula for calculating interest** is as follows:

Interest = Principal x Rate x Time

The principal is the face value of the note, the rate is the annual interest rate, and the time is a fraction (in terms of one year). *The interest on a $12,000, three-month note with an interest rate of 4 percent is $120*, calculated as follows:

$120 = $12,000 x 4% x 3/12 months

- A **note receivable** is *recorded at its principal value, and no interest revenue is recorded when the note is accepted* because the revenue recognition principle does not recognize revenue until earned. *If a note is accepted in settlement of an open account,* then the entry is a debit to Notes Receivable and a credit to Accounts Receivable. *If a note is exchanged for cash,* then the entry is a debit to Notes Receivable and a credit to Cash. Notes are normally held to their maturity date, at which time, the principal value plus accrued interest is due. Occasionally, a **maker defaults on a note**.

- A **note is honoured** if it is *paid in full at the maturity date.* Consider again the note mentioned above: $12,000, three-month note with an interest rate of 4 percent with total interest of $120 due at maturity. On the maturity date, the holder records the following journal entry:

Cash	12,120	
Notes Receivable		12,000
Interest Revenue		120
(To record collection of note)		

If the note had been issued on December 1 and the holder had a December 31 year end, then the holder would have accrued interest on December 31 with the following entry:

Interest Receivable	40	
Interest Revenue		40
(To record accrued interest: $12,000 x 4% x 1/12)		

On the maturity date, March 1, the following entry would be recorded:

Cash	12,120	
Notes Receivable		12,000
Interest Receivable		40
Interest Revenue		80

- A **note is dishonoured** if it *is not paid in full at maturity.* If the $12,000, 4 percent, three-month note had not been paid on March 1, then the following journal entry would have been required:

Accounts Receivable	12,120	
Notes Receivable		12,000
Interest Revenue		120

While the note no longer has legal validity on the due date, the holder of the note records the entire amount as a receivable, signalling his intention to try to collect from the maker of the note. If the holder later determines that the account is not collectible, then he will write off the account by debiting the Allowance account and crediting Accounts Receivable.

Like accounts receivable, notes receivable are *reported at their net realizable value.* Valuing short-term notes receivable is the same as valuing accounts receivable. The calculations and estimations involved in determining net realizable value and in recording the proper amount of bad debts expense and related allowance are similar.

study objective 4

Explain the
statement
presentation of
receivables.

- **Short-term receivables** are reported in the Current Assets section of the balance sheet following cash Cash and Short-term Term Investments. Although only the net realizable value must be disclosed, it is helpful to report both the gross amount of receivables and the allowance for doubtful accounts either on the balance sheet or in the notes to the financial statements.

- **Bad Debts Expense** appears on the statement of earnings as an operating expense. **Interest Revenue** is shown under other revenues in the non-operating section of the statement of earnings item.

- A **company must disclose any particular problem with receivables, such as significant risk of uncollectible accounts.**

study objective 5

Apply the
principles of sound
accounts receivable
management.

- **Managing receivables** involves *five steps*:
  1. Determining who to extend credit to.
  2. Establishing a payment period.
  3. Monitoring collections.
  4. Establishing the liquidity of receivables.
  5. Accelerating cash receipts from receivables, when necessary.

- **Determining who receives credit** is a *critical issue for a company*. If a credit policy is too generous, then the company may extend credit to risky customers. If the policy is too tight, then it may lose sales. If a **company requires references from new customers**, then it must check out the references before it extends credit and, after credit is extended, continue to monitor the financial health of customers.

- When a company **establishes a payment period**, it must make sure to communicate the policy to customers. The payment period should be consistent with the period offered by competitors.

- A company needs to **monitor collections**. An *aging schedule* helps to do this in the following ways: it helps to establish the allowance for bad debts, it aids in the estimation and timing of future cash inflows, it provides information about the collection experience of the company, and it identifies problem accounts. If a company has significant **concentrations of credit risk**, it is required to disclose this risk in the notes to the financial statements. A **concentration of credit risk** is a *threat of nonpayment from a single customer or class of customers that could adversely affect the company's financial health.*

- To help **evaluate its receivables balance, a company calculates the receivables turnover ratio** by *dividing net credit sales by average gross accounts receivable.* (Average receivables are calculated by adding together the beginning and ending balances of receivables and dividing the sum by two.) If net credit sales total $25,000 and average receivables total $5,000, then the receivables turnover is five times, meaning that the company collects its receivables five times during the accounting period.

- This *ratio measures the number of times receivables are collected during the period.* A decreasing ratio should be of concern to a company, particularly if its competitors' ratios are holding steady or increasing.

- To calculate the **average collection period**, the company *divides the receivables turnover into 365 days*. Using the numbers above, the average collection period is 73 days (365 ÷ 5). A *general rule is that the collection period should not greatly exceed the credit-term period.*

- A company can borrow money from a bank by **using its accounts receivable as collateral**.

- A **company frequently sells its receivables to another company to shorten the cash-to-cash operating cycle**. There are *three reasons for the sale of receivables*: they may be a very large asset that a company wishes to convert to cash; they may be the only reasonable source of cash; and billing and collection are time-consuming and costly for companies.

- A company may sell its receivables to a *factor*, which is a *finance company or bank that buys receivables from businesses for a fee and then collects the payments directly from the customers.*

- A **retailer may allow its customers to use credit cards to charge purchases**, and its acceptance of a national credit card is *another form of selling the receivable* by the retailer. Use of such credit cards translates to more sales with zero bad debts for the retailer.

  Sales resulting from the use of bank credit cards are considered cash sales by the retailer. Issuing banks charge the retailer a fee. If a jewellery store sells $5,000 of jewellery to customers using that use bank credit cards and its bank charges a fee of 4 percent, then the jewellery store records the following entry:

Cash	4,800	
Service Charge Expense	200	
Sales		5,000
(To record credit card sales)		

Chapter Self-Test

As you work through the exercises and problems, remember to use the **Decision Toolkit** discussed and used in the text:

1. *Decision Checkpoints*: At this point, you ask a question.
2. *Info Needed for Decision*: You make a choice regarding the information needed to answer the question.
3. *Tool to Use for Decision*: At this point, you review just what the information chosen in step 2 does for the decision-making process.
4. *How to Evaluate Results*: You conduct an evaluation of information for answering the question.

Note: The notation (SO1) means that the question was drawn from study objective number one.

Multiple Choice

Please circle the correct answer.

(SO1)   1. Accounts and notes receivable that result from sales transactions are called:
    a. other receivables.
    b. non-trade receivables.
    c. trade receivables.
    d. non-current receivables.

(SO1)   2. Interest receivable and loans to company officers are included in:
    a. non-trade receivables.
    b. trade receivables.
    c. notes receivable.
    d. accounts receivable.

(SO1)   3. For a service organization, a receivable is recorded when:
    a. the customer pays the bill.
    b. when service is provided on account.
    c. thirty days after service is provided.
    d. when the bill is sent to the customer one week after service is provided.

(SO1)   4. A subsidiary accounts receivable ledger:
    a. is used by corporations who have subsidiary companies.
    b. provides supporting detail to the general ledger.
    c. replaces the main general ledger accounts receivable account.
    d. is used by all companies.

(SO2)   5. The entry to record estimated uncollectibles is:
    a. Bad Debts Expense
          Accounts Receivable
    b. Allowance for Doubtful Accounts
          Accounts Receivable
    c. Accounts Receivable
          Allowance for Doubtful Accounts
    d. Bad Debts Expense
          Allowance for Doubtful Accounts

(SO2)   6. The entry to record the write-off of an uncollectible account is:
    a. Bad Debts Expense
          Accounts Receivable
    b. Allowance for Doubtful Accounts
          Accounts Receivable
    c. Accounts Receivable
          Allowance for Doubtful Accounts
    d. Bad Debts Expense
          Allowance for Doubtful Accounts

(SO2)   7. Before a write-off of an uncollectible account, Accounts Receivable had a $10,000 balance, and the Allowance for Doubtful Accounts had a $500 balance. After a write-off of $100, the net realizable value is:

a. $10,000.
b. $9,500.
c. $9,400.
d. $9,300.

8. The Allowance for Doubtful Accounts has a $400 credit balance. An aging   (SO2)
schedule shows that total estimated bad debts is $3,600. The adjusting entry will
require a debit and a credit for:
a. $4,000.
b. $3,600.
c. $3,200.
d. some other amount.

9. The Allowance for Doubtful Accounts has a $400 debit balance. An aging   (SO2)
schedule shows that total estimated bad debts is $3,600. The adjusting entry will
require a debit and a credit for:
a. $4,000.
b. $3,600.
c. $3,200.
d. some other amount.

10. When an account is written off using the allowance method for uncollectible   (SO2)
accounts, the:
a. net realizable value of total accounts receivable will increase.
b. net accounts receivable will decrease.
c. allowance account will increase.
d. net accounts receivable will stay the same.

11. A company issues a four-month, 9 percent note for $30,000. The total interest   (SO3)
on the note is:
a. $90.
b. $900.
c. $2,700.
d. $3,000.

12. The journal entry written on the maturity date by the holder of a three-month,   (SO3)
4 percent, $15,000 note will include a:
a. debit to Cash for $15,150.
b. credit to Notes Receivable for $15,150.
c. debit to Interest Revenue for $150.
d. credit to Cash for $15,150.

13. A company holds a four-month, 5 percent, $21,000 note that was not paid in   (SO3)
full on the maturity date. The journal entry on the maturity date will include a:
a. debit to Accounts Receivable for $21,350
b. credit to Notes Receivable for $21,350
c. debit to Cash for $21,350
d. debit to Notes Receivable for $21,000

(SO3)   14. A promissory note has two key parties as follows:
    a.   Debtor and a bank
    b.   Debtor and the sender
    c.   Receiver and the sender
    d.   Payee and the maker

(SO3)   15. The interest on a $5,000, 5 percent, three-month note receivable is:
    a. $62.50
    b. $83.33
    c. $250.00
    d. $125.00

(SO4)   16. Accounts receivable are valued and reported on the balance sheet:
    a.   at the gross amount.
    b.   when customer makes payment.
    c.   at net realizable value.
    d.   in the Other Asset category.

(SO4)   17. Bad Debts Expense is reported on the statement of earnings as:
    a.   an operating expense.
    b.   part of net sales.
    c.   part of cost of goods sold.
    d.   a contra-revenue account.

(SO4)   18. Which of the following is the correct sequence for receivables on the balance sheet?
    a.   Notes receivable, other receivables, accounts receivable
    b.   Accounts receivable, notes receivable, other receivables
    c.   Notes receivable, accounts receivable, other receivables
    d.   Accounts receivable, other receivables, notes receivable

(SO5)   19. A threat of nonpayment from a single customer or class of customers that could adversely affect the financial health of a company is called:
    a.   accounts receivable concentration risk.
    b.   notes receivable concentration risk.
    c.   credit risk.
    d.   a concentration of credit risk.

(SO5)   20. Net credit sales are $800,000, average gross receivables total $150,000, average inventory totals $200,000, and the allowance for doubtful accounts totals $8,000. The receivables turnover is:
    a.   100 times.
    b.   5.33 times.
    c.   4.00 times.
    d.   1.33 times.

(SO5)   21. Please use the information from number 20. The average collection period is:
    a.   100 days.
    b.   75.0 days.
    c.   68.5 days.
    d.   5.33 days.

22. Kerrison Corporation sold $6,000 of merchandise to customers who charged   (SO5)
    their purchases with a bank credit card. Kerrison's bank charges it a 4 percent
    fee. The journal entry to record the credit card sales will include a:
    a.   debit to Cash for $5,760.
    b.   credit to Sales for $5,760.
    c.   debit to Cash for $6,000.
    d.   credit to Service Charge Expense for $240.

23. The receivables turnover ratio is used to analyze: (SO5)
    a.   credit worthiness.
    b.   profitability.
    c.   solvency.
    d.   liquidity.

Problems

1. Please record journal entries for the following items for Morrison Corporation:
    a.   At the end of the accounting period on June 30, Morrison prepares an   (SO2)
         aging schedule of accounts receivable that shows total estimated bad debts
         of $5,200. On this date, the Allowance for Doubtful Accounts has a debit
         balance of $300, and Accounts Receivable has a balance of $85,000.

    b.   On July 5, Morrison receives word that Sperry Ltd. has declared bankruptcy,   (SO2)
         and Morrison writes off its account receivable of $800.

    c.   On September 12, Sperry Ltd. notifies Morrison that it can pay its $800   (SO2)
         debt and includes a cheque for the entire amount.

    d.   What is the net realizable value of accounts receivable after the entry in (a)   (SO2)
         is written? What is the net realizable value after the write-off in (b)?

a–c

Date	Account Titles	Debit	Credit

d.

2.   A company's partial balance sheet, at December 31, appears as follows before adjusting entries for 2007 have been made:

Current Assets		2007		2006
Cash and cash equivalents		$50,000		$60,000
Short-term investments		40,000		30,000
Note receivable		80,000		75,000
Accounts receivable	$90,000		$80,000	
Less: Allowance for doubtful accounts	15,000	75,000	10,000	70,000
Other current assets		90,000		95,000
Total current assets		$335,000		$330,000

(SO3)   **Required:**

a.   The $80,000 note shown above for 2007 represents a three-month, 4.5 percent interest bearing note issued on November 1, 2007. Prepare any required adjusting entry.

(SO3)

b.   Journalize the entry that would be required when the note is collected at maturity in 2008, assuming that the adjusting entry in (a) was made.

(SO2)

c.   An aging of accounts receivable prepared on December 31, 2007, indicates that bad debts are estimated to be $77,000. Prepare any required adjusting entry.

(SO5)

d.   Calculate the receivables turnover and the average collection period for 2007, assuming net credit sales for 2007 are $501,500.

3.   The following accounts appear in the general ledger of Majestic Corporation at December 31, 2006 with the following balances:

Accounts Receivable	$125,000
Accumulated Amortization	60,000
Allowance for Doubtful Accounts	18,000
Amortization Expense	10,000
Cash	90,000
Dividends	8,000
Equipment	200,000
Merchandise Inventory	100,000
Notes Payable	50,000
Office Supplies	1,000
Prepaid Expenses	12,000
Sales	250,000
Sales Returns and Allowances	10,000
Short-Term Notes Receivable	75,000
Short-Term Investments	80,000

(SO4)   **Required:**

Prepare the partial balance sheet presentation for current assets of Majestic Corporation.

4.   Please refer to the Domtar and Cascades financial statements for information for answering the following questions. **Don't** forget to use the **Decision Toolkit** approach for help in the problem solving.

a. What is the percentage increase or decrease in accounts receivable from 2003 to 2004?   (SO1)

b. For both Domtar and Cascades, calculate the receivables turnover and average collection period for 2004.   (SO5)

c. Compare your results obtained in (b).   (SO5)

Solutions to Self-Test

Multiple Choice

1. c Other and nontrade receivables are basically the same thing and arise from such items as interest and loans to company officers. Accounts receivable are always current assets.

2. a Trade receivables arise from sales transactions, notes receivable are written promises and usually include interest, and accounts receivable are amounts owed by customers on account.

3. b A receivable is recorded before the customer pays the bill. The receivable should be recorded when the service is performed, not at some other specific date.

4. b.

5. d The answer in (a) is the write-off of a debt under the direct write-off method. The answer in (b) is the write-off of a debt under the allowance method. The answer in (c) is the reinstatement of a written-off account under the allowance method.

6. b

7. b The net realizable value is $9,500 ($10,000 – $500) before the write off and $9,500 ($9,900 – $400) after.

8. c $3,600 is the amount that must be in the Allowance account after adjustment. Since it already has a credit balance of $400, only $3,200 is needed to raise the balance to $3,600.

9. a $3,600 is the amount that must be in the Allowance account after adjustment. Since it has a debit balance of $400, $4,000 is needed to raise the balance to $3,600.

10. d

11. b $30,000 x 9% x 4/12 months

12. a The journal entry is:

Cash	15,150	
Notes Receivable		15,000
Interest Revenue		150
($15,000 x 4% x 3/12 = $150)		

13. a The journal entry is:

Accounts Receivable	21,350	
Notes Receivable		21,000
Interest Revenue		350
($21,000 x 5% x 4/12 = $350)		

14. d

15. a $5,000 x 5% x 3/12 = 62.50

16. c
17. a
18. c
19. d
20. b   Net credit sales ÷ Average gross receivables = $800,000 ÷ $150,000 = 5.33 times
21. c   365 ÷ Receivables turnover = 365 ÷ 5.33 = 68.5 days
22. a   The journal entry is:

Cash	5,760	
Service Charge Expense	240	
Sales		6,000

23. d

Problems

1. a.   June 30

Bad Debts Expense	5,500	
Allowance for Doubtful Accounts		5,500

(To record the estimate of uncollectible accounts: $300 + $5,200)

b.   July 5

Allowance for Doubtful Accounts	800	
Accounts Receivable—Sperry		800

(To write off the Sperry account)

c.   Sep. 12

Accounts Receivable—Sperry	800	
Allowance for Doubtful Accounts		800

(To reinstate Sperry account)

Cash	800	
Accounts Receivable—Sperry		800

(To record collection on Sperry account)

d.

	Before Write off	After Write off
Accounts receivable	$85,000	$84,200
Less: Allowance Doubtful Accounts	5,500	4,700
Net realizable value	$79,500	$79,500

The net realizable value does not change because both accounts are reduced by the same amount.

2.

a.   Dec. 31, 2007

Interest Receivable	600	
Interest Revenue		600

$80,000 x .045 x 2/12

b.   Feb. 1, 2008

Cash	80,900	
Interest Receivable		600
Interest Revenue		300
Notes Receivable		80,000

Interest Revenue = $80,000 x .045 x 1/12 = $300

c. Dec. 31, 2007   Bad Debts Expense   2,000
                          Allowance for Doubtful Accounts   2,000
                          $77,000 − $75,000

d. Receivables turnover $$\frac{\$501,500}{(\$90,000 + \$80,000) \div 2} = 5.9 \text{ times}$$

Average collection period $$\frac{365}{5.9} = 61.9 \text{ days}$$

3.

MAJESTIC CORPORATION
Balance Sheet (Partial)
December 31, 2006

Current assets		
Cash		$ 90,000
Short-term investments		80,000
Accounts receivable	$125,000	
Less: Allowance for doubtful accounts	18,000	107,000
Short-term notes receivable		75,000
Merchandise inventory		100,000
Office supplies		1,000
Prepaid expense		12,000
Total current assets		$465,000

4. (all dollar amounts are in millions)

a. Domtar: The amount has increased by 18.3%.
    $233 − $197 = $36 ÷ $197
    Cascades: The amount has increased by 6.7%.
    $527 − $494 = $33 ÷ $494

    Domtar:
    Average receivables = ($233 + $197) ÷ 2 = $215.00
    Receivables turnover = net credit sales ÷ average receivables
    $5,115 ÷ $215.00 = 23.79 times
    Average collection period = 365 ÷ receivables turnover
    365 ÷ 23.79 = 15.34 days

    Cascades:
    Average receivables = ($527 + $494) ÷ 2 = $510.50
    Receivables turnover = net credit sales ÷ average receivables
    $3,254 ÷ $510.50 = 6.4 times
    Average collection period = 365 ÷ receivables turnover
    365 ÷ 6.4 = 57.03 days

b. The average collection period for Cascades is much longer than it is for Domtar
    (57.03 days compared to with 15.34 days). To further evaluate the effectiveness
    of the accounts receivable collection policy, the credit period granted to

customers would have to be examined. For example, if Cascades has a 30-day collection period, then the average collection period of 57.03 days in 2004 would represent a poor collection record.

chapter 9

Reporting and Analyzing Long-Lived Assets

Chapter Overview

In this chapter, you will learn how to account for long-lived assets. You will learn about the amounts at which they are recorded in the accounting records and how to allocate their cost to expense using different amortization methods. You will learn how to dispose of long-lived assets and methods used by companies for evaluating their use. Finally, you will learn how to report long-lived assets on the balance sheet.

Review of Specific Study Objectives

- Long-lived, **tangible assets** are *resources that have physical substance, are used in the operations of a business, and are not intended for sale to customers.* The term "property, plant, and equipment" is used to identify tangible long-lived assets.

- **Property, plant, and equipment are recorded at cost**, which consists of *all expenditures necessary to acquire the asset and make it ready for its intended use.*

- **Operating expenditures** *are costs that benefit the current period and are expensed.*

- **Capital expenditures** *are costs that benefit future periods and are included in a long-lived asset account.*

- Property, plant, and equipment are often divided into four classes:

  1. Land, such as a building site.
  2. Land improvements, such as driveways, parking lots, fences, and underground sprinkler systems.
  3. Buildings, such as stores, offices, factories, and warehouses.
  4. Equipment, such as store checkout counters, office furniture, cash registers, coolers, factory machinery, and delivery equipment.

- **The cost of land** includes *the cash purchase price and closing costs, such as survey and legal fees.* All costs incurred in making land ready for its intended use increase the Land account: clearing, draining, filling, grading, and razing old buildings are included. If the land has a building on it that must be removed to make the site suitable for construction of a new building, all demolition and removal costs, less any proceeds from salvaged materials, are chargeable to the Land account. Once the land is ready for its intended use, recurring costs, such as annual property taxes, are expensed. Its cost is not amortized over the life of the asset because land has an unlimited useful life.

- The **cost of land improvements** includes *all expenditures necessary to make the improvements ready for their intended use.* For example, constructing a parking lot includes paving, fencing, and lighting. Land improvements require maintenance and replacement to maintain their value to the company. Because of this, the cost of land improvements is amortized over their limited useful lives.

- The **cost of buildings** includes *all expenditures relating to the purchase or construction of a building.* If a **building is purchased**, then the costs include the purchase price and closing costs. In addition, any cost required to make the building ready for its intended use are also charged to the Building account. Such costs include remodelling rooms and offices and replacing or repairing the roof, floors, electrical wiring, and plumbing. If a **building is constructed**, then costs include the contract price, architects' fees, building permits, excavation costs, and interest costs incurred to finance the project (the inclusion of the latter is limited to the construction period).

- The **cost of equipment** includes *the cash purchase price, freight charges, and insurance during shipping (if paid by the purchaser), as well as assembling, installing, and testing the unit.* Fees, which occur after the equipment is operational, such as vehicle licences and accident insurance, are debited to an expense account or treated as a prepaid asset.

- **Companies often lease assets.** In a lease, a **lessor** agrees to allow another party, the **lessee**, to use the asset for an agreed period of time at an agreed price. Some **advantages of leasing** include *reduced risk of obsolescence, low down payment, tax advantages, and non-reporting of assets and liabilities.* In an **operating lease**, the lessee uses the asset but does not record an asset or a liability. Instead, periodic lease payments are recorded as rent expense (or prepaid rent). Under a **capital lease**, the lessee uses the asset and does record an asset and a liability.

- **Amortization** is the *process of allocating the cost of a long-lived asset to expense over its useful (service) life in a rational and systematic way.* Such cost allocation is designed to properly match expenses with revenues in accordance with the matching principle.

- The **journal entry to record amortization** is:

> Amortization Expense
> Accumulated Amortization

Amortization Expense appears on the statement of earnings, and the Accumulated Amortization account is a contra asset account, subtracted from the asset's original cost to give its net book value.

- **Recognizing amortization for an asset does not result in the accumulation of cash for the replacement of the asset.**

- **Amortization is a process of cost allocation**, *not a process of asset valuation. Thus, the net book value (cost less accumulated amortization) may differ significantly from the fair market value of the asset.*

- **Land improvements, building, and equipment are amortizable assets**, but *land* is not. Land has an indefinite useful life and often appreciates in value.

- **Amortizable assets lose their utility** because of *wear and tear and obsolescence*, the process by which an asset becomes out of date before it physically wears out.

- **Three factors** affect the calculation of amortization: *cost, useful life* (an estimate of the productive, or service, life of the asset, expressed in terms of time, units of activity, or units of output), and *salvage value* (an estimate of the asset's value at the end of its useful life).

- The **straight-line, declining-balance, and units-of-activity methods** of amortization are *all acceptable under generally accepted accounting principles.* Management of a company chooses the method that it feels best measures the asset's contribution to revenue and then applies that method consistently. The *straight-line method is the most widely used because it is simple to apply and understand.*

- Under the **straight-line method**, an equal amount of amortization is expensed each year of the asset's useful life. *Amortizable cost*, which is the asset's cost less its salvage value, *is divided by the useful life* to give the annual amortization expense. A straight-line rate can also be calculated (100% ÷ useful life) and multiplied by the amortizable cost to give the annual amortization expense.

  Consider the **following example.** A company purchased a truck on January 2 for $58,000. The truck has a useful life of 5 years and a salvage value of $8,000. The amortizable cost is $50,000 ($58,000 – $8,000), and annual amortization is $10,000 (50,000 ÷ 5 years). The straight-line rate is 20 percent (100% ÷ 5 years); multiplying $50,000 by 20 percent also yields $10,000 per year. After 5 years, the total accumulated amortization is $50,000, and the book value of the asset is $8,000 ($58,000 – $50,000). Note that *the net book value equals the salvage value after all amortization is taken.* If this asset had been purchased on July 1, then amortization for the year ended December 31 would have been $5,000 ($10,000 x 6/12).

> **study objective 2**
>
> Explain the concept of, and calculate, amortization.

- The **declining-balance method** is called an *accelerated method because it results in more amortization in the early years of an asset's life than does the straight-line method.* The amortization expense is lower than under the straight-line method in the later years of the asset's life. However, the total amount of amortization (the amortizable cost) taken over an asset's life is the same, regardless of the method of amortization used. A common way to apply the declining-balance method is to use a rate that is double the straight-line rate, thus producing double declining balance. Just as is true for the straight-line method, amortization under this method is a function of time.

- Under the **units-of-activity method**, *useful life is expressed in terms of the total units of production or the use expected from the asset.* Units of output, machine hours, kilometres driven, and hours flown can all be used. This method is excellent for factory machinery, vehicles, and airplanes.

- **Under all three methods total amortization is the same.** The only thing that differs is the timing at which the expense is taken.

study objective 3

Describe other accounting issues related to amortization.

- The Canada Revenue Agency (CRA) allows corporate taxpayers to deduct a specified amount of amortization expense when calculating taxable income. The amortization allowed for income tax purposes is calculated on a class (group) basis, using the single-declining method, and is termed **capital cost allowance (CCA). For accounting purposes**, a company should choose the amortization method that best matches revenue to expense.

- In some instances, the market value of a long-lived asset may fall significantly below the net book value of the asset and is not expected to be recovered. Such a permanent decline in the market value of the asset is referred to as an **impairment loss**. The journal entry to record an impairment loss is:

  Loss on Impairment
      Accumulated Amortization

- The impairment loss is recorded on the statement of earnings as part of continuing operations and not under "other expenses."

- Unlike inventories, the lower of cost or market rule does not apply automatically to property, plant, and equipment. Because inventory is expected to be converted into cash within the year, it is important to value it annually at the lesser of its cost or market value. In contrast, property, plant, and equipment are used in operations over a longer term and are not available for resale. The going-concern assumption assumes that a company will recover at least the cost of its long-lived assets. So, when a permanent impairment occurs in the value of the asset, its book value should be written down to market. This does not happen often.

- **Amortization should be changed** if *wear and tear or obsolescence indicates that annual amortization is inadequate or excessive.*

- The **change in amortization** is *made in current and future years but not in prior periods.* This means that prior years' financial statements do not have to be restated. Continual restatement would undermine confidence in the financial statements. The revised amortization is calculated using the net book value at the time of the change in the estimate, the revised salvage value, and the remaining useful life.

- **Significant changes** in estimates must be disclosed in the financial statements.

- Regardless of the method of disposal, **amortization must be brought up to date, if necessary**. Then, when the disposal journal entry is written, the *asset account is credited for its cost, and the related Accumulated Amortization account is debited.*

- If the **disposal is a sale**, then the *book value of the asset is compared with the proceeds of the sale.* If the proceeds exceed the book value, then there is a **gain on the sale**. If the proceeds are less than the book value, then there is a **loss on the sale**.

- Consider the **following example**. A *company sells a piece of machinery* that cost it $10,000 and which has accumulated amortization of $6,000 *for $5,000*. The journal entry to record the sale is as follows:

Cash	5,000	
Accumulated Amortization	6,000	
Machinery		10,000
Gain on Disposal		1,000
(To record sale of machinery at a gain)		

The book value of the asset is $4,000 ($10,000 – $6,000). Since the company received $5,000 for the asset, it sold the asset for a $1,000 gain. **Gain on Disposal** appears in the "Other Revenues" section of the statement of earnings.

If the company had sold the asset for $2,000, then it would have incurred a loss of $2,000 ($4,000 book value – $2,000 cash proceeds). The journal entry is as follows:

Cash	2,000	
Accumulated Amortization	6,000	
Loss on Disposal	2,000	
Machinery		10,000
(To record sale of machinery at a loss)		

Loss on Disposal appears in the "Other Expenses" section of the statement of earnings.

- If the **disposal is a retirement**, then it is *recorded as a sale in which no cash is received*. The asset is credited for its cost, Accumulated Amortization is debited for the proper amount, and a loss is debited for the book value of the asset on the date of retirement. A retirement will never result in a gain. If the asset sold in the two journal entries above is simply retired, then the journal entry is as follows:

Accumulated Amortization	6,000	
Loss on Disposal	4,000	
Machinery		10,000
(To record retirement of machinery)		

- In an exchange of assets, a new asset is typically purchased by trading in an old asset, on which a trade-in allowance is given toward the purchase price of the new asset. An additional cash payment is usually also required for the difference between the trade-in allowance and the purchase price of the new asset. Accounting for exchange transactions is complex and is left for more advanced accounting courses.

study objective 4

Explain how to account for the disposal of property, plant, and equipment.

study objective 5

Identify the basic issues related to accounting for intangible assets.

- **Intangible assets** are *rights, privileges, and competitive advantages that result from ownership of long-lived assets that do not possess physical substance.* Intangibles must be evidenced by contracts, licenses, and other documents. Intangibles may arise from the following sources:

  1. Government grants, such as patents, copyrights, franchises, trademarks, and trade names.
  2. Acquisition of another business, in which the purchase price includes a payment for goodwill.
  3. Private monopolistic arrangements arising from contractual agreements, such as franchises and leases.

- **Intangible assets are recorded at cost**. If an intangible asset has a **limited life**, its amortizable cost (cost less salvage value) should be allocated over the shorter of the (1) estimated useful life, and (2) legal life. The straight-line method of amortization is typically used. The **journal entry to record amortization** includes a *debit to amortization expense and a credit to accumulated amortization.* If an intangible asset has an **indefinite life**, it is not amortized. However, its cost is reviewed and tested for an impairment loss annually or, more often, as circumstances dictate. If any impairment is evident, that is, if the asset's market value permanently falls below its book value, the asset must be written down to its market value and an impairment loss recorded. If no impairment has occurred, the asset remains at its current value until the following year, when it is evaluated again.

- As mentioned above, intangible assets are segregated into two categories—those with limited lives and those with indefinite lives—in order to determine whether or not the intangible assets should be amortized. The following represent intangible assets with limited lives:

  - A **patent** is an *exclusive right issued by the Canadian Intellectual Property Office of Industry Canada that enables the recipient to manufacture, sell, or otherwise control an invention for a period of 20 years from the date of the application.* The **initial cost** of *a patent is the cash or cash equivalent price paid to acquire the patent.* The cost of the patent should be amortized over its 20-year legal life or its useful life, whichever is shorter. If the owner of a patent successfully defends the patent in a lawsuit, then the costs of the lawsuit are debited to the Patent account and amortized over the remaining life of the patent.

  - A **copyright** is *granted by the Canadian Intellectual Property Office, giving the owner the exclusive right to reproduce and sell an artistic or published work.* The **legal life** of a copyright is the life of the creator plus 50 years, and the **cost** is the *cost of acquiring and defending* it. Generally, the useful life of a copyright is significantly shorter than its legal life, and the copyright is therefore amortized over its useful life.

  - **Research and development (R & D) costs** are not intangible assets, per se. But, they may lead to patents, copyrights, new processes, and new products. There are many uncertainties in identifying the extent and timing of the future benefits of these expenditures. As a result, research costs are **always recorded as an expense when incurred**, whether the research and development are successful or not. Certain development costs can be capitalized if it is reasonably certain that they will provide future benefits; otherwise, they too must be expensed.

- The following represent intangible assets with indefinite lives:

    - A **trademark or trade name** is a *word, phrase, jingle, or symbol that distinguishes or identifies a particular enterprise or product*. Trademarks and trade names have tremendous value to companies and are vigorously defended. The creator or original user may obtain the exclusive legal right to trademark or trade name by registering it with the Canadian Intellectual Property Office. Such registration provides continuous protection and may be renewed every 15 years as long as the trademark or trade name is in use. If they are **purchased**, then *the cost is the purchase price*. If they are **developed** by the enterprise itself, the *cost includes lawyer's fees, registration fees, design costs, successful legal defence costs, and other such expenditures*. Because trademarks and trade names normally have indefinite lives, they are not amortized. The book value must be tested annually for impairment and a loss recognized, if appropriate.

    - A **franchise** is a *contractual agreement under which the franchisor grants the franchisee the right to sell certain products, to render specific services, or to use certain trademarks or trade names, normally within a designated geographic area*. Another type of franchise is granted by a governmental body and permits an enterprise to use public property in performing its services. This operating right is called a **licence**. Both franchises and licences may be granted for a definite period of time, an indefinite period, or in perpetuity. **Initial costs associated with the acquisition** are *debited to the asset account*; after that, annual recurring costs are recorded as operating expenses. In the case of a limited life, the cost of a franchise (or licence) should be amortized over the useful life. If the life is indefinite, it is not amortized but is tested annually for impairment.

    - **Goodwill** represents the value of all favourable attributes that relate to a company. These include excellent management, a desirable location, skilled employees, good customer relations, high-quality products, fair pricing policies, and harmonious relations with labour unions. Unlike other assets, such as investments or property, plant, and equipment, which can be sold individually in the marketplace, goodwill can be identified only with the business *as a whole*. Goodwill is **recorded only when there is an exchange transaction that involves the purchase of an entire business**. Because goodwill has an indefinite life, it is not amortized. Since goodwill is measured using the market value of a company, a subjective evaluation that can easily change, it must be tested annually for impairment and a loss recognized, if appropriate.

- Long-lived assets are normally reported under the headings *Property, Plant, and Equipment and Intangible Assets*. Sometimes, intangible assets are listed separately, following Property, Plant, and Equipment, with no separate caption. Goodwill must be separately disclosed; other intangibles can be grouped together for reporting purposes.

- There should be **disclosure in the financial statements or in the notes to the statements** of *the balances of the major classes of assets and accumulated amortization by major classes or in total. Amortization methods used should be disclosed, as should the amount of expense for the period.*

> **study objective 6**
>
> Indicate how long-lived assets are reported in the financial statements.

- The amortization expense and impairment losses are reported in the operating section of the statement of earnings. The cash flows resulting from the purchase or sale of long-lived assets are reported in the investing section of the cash flow statement.

- **Two measures** are used to analyze assets: return on assets and asset turnover.

- The **return on assets** ratio measures the overall profitability of a company. It is calculated by dividing net earnings by average total assets. The return on assets ratio indicates the amount of net earnings generated by each dollar invested in assets. Thus, the higher the return on assets, the more profitable the company is.

- The **asset turnover** ratio indicates how efficiently a company is able to generate sales with a given amount of assets. It is calculated by dividing net sales by average total assets. It shows how many dollars of sales are generated by each dollar invested in assets. The higher the ratio, the more efficiently the company is operating. If the ratio is 1.25 times, then this means that for each *dollar invested in assets*, the company generates sales of $1.25. Asset turnover ratios vary considerably among industries.

- To complete the analysis of the sales-generating ability of a company's assets, the **profit margin**, discussed in Chapter 5, can be used in conjunction with the **asset turnover ratio** to explain the **return on assets ratio**. The relationship is as follows:

Profit Margin	x	Asset Turnover	=	Return on Assets
↓		↓		↓
$\dfrac{\text{Net Earnings}}{\text{Net Sales}}$	x	$\dfrac{\text{Net Sales}}{\text{Average Total Assets}}$	=	$\dfrac{\text{Net Earnings}}{\text{Average Total Assets}}$

This relationship has important implications for management. If a company wants to increase its return on assets, it can do so either by increasing the margin it generates from each dollar of goods that it sells (profit margin) or by trying to increase the volume of goods that it sells (asset turnover).

- Under the **declining-balance method**, amortization expense is calculated by *multiplying the book value of the asset by the straight-line rate*. **Salvage value is initially ignored in the calculations**. Later, amortization stops when the net book value reaches the salvage value. Double declining balance is one of the forms of the declining-balance method: the rate is the straight-line rate multiplied by two. If an asset has a useful life of four years, then the straight-line rate is 25 percent (100% ÷ 4 years). Double that rate is 50 percent.

Assume that the asset with a four-year useful life originally cost $50,000 and has a salvage value of $5,000. Amortization expense for the four years will be:

Year	Book Value		Rate		Amortization Expense
1	$50,000	x	50%	=	$25,000
2	25,000	x	50%	=	12,500
3	12,500	x	50%	=	6,250
4	6,250	x	50%	=	1,250
					$45,000

Note that in year four, only $1,250 of amortization was taken, even though the book value of $6,250 multiplied by 50 percent yields $3,125. Remember that book value must equal salvage value at the end of the four years, and $3,125 would have violated that. In the final year, only amortization that will make the total amortization $45,000 ($50,000 – $5,000) is taken.

Amortization under this method is a function of time. Therefore, an asset purchased during the year must have its amortization prorated. If the asset above had been purchased on April 1, then amortization for year 1 would have been $18,750 ($50,000 x 50% x 9/12). Book value for year two would have been $31,250 ($50,000 – $18,750).

- Under the **units-of-activity method**, amortizable cost *per unit is calculated and applied to actual units during the accounting period.*

- A company purchased an asset with a cost of $30,000, a salvage value of $5,000, an estimated useful life of five years, and estimated units of output of 50,000. In year one, the asset produced 12,000 units. Amortization is calculated as follows:

$30,000 – $5,000 = $25,000 amortizable cost
$25,000 ÷ 50,000 units = $0.50 per unit
$0.50 per unit x 12,000 actual units = $6,000

Note that the useful life in years is not used in the calculation. Note, too, that this method starts with the amortizable cost, just as straight-line amortization does. Since the units-of-activity method is a function of usage and not of time, it is not necessary to prorate amortization if the asset is purchased at a time other than the beginning of the accounting period.

- Remember that **all three methods produce the same total amount of amortization over the life of an asset**. It is the timing of the expense that differs among the methods.

Chapter Self-Test

As you work through the exercises and problems, remember to use the **Decision Toolkit** discussed and used in the text:
1. *Decision Checkpoints*: At this point, you ask a question.
2. *Info Needed for Decision*: You make a choice regarding the information needed to answer the question.
3. *Tool to Use for Decision*: At this point, you review just what the information chosen in step 2 does for the decision-making process.
4. *How to Evaluate Results*: You conduct an evaluation of information for answering the question.

Note: The notation (SO1) means that the question was drawn from study objective number one.

Multiple Choice

Please circle the correct answer.

(SO1)   1. A company purchases a used delivery van for $20,000. The logo of the company is painted on the side of the van for $600. The van licence is $60. The van undergoes safety testing for $110. What does the company record as the cost of the new van?
a. $20,600
b. $20,660
c. $20,710
d. $20,770

(SO1)   2. Massey Corporation purchased a piece of land for $50,000. It paid legal fees of $9,000. An old building on the land was torn down at a cost of $2,000, and proceeds from the scrap were $500. The total to be debited to the Land account is:
a. $61,000.
b. $60,500.
c. $59,000.
d. $50,000.

(SO1)   3. Newcome Corporation installed a new parking lot for its employees at a cost of $10,000. The $10,000 should be debited to:
a.   Repairs and Maintenance Expense.
b.   Land.
c.   Land Improvements.
d.   Parking Lot.

(SO1)   4. Oliver Corporation purchased a piece of equipment for $20,000. It paid shipping charges of $500 and insurance during transit of $200. Installation and testing of the new equipment cost $1,000. The total to be debited to the Equipment account is:
a. $20,000.
b. $20,500.
c. $20,700.
d. $21,700.

(SO2)   5. Which of the following is not an amortizable asset?
a.   Land
b.   Building
c.   Driveway
d.   Equipment

(SO2)   6. Which of the following is a way to express the estimated useful life of an amortizable asset?
a.   Five years
b.   Ten thousand machine hours
c.   Thirty thousand units
d.   All of the above are expressions of useful life

7. At the beginning of the year, Powers Corporation purchased a piece of   (SO2)
    machinery for $50,000, with a salvage value of $5,000, an estimated useful life
    of nine years, and estimated units of output of 90,000 units. Actual units
    produced during the first year were 11,000. Amortization expense for the first
    year under the straight-line method is:
    a. $5,556.
    b. $5,500.
    c. $5,300.
    d. $5,000.

8. Which of the following statements is correct?   (SO2)
    a.   Straight-line amortization is an accelerated method of amortization.
    b.   The total amount of amortization for an asset is the same, regardless of
         the method used.
    c.   The total amount of amortization for an asset differs depending on the
         method used.
    d.   In the later years of an asset's useful life, straight-line amortization gives a
         lower expense than does declining-balance amortization.

9. Which of the following statements is correct?   (SO3)
    a.   Once amortization expense is set, it may never be changed for an asset.
    b.   When a change in estimate for amortization is required, the change is
         made to prior periods.
    c.   When a change in estimate for amortization is required, the change is
         made in current and future years but not to prior periods.
    d.   When a change in estimate for amortization is required, the change is
         made to prior periods and in current and future years.

10. A permanent decline in the market value of an asset is called: (SO3)
    a.   an impairment.
    b.   a write-down.
    c.   earnings management.
    d.   a capital expenditure.

11. Which of the following methods will result in the highest amortization in the (SO3)
    first year?
    a.   Units-of-activity
    b.   Time valuation
    c.   Straight-line
    d.   Declining-balance

12. A company sold for $3,000 a long-lived asset, which had a cost of $10,000 and (SO4)
    accumulated amortization of $7,500. The company had a:
    a.   loss of $500.
    b.   gain of $500.
    c.   gain of $3,000.
    d.   loss of $7,000.

(SO4)   13. A company sold for $2,000 a long-lived asset, which had a cost of $10,000 and accumulated amortization of $7,500. The company had a:
     a.   loss of $500.
     b.   gain of $500.
     c.   gain of $2,000.
     d.   loss of $8,000.

(SO4)   14. Quick Corporation retired a piece of equipment, which had a cost $8,000 and accumulated amortization of $7,000. The journal entry to record the retirement will include a:
     a.   debit to Gain on Disposal for $1,000.
     b.   credit to Gain on Disposal for $1,000.
     c.   credit to Loss on Disposal for $1,000.
     d.   debit to Loss on Disposal for $1,000.

(SO5)   15. Which of the following gives the recipient the right to manufacture, sell, or otherwise control an invention for a period of 20 years?
     a.   Patent
     b.   Copyright
     c.   Trademark
     d.   Licence

(SO1)   16. A company successfully defended its copyright on a piece of literature at a cost of $75,000. The journal entry to record that cost includes a debit to:
     a.   Legal Fees Expense for $75,000.
     b.   Intangible Assets for $75,000.
     c.   Copyright for $75,000.
     d.   Research and Development Expense for $75,000.

(SO5)   17. At the beginning of the year, Righter Corporation purchased for $10,000 a patent with a legal life of eight years. Righter estimates that the useful life of the patent will be four years. Amortization expense on the patent for the year is:
     a. $2,500.
     b. $1,250.
     c. $588.
     d. $250.

(SO6)   18. With respect to long-lived assets, which of the following must be disclosed in the financial statements or notes to the financial statements?
     a.   The balances of major classes of assets
     b.   Accumulated amortization by major classes of assets
     c.   Amortization methods used
     d.   All of the above must be disclosed

(SO6)   19. An impairment loss is reported:
     a.   as a note to the financial statements.
     b.   in the operating activities section in the cash flow statement.
     c.   as a special item in the statement of retained earnings.
     d.   in the operating expenses section in the statement of earnings.

20. A company's average total assets is $200,000, amortization expense is $10,000,   (SO7)
    and accumulated amortization is $60,000. Net sales total $250,000. The asset
    turnover is:
    a.   0.8 times.
    b.   1.25 times.
    c.   3.33 times.
    d.   4.17 times.

21. The return on assets ratio: (SO7)
    a.   indicates how efficiently a company uses its assets.
    b.   measures the overall profitability of a company.
    c.   indicates whether assets should be replaced.
    d.   measures the liquidity of a company.

22. A company can increase its return on assets by: (SO7)
    a.   decreasing its average assets and holding its net sales and net earnings
         constant.
    b.   increasing its average assets and holding its net sales and net earnings
         constant.
    c.   increasing its net sales and holding its net earnings and average total assets
         constant.
    d.   decreasing its net earnings and holding its net sales and average total
         assets constant.

23. On January 3, 2006, Powers Corporation. purchased a piece of machinery for   (SO8)
    $50,000. It has a salvage value of $5,000, an estimated useful life of nine years,
    and estimated units of output of 90,000 units. Actual units produced during
    the first year were 11,000. Amortization expense for 2006 under the units-of-
    activity method is:
    a. $5,556.
    b. $5,500.
    c. $5,300.
    d. $5,000.

24. On January 4, 2006, Sacks Corporation purchased a piece of equipment for   (SO8)
    $20,000. It has a salvage value of $4,000 and an estimated useful life of eight
    years. Amortization expense for 2006 under the double declining-balance
    method is:
    a. $5,000.
    b. $4,000.
    c. $2,000.
    d.   None of the above is the correct amount.

Problems

(SO4)   1.   Townsend Corporation owns a piece of machinery that it had purchased three years ago for $40,000. The machinery has an estimated salvage value of $5,000 and an estimated useful life of 10 years. At the end of 2005, the Accumulated Amortization account had a balance of $10,500. On April 1, 2007, the corporation sold the machinery for $27,000.

Required:
Record the following journal entries:
   a.   The amortization entry on December 31, 2006.
   b.   The entry or entries to record the sale on April 1, 2007.
   c.   If Townsend had simply retired the machinery on April 1, 2007, then what would the journal entry or entries have been?

Date	Account Titles	Debit	Credit

(SO2,3,4)   2.   The Sligo Corporation adjusts and closes its account the end of each calendar year and uses the straight-line method of amortization on all its machinery equipment. On January 2, 2004, machinery was purchased for cash at a cost of $45,000. Useful life was estimated to be 10 years and salvage value $8,000.

On June 29, 2007, Sligo decided to lease new, more efficient machinery; consequently, the machinery described above was sold on this date for $33,350 cash.

Required:
Prepare the following journal entries:
- a. to record the purchase of the machinery.
- b. to record amortization for 2004, 2005, and 2006.
- c. to record the disposal of the machinery on June 29, 2007.

Date	Account Titles	Debit	Credit

3. The following account balances are provided for the Vic Corporation as of   (SO6)
   December 31, 2006:

Cash	$200,000
Accounts Receivable	260,000
Accumulated Amortization-Equipment	300,000
Accumulated Amortization-Building	370,000
Accumulated Amortization-Patents	10,000
Allowance for Doubtful Accounts	70,000
Building	900,000
Patents	40,000
Equipment	800,000
Goodwill	150,000
Inventories	180,000
Land	700,000
Prepaid Expenses	30,000
Short-Term Investments	90,000

Required:

Prepare the assets section of the balance sheet for Vic Corporation as December 31, 2006.

4. Please refer to the Domtar and Cascades financial statements for information for answering the following questions. Do not forget to use the **Decision Toolkit** approach for help in the problem solving.

(SO1,2,6)   a.   What line items concerning property, plant, and equipment and amortization can be found on Cascades' statement of earnings, balance sheet, and cash flow statement for 2004?

(SO6)   b.   In Domtar's notes to financial statements, what does Note 1 disclose about property, plant, and equipment?

(SO6)   c.   In Cascades' notes to financial statements, what does Note 5 disclose about property, plant, and equipment?

(SO7)   d.   Calculate the profitability of both companies for 2004 breaking down each company's return on assets ratio into its profit margin and asset turnover components.

(SO8)   e.   Compare the performance of Domtar and Cascades for 2002 using the information obtained in (d). The return on assets for the industry in 2004 was 1.6 percent.

Solutions to Self-Test

Multiple Choice

1. c $20,000 + $600 + $110 = $20,710

2. b $50,000 + $9,000 + $2,000 − $500

3. c   Using an expense account is incorrect because the parking lot will benefit future periods, and land does not have a limited useful life, as does a parking lot. Typically, a company will not call an account "Parking Lot" but will use "Land Improvements."

4. d $20,000 + $500 + $200 + $1,000

5. a   The other three are amortizable.

6. d

7. d   ($50,000 − $5,000) ÷ 9 years = $5,000

8. b   Straight-line gives an even amount of amortization for each year of an asset's useful life. In the later year of an asset's useful life, straight-line amortization gives a higher expense than does declining-balance amortization.

9. c   Amortization methods may be changed. A change in estimate never affects prior periods, only current and future periods.

10. a   Earnings management involves timing the recognition of gains and losses to achieve certain results. A capital expenditure is money spent on an asset after its purchase. A write-down is what is done when there is an impairment.

11. d

12. b   Book value is $2,500 ($10,000 − $7,500). Since the proceeds exceed the book value by $500, there is a gain.

13. a   Book value is $2,500 ($10,000 – $7,500). Since the book value exceeds the proceeds by $500, there is a loss.

14. d   Since the book value is $1,000 ($8,000 – $7,000), there is a Loss on Disposal, and losses are always debited.

15. a   A copyright protects literary and artistic works. A trademark is a word, phrase, jingle, or symbol that distinguishes or identifies an enterprise or product. A licence is an operating right.

16. c   The money spent for a successful legal defence of an intangible asset is debited to the asset account. Use of an expense account is inappropriate.

17. a $10,000 ÷ 4 years. The shorter period is used.

18. d

19. d

20. b   Asset turnover = net sales ÷ average total assets; $250,000 ÷ $200,000 = 1.25 times

21. b

22. a   Return on assets = profit margin x asset turnoverDecreasing the average assets increases the asset turnover and therefore the return on assets ratio.

23. b $50,000 - $5,000 = $45,000 ÷ 90,000 units = $0.50/unit
         $0.50/unit x 11,000 actual units = $5,500

24. a   The double-declining-balance rate is 25 percent [(100% ÷ 8 years) x 2], and $20,000 x 25% = $5,000.

Problems

1. a. and b.

Dec. 31, 2006	Amortization Expense		3,500
	Accumulated Amortization—Machinery	3,500	
	(To record annual amortization)		
	$40,000 – $5,000 = $35,000 ÷ 10 years = $3,500		

Apr. 1, 2007	Amortization Expense	875	
	Accumulated Amortization—Machinery		875
	(To bring amortization up to date)		
	$3,500 annual amortization x 3/12 = $875		

	Cash	27,000	
	Accumulated Amortization—Machinery	14,875	
	Machinery		40,000
	Gain on Disposal		1,875
	(To record disposal at a gain)		
	Accumulated amortization =		
	$10,500 + $3,500 + $875 = $14,875		
	Book value = $40,000 – $14,875 = $25,125		
	Gain = $27,000 – $25,125 = $1,875		

c.

| Apr. 1, 2007 | Amortization Expense | 875 | |
| | Accumulated Amortization—Machinery | | 875 |

(To bring amortization up to date)

$3,500 annual amortization x 3/12 = $875

	Loss on Disposal	25,125	
	Accumulated Amortization—Machinery	14,875	
	Machinery		40,000

(To record retirement of asset)

Accumulated Amortization =

$10,500 + $3,500 + $875 = $14,875

Book value = $40,000 − $14,875 = $25,125

The loss on disposal equals the book value of the machinery.

2.   a.

| Jan. 2, 2004 | Machinery | 45,000 | |
| | Cash | | 45,000 |

(To record purchase of machinery)

b.

| Dec. 31, 2004 | Amortization Expense | 3,700 | |
| | Accumulated Amortization—Machinery | | 3,700 |

(To record amortization for 2004)

$45,000 − $8,000) = $37,000 ÷ 10 years = $3,700

| Dec. 31, 2005 | Amortization Expense | 3,700 | |
| | Accumulated Amortization—Machinery | | 3,700 |

(To record amortization for 2005)

| Dec. 31, 2006 | Amortization Expense | 3,700 | |
| | Accumulated Amortization—Machinery | | 3,700 |

(To record amortization for 2006)

c.

| June 29, 2007 | Amortization Expense | 1,850 | |
| | Accumulated Amortization—Machinery | | 1,850 |

(To bring amortization up to date prior to
disposal of machinery: $3,700 ÷ 2 = $1,850)

	Cash	33,350	
	Accumulated Amortization-Machinery	12,950	
	Machinery		45,000
	Gain on Disposal		1,300

(To record disposal at a gain)

Accumulated amortization = $3,700 + $3,700 +
$3,700 + $1,850 = $12,950

Net book value = $45,000 − $12,950 = $32,050

Gain = $33,350 − $32,050 = $1,300

3.

Vic Corporation
Balance Sheet (Partial)
December 31, 2006

Current Assets

Cash		$200,000
Accounts receivable	$260,000	
Less: Allowance doubtful accounts	70,000	190,000
Short-term investments		90,000
Inventories		180,000
Prepaid expenses		30,000
Total current assets		690,000

Property, Plant, and Equipment

Land		700,000
Building	$900,000	
Less: Accumulated amortization	370,000	530,000
Equipment	$800,000	
Less: Accumulated amortization	300,000	500,000
Total Property, Plant, and Equipment		1,730,000

Intangible Assets

Goodwill		150,000
Copyrights	40,000	
Less: Accumulated amortization	10,000	30,000
Total Intangible Assets		180,000
Total assets		$2,600,000

4. a.   Amortization of $159 million on the consolidated statement of earnings; property, plant, and equipment of $1,700 million on the consolidated balance sheet; and the purchase of property, plant, and equipment of $121 million on the consolidated statement of cash flows.

b.   Note 1 describes how property, plant, and equipment are recorded and what amortization methods are used.

c.   Note 5 describes the original cost, the amount of accumulated amortization, and the net book value of each type of property, plant, and equipment asset.

d.   ($ in millions)

Profit Margin   x   Asset Turnover   =   Return on Assets

$\dfrac{\text{Net Earnings}}{\text{Net Sales}}$ x $\dfrac{\text{Net Sales}}{\text{Average Total Assets}}$ =   Return on Assets

Domtar: $\dfrac{(\$42)}{\$5,115}$ x $\dfrac{\$5,115}{(\$5,688 + \$5,848) \div 2}$

(0.82%)   x   0.89 times   =   (0.73%)

Cascades: $\dfrac{\$23}{\$3,254}$ x $\dfrac{\$3,254}{(\$3,144 + \$2,927) \div 2}$

0.71%   x   1.07 times   =   0.76%

e.   Both companies' returns on assets were below the industry average of 2.9 percentage in 2004; however, Cascades' low profit margin and slightly higher asset turnover were higher than Domtar's negative profit margin and lower asset turnover, resulting in a slightly higher return on assets for Cascades.

chapter 10

Reporting and Analyzing Liabilities

Chapter Overview

Chapter 10 discusses the two basic types of liabilities—current and long-term. In the former category, you will learn about an operating line of credit, notes payable, sales taxes payable, property taxes payable, payroll, and current maturities of long-term debt. In the latter category, you will learn about notes payable and bonds payable. For both categories, you will learn about financial statement presentation and analysis. Finally, you will learn how to apply the straight-line and effective-interest methods of amortizing bond discounts and premiums.

Review of Specific Study Objectives

- A current **liability** is a *debt that will be paid (1) from existing current assets or through the creation of other current liabilities, and (2) within one year.* A debt that does not meet both criteria is classified as a long-term liability.

- **Current liabilities** *include notes payable; accounts payable; unearned revenue; accrued liabilities, such as taxes, salaries and wages, and interest; and the current portion of long-term debt.* All material current liabilities should be reported on the balance sheet.

> **study objective 1**
>
> Explain the accounting for current liabilities.

- **An operating line of credit** is set up at a company's bank to help the company manage its temporary cash shortfalls. This means that the company has been pre-authorized by the bank to borrow money, up to pre-set limit, when it is needed. Security, called collateral, is usually required by the bank as protection in the event of a default on the loan. Collateral normally includes some or all of the company's current assets. Line of credit borrowings are normally on a short-term basis, repayable immediately upon request—that is, on demand, by the bank.

- A number of companies show a negative, or overdrawn, cash balance at year end as a result of using their line of credit. This amount is usually termed **bank indebtedness, bank overdraft**, or **bank advances**. No special entry is required to record the overdrawn amount. The normal credits to cash will simply accumulate and be reported as a current liability with a suitable note disclosure.

- **Notes payable** are *obligations in the form of written notes.* They give written documentation of a liability and usually require the borrower to pay interest. If a note is due for payment within one year of the balance sheet, then it is classified as a current liability.

- Consider the **following example**. Robinson Ltd. borrows $20,000 and issues a three-month, 6-percent note on May 1. Interest and plus principal is repayable at maturity. The *entry on May 1* is:

Cash	20,000	
Notes Payable		20,000
(To record issue of note)		

If Robinson prepares financial statements on June 30, necessitating adjusting entries, then the adjusting entry for accrued interest is:

Interest Expense	200	
Interest Payable		200
(To record accrued interest: $20,000 x 6% x 2/12)		

On the *maturity date, August 1,* the following entry is recorded:

Notes Payable	20,000	
Interest Payable	200	
Interest Expense	100	
Cash		20,300
(To record payment of note plus interest)		

Total interest on the note is $300, and the maturity value is $20,300. The interest payable of $200 must be taken off the books, since it is no longer payable, and the interest expense is the third month's interest ($20,000 x 6% x 1/12).

- There are usually **sales taxes (GST, PST, and/or HST) on items sold**. The retailer serves as a collection agent for the taxing authority, usually the provincial and federal governments, and must periodically remit to these governments the sales taxes collected. *When an item is sold, the amount of the sale and the amount of each of the sales taxes collected are usually rung up separately on the cash register.* If $500 of merchandise is sold, the GST percentage is 7 percent, and the PST percentage is 8 percent, then and the following entry records the sale:

Cash		575	
Sales			500
GST Payable			35
PST Payable			40
(To record sales and sales taxes)			

When these two sales taxes are remitted to the governments, the entry is:

GST Payable		35	
PST Payable		40	
Cash			75
(To remit sales taxes to tax agencies)			

- Businesses pay **property taxes** annually. It is difficult to determine the property tax expense because the amount due for the current year is unknown until the bill is received, usually sometime in the spring of each year.

To illustrate, assume that a company's year end is December 31 and that it makes adjusting entries only annually. This company receives its property tax bill of $8,400 on March 1, and it is due to be paid on May 31. On March 1, when the property tax bill is received, the company records the liability owed for its property taxes. It also records the property tax expense for the two months that have already passed.

Mar. 1	Property Tax Expense [($8,400 ÷ 12) x 2]	1,400	
	Prepaid Property Tax [($8,400 ÷ 12) x 10]	7,000	
	Property Tax Payable		8,400

At this point, the company has both a prepaid asset (Prepaid Property Tax) and a liability (Property Tax Payable).

The property tax payable liability will be eliminated when paid on May 31, as follows:

May 31	Property Tax Payable	8,400	
	Cash		8,400

At year-end, when the company prepares its adjusting entries, it will record the property tax expense that has expired for 10 months March through December.

Dec. 31	Property Tax Expense	7,000	
	Prepaid Property Tax		7,000

At year end, the Prepaid Property Tax and Property Tax Payable accounts will have a zero balance. The Property Tax Expense account will have a balance of $8,400.

Some companies make monthly adjusting entries. In such cases, they normally use the prior period's property tax amount to record the property tax expense for the first few months of the year. Once they receive the current period's property tax bill, they adjust for any discrepancies.

- **Every employer incurs liabilities relating to employees' salaries and wages.** Amounts withheld from employees' pay cheques, called withholding taxes, must be remitted to the appropriate authorities. Withheld amounts include *federal and provincial income taxes, Canada Pension Plan (CPP) contributions, Employment Insurance (EI) premiums, and other amounts specified by employees, such as charitable contributions, union dues, and health insurance.*

- **Every employer incurs a second type of payroll-related liability.** With every payroll, the employer incurs liabilities to pay various payroll costs that are levied, such as the employer's share of CPP and EI. In addition, the provincial governments mandate employer funding of a workplace health, safety, and compensation plan. Each of these contributions, plus such items such as paid vacations and employer-sponsored pensions, are collectively referred to as **employee benefits**.

- **Payroll and payroll tax liability accounts** are *classified as current liabilities* because they must either be paid to employees or remitted to government authorities or other third parties both periodically and in the near-term.

- Companies often have **long-term debt of which a portion is due in the current period**. If a company has a 10-year mortgage, then the portion due in the current period must be classified as current. These items are often *identified on the balance sheet as "long-term debt due within one year."* No adjusting entry is required. The proper classification is recognized when the balance sheet is prepared.

- **Long-term liabilities** are *obligations that are expected to be paid after one year. They are often in the form of bonds or long-term notes.*

study objective 2

Explain the accounting for long-term notes payable.

- **Long-term notes payable** are similar to short-term notes payable, except that the terms of the note exceed one year.

- The following are **types of notes**:

  a. *Secured notes* have specific assets of the issuer pledged as collateral for the notes. Secured notes are also known as mortgages.
  b. *Unsecured notes* are issued against the general credit of the borrower. These are also known as debentures and are issued by corporations with good credit ratings.
  c. *Convertible debt* may be converted into common shares.

- A long-term note may be unsecured or secured. Secured notes are commonly known as mortgages. A **mortgage note payable** is widely used by individuals to purchase homes or by companies to acquire property, plants, and equipment.

- Most long-term notes are repayable in a series of periodic payments. These payments are known as **instalments** and are paid monthly, quarterly, semi-annually, or at another defined period. Each payment consists of (1) interest on the unpaid balance of the loan, and (2) a reduction of the loan principal. Payments generally take one of two forms: (1) fixed principal payment plus interest, or (2) blended principal and interest payments.

- Instalment notes with **fixed principal payments** are repayable in equal periodic amounts, **plus interest**. Interest may be either fixed or floating. A fixed interest rate will be constant over the term of the note. A floating (or variable) interest rate will change with fluctuating market rates. Floating rates are generally tied to changes in the prime rate.

- Instalment notes with **blended principal and interest payments** are repayable in equal periodic amounts, **including interest**. Blended principal and interest payments result in changing amounts of interest and principal applied to the loan. With fixed principal payments, the interest decreases each period (as the principal decreases). In contrast, with blended principal and interest payments, the portion applied to the loan principal increases each period.

- **A bond** *is a form of interest-bearing note payable issued by corporations, universities, and governmental agencies.* Bonds are issued in small denominations (usually $1,000 or multiples of $1,000) and attract many investors.

- The following are **types of bonds**:

  a. *Secured bonds* have specific assets of the issuer pledged as collateral for the bonds.
  b. *Unsecured bonds* are issued against the general credit of the borrower. These are also known as debentures and are issued by corporations with good credit ratings.
  c. *Convertible bonds* may be converted into common shares.
  d. *Redeemable (callable) bonds* are subject to retirement at a stated dollar amount prior to maturity at the option of the issuer.

- A **bond certificate** is issued to investors to provide evidence of an investor's credit claim against the company. The certificate provides such information such as the name of the issuer, the **face value**, the contractual interest rate, and the maturity date of the bond. The face value is the amount of principal due at the **maturity date**. The maturity date is the date that the final payment is due to the investor from the company. The **contractual interest rate** is the rate used to determine the amount of cash interest the borrower pays and the investor receives.

- **Bonds may be issued** *at face value, at a discount (below face value), or at a premium (above face value).*

- **Bond prices** are *quoted as a percentage of the face value of the bond,* such as 97 or 101. If a $1,000 bond sells at 97, then the issuing corporation receives 97 percent of the face value, or $970. If the bond sells at 101, then the corporation receives $1,010.

- When a **bond sells at face value (the contractual rate of interest equals the market interest rate)**, the journal entry to record the issue is a *debit to Cash and a credit to Bonds Payable.* When **bond interest is paid**, the *debit is to Bond Interest Expense, and the credit is to Cash.* If **interest is accrued**, then the *debit is to Bond Interest Expense, and the credit is to Bond Interest Payable.* Bonds Payable is reported as a long-term liability, and Bond Interest Payable is a current liability.

- When a bond is issued, if **the contractual rate of interest exceeds the market rate of interest**, then the bond is *issued at a premium.* If the **contractual rate of interest is lower than the market rate of interest**, then the bond is *issued at a discount.*

- Consider the **following example**. The Jays Corporation issued $500,000, five-year, 5-percent bonds at 96 on January 1, 2006, with interest payable each July and January 1. The **journal entry on January 1, 2006**, is as follows:

Cash ($500,000 x 96%)	480,000	
Discount on Bonds Payable	20,000	
Bonds Payable		500,000
(To record issue of bonds)		

Note that Bonds Payable is always credited for the face amount of the bonds. **Discount on Bonds Payable** is a *contra account*, deducted from Bonds Payable. After issue, the balance sheet presentation of the bond is:

Long-term liabilities	
Bonds payable	$500,000
Less: Discount on bonds payable	20,000
	$480,000

The $480,000 is the carrying (or book) value of the bonds.

The **discount** is an additional cost of borrowing and, according to the matching principle, should be recorded as bond interest expense over the life of the bonds. This is referred to as **amortizing the discount**. Amortizing a discount results in an increase in interest expense. Procedures for amortizing bond discounts are discussed in the Appendix (10A) to this chapter.

- Let us now assume that the Jays Corporation issued $500,000, five-year, 5-percent bonds at 102 on January 1, 2006, with interest payable each July and January 1. The **journal entry on January 1, 2006**, is as follows:

Cash ($500,000 x 102%)	510,000	
Premium on Bonds Payable		10,000
Bonds Payable		500,000
(To record issue of bonds)		

Note again that Bonds Payable is always credited for the face amount of the bonds. **Premium on Bonds Payable** is an *adjunct account*, added to Bonds Payable. After issue, the balance sheet presentation of the bond is:

Long-term liabilities	
Bonds payable	$500,000
Add: Premium on bonds payable	10,000
	$510,000

The $510,000 is the carrying (or book) value of the bonds.

The **premium** is a *reduction in the cost of borrowing, and it reduces bond interest expense over the life of the bonds*. Amortizing a premium results in a decrease in interest expense. Procedures for amortizing bond premiums are discussed in the Appendix (10A) to this chapter.

- **At maturity, the book value of bonds equals the face value**, and the journal entry to redeem the bonds involves a debit to Bonds Payable and a credit to Cash.

- If **bonds are redeemed before maturity**, it is necessary to (1) update any unrecorded interest, (2) eliminate the carrying value of the bonds at the redemption date, (3) record the cash paid, and (4) recognize the gain or loss on redemption. If $500,000 of bonds with a carrying value of $496,000 are redeemed at 101 by the company, the following entry is required:

Bonds Payable	500,000	
Loss on Redemption	9,000	
Discount on Bonds Payable		4,000
Cash		505,000
(To record redemption of bonds)		

Discount is calculated as follows: $500,000 – $496,000
Cash is calculated as follows: $500,000 x 101%
Loss is calculated as follows: $505,000 – $496,000

The **loss or gain on bond redemption** is *reported in the statement of earnings, as Other Expenses or Revenues.*

- **Current liabilities** are reported as the first category in the liabilities section of the balance sheet. Each of the principal types of current liabilities is listed separately within the category, and important data relating to them are disclosed in the notes to the financial statements. Similar to current assets, current liabilities are generally listed in their order of maturity.

- **Long-term liabilities** are reported separately immediately following current liabilities. Summary data regarding debts may be presented in on the balance sheet, while detailed data (such as interest rates, maturity dates, conversion privileges, and assets pledged as collateral) should be shown in a supporting schedule in the notes.

- Information regarding cash inflows and outflows during the year that resulted from the principal portion of debt transactions is provided in the financing activities in the **cash flow statement**. Interest expense is reported in the operating activities section, even though it resulted from debt transactions.

- **Liquidity ratios** measure the short-term ability of a company to pay its maturing obligations and to meet unexpected needs for cash. A commonly used measure of liquidity is the **current ratio** (current assets divided by current liabilities). The current ratio can be misleading because some items, such as receivables and inventory may not be very liquid and are included in the numerator. Consequently, the current ratio should be supplemented by other ratios, such as the receivables turnover and inventory turnover.

- Many companies keep few liquid assets on hand because they cost too much to hold and, thus, must rely on other sources of liquidity. One such source is an **operating bank line of credit**, as discussed earlier in this chapter.

- **Solvency ratios** measure the ability of a company to repay its long-term debt and survive over a long period of time. One solvency ratio is **debt to total assets**, calculated by dividing total liabilities by total assets. This ratio indicates the extent to which a company's debt could be repaid by liquidating its assets. To supplement the information provided by the debt-to-total-assets ratio, the **times interest earned ratio** is used. It is calculated as follows: earnings before interest expense and income tax expense (EBIT) by interest expense. This ratio calculates how many times the company has earned its interest payments in an accounting period, thus providing an indication of a company's ability to meet interest payments as they come due.

- A concern for analysts when they evaluate a company's liquidity and solvency is whether that company has properly recorded all of its obligations. **Contingent liabilities and off-balance sheet financing** are two examples of unrecorded debt.

- **Contingent liabilities** are events with uncertain outcomes. A good example of a contingency is a lawsuit, and other contingencies are product warranties and environmental problems. If it is probable that the contingency will occur and the company can reasonably estimate the expected loss, then the **company should accrue the loss** by debiting a loss account and crediting a liability account. If both conditions are not met, then the **company discloses the loss in the notes to the financial statements.**

- **Off-balance sheet financing** refers to a situation where liabilities are not recorded on the balance sheet. One very common type of off–balance sheet financing results from leasing transactions, which were discussed in Chapter 9.

study objective 5

Apply the straight-line and effective-interest methods of amortizing bond discounts and premiums (Appendix 10A).

- To follow the matching principle, bond discounts or premiums must be allocated to expense in each period in which the bonds are outstanding. There are two commonly used amortization methods to do so: the straight-line method and the effective-interest method.

The straight-line method allocates the same amount to interest in each interest period. To illustrate the straight-line method, the Jays Corporation, illustrated earlier, is used. You will recall that the Jays Corporation issued $500,000, five-year, 5% -percent bonds at 96 on January 1, 2006, with interest payable each July and January 1. In this example, the discount is $20,000. Amortization of this discount using the straight-line method is $2,000 every six-month period ($20,000 ÷ 10 interest payment periods, as the bond is a five-year bond that pays interest twice a year).

On **July 1, 2006, the following entry is recorded:**

Bond Interest Expense	14,500	
Discount on Bonds Payable		2,000
Cash		12,500

(To record payment of interest and amortization of discount)

Cash is calculated as follows: $500,000 x 5% x 6/12
Discount is calculated as follows: $20,000 ÷ 10 interest payment periods Bond interest expense is simply the sum of the two credits.

On **December 31, 2006, the following entry is recorded:**

Bond Interest Expense	14,500	
Discount on Bonds Payable		2,000
Bond Interest Payable		12,500

(To accrue interest and discount amortization)

These **same two entries will be written over the next four years**, eventually reducing the balance in the discount account to zero. On the maturity date, the carrying value of the bonds will be $500,000, their face value, which is correct because that is the amount that must be paid back on that date.

- The amortization of bond premium parallels that of bond discount. Again the Jays Corporation example is used, where it issued $500,000, five-year, 5-percent bonds at 102 on January 1, 2006, with interest payable each July 1 and January 1. In this case, the premium is $10,000. Amortization of this premium using the straight-line method is $1,000 every six-month period ($20,000 ÷ 10 interest payment periods).

On **July 1, 2006, the following entry is recorded:**

Bond Interest Expense	11,500	
Premium on Bonds Payable	1,000	
Cash		12,500

(To record payment of interest and amortization of premium)

Cash is calculated as follows: $500,000 x 5% x 6/12
Premium is calculated as follows: $10,000 ÷ 10 interest payment periods (the bond is a five-year bond that pays interest twice a year).
Bond interest expense is simply the difference between the cash and the premium.

On **December 31, 2006, the following entry is recorded:**

Bond Interest Expense	11,500	
Premium on Bonds Payable	1,000	
Bond Interest Payable		12,500

(To accrue interest and premium amortization)

These **same two entries will be written over the next four years**, eventually reducing the balance in the premium account to zero. Once again, on the maturity date, the carrying value of the bonds will be $500,000, their face value, which is correct because that is the amount that must be paid back on that date.

- The effective-interest method of amortization calculates interest expense by multiplying the carrying value of the bonds by the market interest rate in effect at the time the bonds were issued. This market rate is also known as the **effective interest rate.**

Under the effective-interest method, the amortization of a bond discount or premium results in periodic interest expense equal to a percentage of the carrying value of the bonds. The effective-interest method results in varying amounts of amortization and interest expense per period but a constant percentage rate. The effective-interest method is considered conceptually superior to the straight-line method.

Both the straight-line and the effective-interest methods of amortization result in the same total amount of interest expense over the term of the bonds. However, **when amounts are materially different each interest period, the effective-interest method is required under generally accepted accounting principles.**

The following steps are required under the effective-interest method:
1. Calculate the **bond interest expense**: Multiply the carrying value of the bonds at the beginning of the interest period by the effective interest rate.
2. Calculate the **bond interest paid** (or accrued): Multiply the face value of the bonds by the contractual interest rate.
3. Calculate the **amortization amount**: Determine the difference between the amounts calculated in steps (1) and (2).

To illustrate the effective-interest method, the Jays Corporation continues to be used. Assume that Jays Corporation issues its $500,000, five-year, 5-percent bonds on January 1, 2006, with interest payable each July 1 and January 1. Also assume that the bonds are issued to yield a market rate of interest of 6 percent. Using time value of money techniques, it is determined that the bonds will sell for $478,678. This sale price results in a discount of $21,322. The bond discount amortization schedule is shown below. All figures have been rounded to the nearest dollar for simplicity.

Jays Corporation
Bond Discount Amortization Table
Effective-Interest Method

Semi-Annual Interest Period	(A) Interest Payment ($500,000 x 5% x 6/12)	(B) Interest Expense (Preceding Bond Carrying Value x 6% x 6/12)	(C) Discount Amortization (B-A)	(D) Unamortized Discount (D-C)	(E) Bond Carrying Value (500,000 – D)
Issue Date				$21,322	$478,678
1	$12,500	$14,360	$1,860	19,462	480,538
2	12,500	14,416	1,916	17,546	482,454
3	12,500	14,474	1,975	15,572	484,428
4	12,500	14,533	2,033	13,539	486,461
5	12,500	14,594	2,094	11,445	488,555
6	12,500	14,657	2,157	9,288	490,712
7	12,500	14,721	2,221	7,067	492,933
8	12,500	14,788	2,288	4,779	495,221
9	12,500	14,857	2,357	2,422	497,578
10	12,500	14,927	2,422*	0	500,000

*$5 difference due to cumulative rounding.

The journal entry for the first interest date on July 1, 2006, is as follows:

Bond Interest Expense	14,360	
Discount on Bonds Payable		1,860
Cash		12,500

(To record payment of interest and amortization of discount)

The journal entry for the second interest date on December 31, 2006, is made. While the interest expense and amortization amounts vary, the cash payment remains a constant $12,500 every interest period.

Bond Interest Expense	14,416	
Discount on Bonds Payable		1,916
Cash		12,500

(To record payment of interest and amortization of discount)

Note that the amount of periodic interest expense increases over the life of the bond when the effective-interest method is applied to bonds issued at a discount. The reason is that a constant percentage is applied to an increasing bond carrying value to calculate interest expense. The carrying value is increasing because of the amortization of the discount.

The bond amortization table would be constructed in the same manner for a bond issued at a premium. The only difference would be that periodic interest expense decreases over the life of the bond when the effective-interest method is applied to bonds issued at a premium. The reason is that a constant percentage is applied to a decreasing bond carrying value to calculate interest expense. The carrying value is decreasing because of the amortization of the premium.

Chapter Self-Test

As you work through the exercises and problems, remember to use the **Decision Toolkit** discussed and used in the text:

1. *Decision Checkpoints*: At this point, you ask a question.
2. *Info Needed for Decision*: You make a choice regarding the information needed to answer the question.
3. *Tool to Use for Decision*: At this point, you review just what the information chosen in step 2 does for the decision-making process.
4. *How to Evaluate Results*: You conduct an evaluation of information for answering the question.

Note: The notation (SO1) means that the question was drawn from study objective number one.

Multiple Choice

Please circle the correct answer.

1. The journal entry to record the accrual of the employer's share of Canada Pension Plan (CPP) would include a: (SO1)
   a.   credit to CPP Payable.
   b.   debit to CPP Expense.
   c.   credit to Payroll Tax Expense.
   d.   debit to CPP Payable.

(SO1)   2. A retailer who collects GST from its customers would:
    a. debit GST Payable.
    b. debit GST Expense.
    c. credit GST Payable.
    d. credit GST Revenue.

(SO1)   3. Which of the following is a criterion for the classification of a liability as current?
    a. It is a debt that can be paid from existing current assets.
    b. It is a debt that can be paid through the creation of other current liabilities.
    c. It must be paid within one year.
    d. All of the above are criteria for the classification of a liability as current.

(SO2)   4. Monthly payments on an instalment note consist of:
    a. interest expense only.
    b. principal repayment only.
    c. interest expense and principal repayment.
    d. neither interest expense nor principal repayment.

(SO2)   5. The interest charged on a $80,000 note payable, at the rate of 5% percent on a 6six-month note would be:
    a. $4,000.
    b. $2,000.
    c. $3,000.
    d. $1,000.

(SO2)   6. A corporation issued a $50,000, 6-percent, four-month note payable on July 1. Interest is payable at maturity. If the corporation's year end is September 30, then the adjusting entry for interest on that date is:

a.	Interest Expense	750	
	Notes Payable		750
b.	Interest Expense	750	
	Interest Payable		750
c.	Interest Expense	1,000	
	Notes Payable		1,000
d.	Interest Expense	1,000	
	Interest Payable		1,000

(SO2)   7. When the corporation in (6) pays the amount due on the maturity date, the journal entry will include a:
    a. debit to Notes Payable for $51,000.
    b. credit to Cash for $50,000.
    c. debit to Interest Expense for $1,000.
    d. debit to Interest Payable for $750.

8. On November 1, 2006, a company issued a note payable of $50,000, of which   (SO2)
   $10,000 is repaid each year. What is the proper classification of this note on the
   December 31, 2006, balance sheet?
   a. $10,000 current liability; $40,000 long-term liability
   b. $50,000 current liability
   c. $50,000 long-term liability
   d. $10,000 long-term liability; $40,000 current liability

9. Notes that are issued against the general credit of the borrower are called: (SO2)
   a.   unsecured notes.
   b.   secured notes.
   c.   mortgage notes.
   d.   convertible notes.

10. A corporation issues $1,000,000 of 4-percent, five-year bonds. The 4-percent   (SO3)
    rate of interest is called the _____ rate.
    a.   yield
    b.   effective
    c.   market
    d.   contractual

11. The current market value of a bond is equal to the: (SO3)
    a.   present value of the principal only.
    b.   present value of the principal and the interest payments.
    c.   present value of interest payments only.
    d.   face value of the principal only.

12. When the contractual rate of interest exceeds the market rate of interest, the   (SO3)
    bond sells at:
    a.   face value.
    b.   a discount.
    c.   a premium.
    d.   some amount other than those listed above.

13. The Premium on Bonds Payable account shown on a balance sheet is: (SO3)
    a.   classified as a revenue account.
    b.   deducted from bonds payable.
    c.   classified as a shareholders' shareholders' equity account.
    d.   added to bonds payable.

14. When calculating the carrying or book value of bonds payable: (SO3)
    a.   premium is subtracted from and discount is added to bonds payable.
    b.   discount is subtracted from and premium is added to bonds payable.
    c.   both discount and premium are subtracted from bonds payable.
    d.   both discount and premium are added to bonds payable.

(SO3)   15. Bonds payable with a face value of $200,000 and a carrying value of $196,000 are redeemed prior to maturity at 102. There is a:
   a.   loss on redemption of $4,000.
   b.   gain on redemption of $4,000.
   c.   loss on redemption of $8,000.
   d.   gain on redemption of $8,000.

(SO4)   16. A gain or loss on the early redemption of bonds payable is classified as a(n):
   a.   operating expense on the statement of earnings.
   b.   addition or subtraction to premium or discount to bonds payable on the balance sheet.
   c.   other expense or other revenue on the statement of earnings.
   d.   long-term liability on the balance sheet.

(SO4)   17. A company's total debt is $250,000, while its total assets are $500,000. Earnings before interest expense and income tax is $300,000, and interest expense is $30,000. The company's times interest earned ratio is:
   a.   10 times.
   b.   2 times.
   c.   50 percent.
   d.   10 percent.

(SO4)   18. Rouse Corporation is being sued by a customer. At the balance sheet date, Rouse's lawyers feel that it is probable that the company will lose the lawsuit and that a reasonable estimate of the loss is $50,000. On the balance sheet date, Rouse should:
   a.   not disclose the lawsuit because a jury has not yet ruled.
   b.   disclose the lawsuit in the notes to the financial statements.
   c.   accrue the loss by debiting an expense and crediting a liability.
   d.   ask for a second opinion from an outside law firm.

(SO4)   19. Some companies finance assets without the liability showing on the balance sheet. This procedure is called:
   a.   fraud.
   b.   capital leasing.
   c.   off-balance sheet financing.
   d.   capitalizing.

(SO4)   20. The ability of a company to survive over a long period of time is measured by:
   a.   liquidity ratios.
   b.   solvency ratios.
   c.   profitability ratios.
   d.   cash management ratios.

(SO4)   21. Which is a very common way to present current liabilities on the balance sheet?
   a.   Notes payable are always being listed first.
   b.   Current maturities of long-term debt are always being listed first.
   c.   By order of magnitude
   d.   By order of maturity date

22. Bonds with a face value of $600,000 and a contractual rate of interest of 4   (SO5)
    percent sold at 102 on January 1. Interest is payable on July 1 and January 1,
    and the bonds mature in 10 years. On July 1, the journal entry to pay interest
    and record straight-line amortization will include a:
    a.   credit to Cash for $12,400.
    b.   debit to Premium on Bonds Payable for $1,200.
    c.   credit to Premium on Bonds Payable for $600.
    d.   debit to Bond Interest Expense for $11,400.

23. What principle does the effective interest method of amortization satisfy?   (SO5)
    a.   Matching principle
    b.   Conservatism principle
    c.   Comparability principle
    d.   Full disclosure principle

Problems

1. The Jansen Corporation incurred the following transactions: (SO1,3)

Required:

   a.   On May 1, the corporation issued a six-month, 6-percent note in the
        amount of $20,000. Interest is payable at maturity. Record the adjusting
        entry for interest on June 30.

   b.   On March 1, the corporation received its $10,020 property tax invoice for
        the calendar year due to be paid on May 15. Record the:
        i)   entry on March 1 to record the receipt of the property tax bill.
        ii) payment of the bill on May 15.
        iii) adjusting entry required on June 30, assuming the company
             makes adjusting entries only annually.

   c.   On July 1, the corporation sold $400,000 of 6-percent, 10-year bonds at
        101. The bonds pay interest every January 1 and July 1. Please record the
        entry for the issue of the bonds.

Date	Account Titles	Debit	Credit

(SO3, SO5)   2. The Dove Corporation issues $100,000 of 10-year, 7-percent bonds for proceeds of 107,473, which reflects a 6-percent market rate of interest. The bonds pay interest semi-annually.

Required:

a. Prepare the journal entry to record the issue of the bond.

b. Prepare the journal entry to record the payment of interest and premium or discount amortization for the first interest period. Assume the effective-interest method of amortization.

c. Refer to (b). Prepare the same entry to record the payment of interest and premium or discount amortization for the first interest period, using the straight-line method of amortization instead of the effective-interest method.

Date	Account Titles	Debit	Credit

3. The following selected general ledger account balances are provided for the   (SO4)
    Rebus Corporation as of December 31, 2006. This is the corporation's first year
    of operations.

Accounts payable	$ 15,000
Accounts receivable	70,000
Accumulated amortization—building	10,000
Advertising expense	1,000
Allowance for doubtful accounts	20,000
Amortization expense	5,000
Bad debt expense	2,000
Bonds payable	100,000
Building	350,000
Cash	140,000
Common shares	234,000
Discount on bonds payable	2,000
Dividends	10,000
Income tax expense	13,000
Interest expense	8,000
Interest payable	13,000
Land	100,000
Mortgage payable	175,000
Notes payable, six-month	40,000

Payroll tax expense	1,000
Provincial sales tax payable	13,000
Retained earnings, January 1	15,000
Service revenue	75,000
Wages expense	10,000
Wages Payable	2,000

Required:

a. Prepare a statement of earnings, a statement of retained earnings, and the balance sheet for Rebus Corporation for 2006, assuming $30,000 of the mortgage is payable next year.

b. Comment on Rebus Corporation's liquidity and solvency.

4. Please refer to the Domtar and Cascades financial statements for information for answering the following questions. Do n't not forget to use the **Decision Toolkit** approach for help in the problem solving.

(SO2)   a. What is Domtar's long-term debt in 2004, and how much did it increase or decrease from 2003? Where are the details of long-debt found?

(SO1)   b. For Cascades, what percentage of total liabilities are current liabilities in 2004? For Domtar?

(SO4)   c. Assess Domtar's and Cascades' solvency using the debt to total assets and times interest earned ratios for 2004 and 2003.

Solutions to Self-Test

Multiple Choice

1. a
2. c
3. d
4. c
5. b $80,000 x 5% x 6/12 = $2,000
6. b $50,000 x 6% x 3/12 = $750
7. d   The journal entry is:

Notes Payable	50,000	
Interest Payable	750	
Interest Expense	250	
Cash		51,000

8. a   The $10,000 is a current maturity of long-term debt.
9. a   Secured notes are secured by some sort of collateral and are also known as mortgage notes. Convertible notes and are convertible into shares of stock at some future date.
10. d   Yield, effective, and market rates are different terms for the same thing.
11. b   Bonds involve two streams of cash flows: principal and interest.
12. c   If the rates are the same, then the bond sells at par value. If the contractual rate is lower than the market rate, then the bond sells at a discount.
13. d

14. b   Premium is added to bonds payable; discount is subtracted from bonds payable.

15. c   The company had to pay $204,000 for bonds with a carrying value of $196,000. The difference between these two numbers is a loss on redemption.

16. c

17. a   The ratio is calculated by dividing earnings before interest expense and income tax by interest expense. In this case, $300,000 ÷ $30,000 = 10 times.

18. c   It is simply disclosed in the notes if both conditions (reasonable estimate and probable) are not met. Only if the possibility of loss is remote does the company do nothing.

19. c   This procedure is allowed under certain circumstances, and capital leases are recorded as liabilities. Off-balance sheet financing should be considered by financial statement analysts.

20. d   Solvency ratios measure the ability of a company to repay its long-term debt and survive over a long period of time.

21. d

22. d   The journal entry is:

Bond Interest Expense	11,400	
Premium on Bonds Payable	600	
Cash		12,000

Premium = $12,000 ÷ 20 interest payment periods
Cash = $600,000 x 4% x 6/12
Bond Interest Expense = $12,000 − $600

23. a

Problems

1. a.

June 30 Interest Expense	200	
Interest Payable		200

(To record interest on note: $20,000 x 6% x 2/12)

   b. i)

Mar. 1 Property Tax Expense		
[($10,020 ÷ 12) x 2]	1,670	
Prepaid Property Tax		
[($10,020 ÷ 12) x 10]	8,350	
Property Tax Payable		10,020

(To record property tax expense and amount owing)

    ii)

May 15 Property Tax Payable	10,020	
Cash		10,020

(To record payment of property tax bill)

    iii)

June 30 Property Tax Expense	3,340	
Prepaid Property Tax		3,340

(To record property tax expense: $10,020 ÷ 12 x 4)

c. July 1   Cash   404,000
                    Bonds Payable   400,000
                    Premium on Bonds Payable   4,000
              (To record sale of bonds at premium)

2. a. Cash   107,743
            Premium on Bonds Payable   7,473
            Bonds Payable   100,000
       (To record issue of bond)

b. Bond Interest Expense   3,224.19
    Premium on Bonds Payable   275.81
         Cash   3,500.00
    Bond interest expense = ($107,473 x 6% x 6/12)
    Premium on bonds payable = ($3,500 − $3,224.19)
    Cash = ($100,000 x 7% x 6/12)

c. Bond Interest Expense   3,126.35
    Premium on Bonds Payable 373.65
         Cash   3,500.00
    Bond interest expense = ($3,500 - $373.65)
    Premium on bonds payable = ($7,473 ÷ 20 interest payments)
    Cash = ($100,000 x 7% x 6/12)

3. a.

Rebus Corporation
Statement of Earnings
Year Ended December 31, 2006

Service revenue		$75,000
Operating expenses		
Wages expense	$10,000	
Payroll tax expenses	1,000	
Amortization expense	5,000	
Advertising expense	1,000	
Bad debt expense	2,000	
Interest expense	8,000	
Total operating expenses		27,000
Earnings before income taxes		48,000
Income tax expense		13,000
Net earnings		$35,000

Rebus Corporation
Statement of Retained Earnings
Year Ended December 31, 2006

Retained earnings balance, January 1	$15,000
Add: Net earnings	35,000
	50,000
Less: Dividends	10,000
Retained earnings balance, December 31	$40,000

Rebus Corporation
Balance Sheet
December 31, 2006

Assets

Current assets		
Cash		$140,000
Accounts receivable	$70,000	
Less: Allowance for doubtful		
accounts	20,000	50,000
Total current assets		190,000
Property, plant, and equipment		
Land		$100,000
Building	$350,000	
Accumulated amortization—		
building	10,000	340,000
Total property, plant, and equipment		440,000
Total assets		$630,000

Liabilities and Shareholders' Equity

Current liabilities		
Accounts payable	$ 15,000	
Wages payable	2,000	
Interest payable	13,000	
Provincial sales tax payable	13,000	
Notes payable, six-month	40,000	
Current portion of mortgage payable	30,000	
Total current liabilities	113,000	
Long-term Liabilities		
Bonds payable	$100,000	
Less: Discount on bonds payable	2,000	98,000
Mortgage payable		145,000
Total long-term liabilities		243,000
Total liabilities		356,000

Shareholders' equity

Common shares	$234,000	
Retained earnings	40,000	
Total shareholders' equity		274,000
Total liabilities and shareholders' equity		$630,000

b. The current ratio is $190,000 ÷ $113,000 = 1.68:1 which means that there are 1.68 times current assets as there are current liabilities. At first glance, it would appear as though the company's liquidity is strong;, however, we would want to prepare additional ratios, such as the receivables turnover ratio, before concluding on the company's liquidity.

The debt to total assets is $356,000 ÷ $630,000 = 56.5% which means that 56.5 percent of total assets are is financed by assets. The times interest earned ratio is used to supplement the debt to total assets ratio and is calculated as follows: ($35,000 + $13,000 + $8,000) ÷ $8,000 = 7 times. (The formula is net earnings + income tax + interest divided by interest). Thus, the current earnings are currently more than sufficient to cover interest expense. Therefore, the solvency position looks favourable.

4. a. Domtar's long-term debt is $2,026 million in 2004 and $2,054 million in 2003, for a reduction of $28 million. Note 15 to the financial statements shows the change in various long-term debt instruments that occurred between 2003 and 2004.

b. Current liabilities divided by total liabilities is as follows ($ in millions):
Cascades: $614 ÷ ($614 + $1,168 + $303) = 29.4%
Domtar: $716 ÷ ($716 + $2,026 + $557 + $343) = 19.7%

c.

Domtar ($ in millions):
Debt to total assets:
2003: ($704 + $2,054 + $562 + $360) ÷ $5,848 = 62.9%
2004: ($716 + $2,026 + $557 + $343) ÷ $5,688 = 64.0%

Times interest earned:
2003: ($-193 + $67 + $169) ÷ $169 = 0.25 times
2004: ($-42 + $52 + $148) ÷ $148 = 1.07 times

Cascades ($ in millions):
Debt to total assets:
2003: $1,871 ÷ $2,927 = 63.9%
2004: $2,085 ÷ $3,144 = 66.3%

Times interest earned:
2003: ($55 + $10 + $80) ÷ $80 = 1.81 times
2004: ($23 + $2 + $76) ÷ $76 = 1.33 times

Both companies increased the amount of assets financed with debt in 2004 from 2003. Domtar increased from 62.9 percent in 2003 to 64 percent in 2004; Cascades increased from 63.9 to 66.3 percent. Domtar's times interest earned ratio improved in 2004, while Cascades' worsened. However, Cascades' times interest earned ratio in 2004 is slightly better than Domtar's. (1.33 versus 1.07 times), even though it has a slightly higher debt to total assets ratio (66.3% versus 64%). This means Cascades is better able to handle its interest payments then than is Domtar.

chapter 11

Reporting and Analyzing Shareholders' Equitty

Chapter Overview

In this chapter, you will learn about the essential features of a corporation and how to account for common shares, preferred shares, and dividends. You will also learn about how to present the shareholders' equity section of the balance sheet. Finally, you will learn how to measure corporate performance using various ratios.

Review of Specific Study Objectives

- A **corporation** is created by law and thus is a *legal entity* with most of the rights and privileges of a person.

- **Corporations** may be *classified in a variety of ways. Two common classifications are by purpose,* such as for-profit or not-for-profit (charitable or medical organizations), and *by ownership* (publicly held, which may have thousands of shareholders, and privately held, which have few shareholders and generally do not offer shares for sale to the public).

- The **income trust** is a relatively new form of corporation in Canada. An income trust is a special or limited purpose company, set up to specifically invest in income-producing assets. The trust pays out most of its earnings to its investors and there is no income tax payable for the trust itself.

study objective 1

Identify and discuss the major characteristics of a corporation and its shares.

- The following are **characteristics of a corporation**:

1. **Separate legal existence**, which means that a *corporation acts under its own name and has most of the same rights as does a person*. It may buy, own, or sell property, borrow money, enter into binding contracts, and sue or be sued, and it pays its own taxes.
2. **Limited liability of shareholders**, which means that the *liability of shareholders is generally limited to the amount of their investment*.
3. **Transferable ownership rights**, which means that a *shareholder may buy or sell shares without approval of the corporation or other shareholders*.
4. **Ability to acquire capital**, resulting from the issue of its shares.
5. **Continuous life**, which means that the *life of the corporation is not affected by the withdrawal, death, or incapacity of a shareholder, employee, or officer*.
6. **Corporation management**, meaning that *shareholders manage the company indirectly through the board of directors*. While professional managers may be hired, some view the separation of ownership and management in a negative fashion.
7. **Government regulation**, both *by federal and provincial governments*, which can be burdensome from both time and money standpoints.
8. **Income taxes** are paid by corporations because they are separate legal entities (with the exception of income trusts). Some argue that corporate earnings are taxed twice (double taxation)—at the corporate level and again at the individual level when dividends are received. This is not quite true, as individuals receive a dividend tax credit to reduce some of the tax burden.

- A **corporation may sell ownership rights** in the form of shares. The shares of a company are divided into different classes, such as Class A, Class B, and so on. The different classes are usually identified by the generic terms **common shares** and **preferred shares**. If it has only one class of shares, then that class is identified as common shares. *Each common shareholder has the following rights:*

1. The **right to vote** in the election of directors and to vote on matters requiring shareholder approval.
2. The **right to share in corporate earnings** through receipt of dividends.
3. The **right to share in distribution of assets upon liquidation of the corporation** in proportion to the shareholder's holdings.

- **Authorized share capital** *is the amount of share capital that a corporation is authorized to sell as indicated in its articles of incorporation*. It may be specified as an unlimited amount or a certain number. If a number is specified, the amount of authorized shares normally anticipates a company's initial and later capital needs. Issued shares are authorized shares that have been sold. No formal journal entry is required for authorized shares, but the *number of shares authorized and issued must be disclosed in the shareholders' equity section of the balance sheet*.

- A **corporation may sell its share capital** *either directly to investors or indirectly through an investment banking firm*. The first time a corporation's shares are offered to the public, the offer is called an *initial public offering (IPO)*. The company receives the cash (less any issue fees) from the sale of the IPO shares whether done by a direct or indirect issue.

Once these shares have been initially issued, they continue trading on the *secondary market*. That is, investors buy and sell shares to each other, rather than from the company. When shares are sold among investors, there is no impact on the company's financial position.

Shares are traded on stock exchanges, such as the Toronto Stock Exchange (TSX).

- **Market value of shares** is established by the interaction between buyers and sellers. In general, the price follows the trend of a company's earnings and dividends. Factors beyond a company's control (such as wars, trade embargoes, elections, and changes in interest rates) can also influence market prices.

- Years ago, *par value or stated value* was used to determine the *legal capital* per share that must remain invested in a business for the protection of corporate creditors. Corporations with par or stated value shares were required to sell their shares at par or stated value or above. Consequently, most companies assigned a very low value to their par or stated value shares a very low value. This value was an arbitrary amount that had nothing to do with the fair market value of the share. Today, the use of par or stated values for shares is either not required or prohibited in Canada.

  No par value shares are *shares that have not been assigned a pre-set legal capital*. When no par value shares are issued, all of the proceeds received are considered to be legal capital.

- **Share capital** is the amount contributed to the corporation by shareholders in exchange for share ownership. Other amounts can also be contributed to the corporation. Together, these other amounts and the share capital form the total **contributed capital** of the corporation.

study objective 2

Record share transactions.

  The following describes the issue of **no par value common shares**. As mentioned earlier, the entire proceeds is are considered to be legal capital of the no par value shares. If 100 common shares are sold for $5 per share, then the journal entry is:

Cash	500	
Common Shares		500

  (To record sale of 100 common shares for $5 per share)

  If another 100 common shares are sold for $7 per share, then the journal entry is:

Cash	700	
Common Shares		700

  (To record sale of 100 common shares for $7 per share)

  Note that in each case, the Common Shares account is credited with the entire proceeds of the sale.

- **Reacquisition of shares** involves companies that purchase their own shares on the open market. A corporation may acquire its own shares to:

  1. increase trading of the company's shares in the securities market in the hopes of enhancing its market value.
  2. reduce the number of shares issued and thereby increase earnings per share.
  3. have additional shares available to issue to officers and employees under bonus and stock compensation plans.

4. have additional shares available for use in acquiring other companies.
5. eliminate hostile shareholders by buying them out.

When a company reacquires its own shares, the repurchased shares must be retired and cancelled which, effectively, restores the shares to the status of authorized but unissued shares.

The difference between the price paid to reacquire the shares and their original cost is, in essence, a "gain" or "loss" on reacquisition. However, companies cannot realize a gain or suffer a loss from share transactions with their own shareholders, and so these amounts are not reported on the statement of earnings. They are seen instead as an excess or deficiency that belongs to the original shareholders and are reported as an increase or decrease in contributed capital.

Assume that a company has 100,000 shares issued and has $400,000 in its common share account and $20,000 in contributed capital. The company decides to reacquire 60,000 of its common shares on the open market. The following journal entry would be made if the company purchases its shares at $3.50 each.

Common Shares ($400,000 ÷ 100,000 x 60,000)	240,000	
Contributed Capital—Reacquisition of Common Shares		30,000
Cash (60,000 x $3.50)		210,000

The average cost of each common share is $4 ($400,000 ÷ 100,000), and so the Common Shares account must be decreased for the cost of each share. The Contributed Capital account is increased by the difference between the cash paid ($3.50 per share) and the average cost of each share ($4 per share).

If the company repurchased its shares at $4.50 each instead of $3.50, the journal entry would be:

Common Shares ($400,000 ÷ 100,000 x 60,000)	240,000	
Contributed Capital—Reacquisition of Shares	20,000	
Retained Earnings	10,000	
Cash (60,000 x $4.50)		270,000

If a company reacquires its shares at a price that is greater than its average cost of the common shares, as shown above, the difference between the purchase price and average cost is first debited to contributed capital, if any exists (the account has a balance of $20,000 in this particular case), and then to retained earnings.

- **Preferred shares** have contractual provisions that may give them *preference or priority over common shares in certain areas*, usually in relation to dividends and to assets in the event of liquidation. Preferred shares usually have no voting rights. If a corporation issues 500 preferred shares for $30 per share, the journal entry is:

Cash	15,000	
Preferred Shares		15,000
(To record sale of 500 shares at $30 per share)		

- **Preferred shares** are *listed before common shares on the balance sheet* because of its their preferences in the areas of dividends and liquidation.

- **Preferred shares have priority over common shares in the matter of dividends.** This does not guarantee that preferred shares will always receive the dividend. The dividend amount is stated as an annual amount per share; for example, $5 preferred shares means that each preferred shares is eligible to receive $5 a year in dividends.

- Preferred shares may contain **a cumulative** dividend feature. This right means that preferred shareholders must be paid both current-year dividends and any unpaid prior-year dividends before common shareholders receive dividends. Preferred dividends not declared in a given period are called *dividends in arrears* and *should be disclosed in the notes* to the financial statements. Dividends in arrears are not a liability. No obligation exists until the board of directors declares the dividend. If a corporation must pay its preferred shareholders $10,000 a year in dividends and has not paid dividends in the past two years, and if it has $50,000 for dividend distribution in the current year, then the distribution will be:

Preferred dividends in arrears	$20,000
Preferred dividends—current year	10,000
Common dividends	20,000
Total dividends distributed	$50,000

The common Common shareholders simply receive the difference between the total of $50,000 and the $30,000, which must be distributed to the preferred shareholders.

- If preferred shares are **non-cumulative**, then *any dividend not declared and paid is forever lost.* Since this is very unattractive to investors, most companies do not issue non-cumulative preferred shares.

- **Preferred shareholders** also have a *preference in the event of liquidation of the corporation.* Creditors must be paid first, then followed by preferred shareholders, and then common shareholders. The preference may be for the legal capital value of the shares or for a specified liquidating value.

- **Convertible preferred shares** allow the shareholder to exchange preferred shares into for common shares at a specified ratio.

- **Redeemable (callable) preferred shares** offer an option for the corporation to repurchase in the future its shares from the shareholder in the future. **Retractable preferred shares** offer the option to the shareholder to resell in the future its shares to the corporation in the future.

- A **dividend** is a *pro rata (equal) distribution of a portion of a corporation's retained earnings to its shareholders.*

- To pay a **cash dividend**, a corporation must have *retained earnings, adequate cash, and dividends declared by the board of directors.* While many companies pay a quarterly dividend, there are companies, called growth companies, that pay no dividends but reinvest earnings in the company so that it can grow.

- There are **three dates of importance for all dividends:** *date of declaration, date of record, and date of payment.* Journal entries are required on the first and third dates. For a **cash dividend**, the journal entry on the *date of declaration* will be as follows if a corporation declares a $0.25 per share cash dividend on 100,000 shares:

study objective 3

Prepare the entries for cash dividends, stock dividends, and stock splits, and understand their financial impact.

| Cash Dividends | 25,000 | |
| Dividends Payable | | 25,000 |

(To declare a cash dividend of
$0.25 per share on 100,000 shares)

Dividends Payable is a current liability. It will normally be paid within the next month.

On the **date of record**, *ownership of the shares is determined for dividend purposes.* No journal entry is required.

On the **date of payment**, the following entry is required:

| Dividends Payable | 25,000 | |
| Cash | | 25,000 |

(To record payment of a cash dividend)

Declaration and payment of a cash dividend reduce both shareholders' equity and total assets.

- A **stock dividend** is *a distribution of the corporation's own shares to shareholders.* A stock dividend results in a decrease in *retained earnings and an increase in share capital. Total shareholders' equity will remain the same* because dollar amounts are simply transferred from retained earnings to share capital accounts. A stock dividend is interesting because an investor really receives nothing extra on the day he receives the shares. His ownership percentage has not changed. In the future, however, if the share price rises, he will have more shares on which there may be price appreciation.

- **Corporations issue stock dividends:**

  1. *to satisfy shareholders' dividend expectations without spending cash.*
  2. *to increase the marketability of the shares by reducing the price per share.*
  3. *to emphasize that a portion of equity has been permanently reinvested in the business and is unavailable for cash dividends.*

- Consider the **following example of a stock dividend.** A corporation has 500,000 common shares issued on the day on which the board of directors declares a 10-percent stock dividend. The fair market value of the shares is $30 per share. Fifty thousand new shares (500,000 x 10%) will be issued. The journal entry on the **date of declaration** is:

Stock Dividends	1,500,000	
Common Stock Dividends		
Distributable		1,500,000

The calculation is as follows: 50,000 shares x $30 = $1,500,000

Common Stock Dividends Distributable is a *shareholders' equity account.* If a balance sheet is prepared after the dividend declaration, then the account will appear directly under the Common Shares account in the share capital section.

On the **date of payment**, the journal entry is:

Common Stock Dividends
Distributable   1,500,000
          Common Shares   1,500,000
(To record distribution of stock dividend)

- Like a stock dividend, a **stock split** involves the *issue of additional shares to shareholders according to their percentage ownership*. Unlike a stock dividend, a stock split *is usually much larger than a stock dividend*. The **purpose of a stock split** is to *increase the marketability of the shares by lowering the market value per share*. A corporation has 200,000 common shares issued; the market price of the shares is $100 per share. The corporation declares a two-for-one stock split. The number of shares will double to 400,000, and the market price will be reduced by half, to $50 per share. Note that the Common Shares account has $1,000,000 in it both before and after the split. A stock split *has no effect on total share capital, retained earnings, and total shareholders' equity*, and no journal entry is required to record it.

- The **balance in retained earnings** is generally available for *dividend declarations*. There may be **retained earnings restrictions** that *make a portion of the balance currently unavailable for dividends*. Restrictions result from legal, contractual, or voluntary causes and are *usually disclosed in the notes* to the financial statements.

<table>
<tr><td>study objective 4</td></tr>
<tr><td>Indicate how shareholders' equity is presented in the financial statements.</td></tr>
</table>

- In the shareholders' equity section of the balance sheet, **contributed capital, retained earnings, and accumulated other comprehensive income** are reported. Within contributed capital, share capital and additional contributed capital are recognized. **Share capital** consists of preferred and common shares, and preferred shares are shown before common shares because of the former's preferential rights. **Additional contributed capital** includes amounts contributed from reacquiring and retiring shares. If a company has a variety of additional sources of contributed capital, it is important to distinguish each one by source.

- **Retained earnings** in on the balance sheet are derived from the statement of retained earnings. Notes to the financial statements are required to explain any restrictions to retained earnings and any dividends that may be in arrears. Just as net earnings is are credited to the Retained Earnings account, so is net loss is debited to the account, even if an overall debit balance in the account results. A *debit balance in Retained Earnings* is called a **deficit** and is reported as a deduction in the shareholders' equity section of the balance sheet.

- **Comprehensive income** includes all changes in shareholders' equity during a period, except for changes that result from the sale or repurchase of shares or from the payment of dividends. It includes:

  1. the revenues, expenses, gains, and losses included in net earnings, and
  2. the gains and losses that bypass net earnings but affect shareholders' equity. This category is referred to as "other comprehensive income." Some examples will be discussed in the next chapter.

Information about cash inflows and outflows during the year that resulted from equity transactions is reported in the financing activities section of the cash flow statement.

study objective 5
Evaluate dividend and earnings performance.

- To **measure a corporation's dividend record**, an investor can *calculate the payout ratio*.

- The **payout ratio** measures *the percentage of earnings distributed in the form of cash dividends to common shareholders*. It is calculated by *dividing total cash dividends to common shareholders by net earnings*. A company with a high growth rate typically has a low payout ratio because it reinvests earnings in the business.

- Another dividend measure is the **dividend yield**. It is calculated by dividing the dividend per share by the share price. It measures the earnings generated by each share for the shareholder, based on the market price of the share.

- The earnings performance of a company is measured in several different ways. It is measured by the earnings per share ratio, discussed in an earlier chapter, and by the **return on shareholders' equity**. The ratio *shows how many dollars were earned for each dollar invested by common shareholders*. It is calculated by *dividing net earnings available to common shareholders (net earnings minus preferred share dividends) by average common shareholders' equity*. The common shareholders' equity is total shareholders' equity, less the legal capital of any preferred shares.

Chapter Self-Test

As you work through the exercises and problems, remember to use the **Decision Toolkit** discussed and used in the text:

1. *Decision Checkpoints*: At this point, you ask a question.
2. *Info Needed for Decision*: You make a choice regarding the information needed to answer the question.
3. *Tool to Use for Decision*: At this point, you review just what the information chosen in step two does for the decision-making process.
4. *How to Evaluate Results*: You conduct an evaluation of information for answering the question.

Note: The notation (SO1) means that the question was drawn from study objective number one.

Multiple Choice

Please circle the correct answer.

(SO1)   1. Which of the following is considered to be a disadvantage of the corporate form of business organization?
     a.   Limited liability of shareholders
     b.   Separate legal existence
     c.   Continuous life
     d.   Provincial and federal government regulations

2. Share capital that has not been assigned a legal value per share in the corporate   (SO1)
    charter is called:
    a. legal capital shares.
    b. par value shares.
    c. no par value shares.
    d. stated value shares.

3. The amount per share that must be retained in the business for the protection   (SO1)
    of corporate creditors is called:
    a. legal capital.
    b. par value.
    c. market value.
    d. stated value.

4. If 3,000 common shares are sold for $6 per share, then the journal entry   (SO2)
    includes a:
    a. credit to Investments for $18,000.
    b. credit to Cash for $18,000.
    c. credit to Retained Earnings for $18,000.
    d. credit to Common Shares for $18,000.

5. If the Common Shares account has a balance of $23,000, and Retained Earnings   (SO2)
    has a balance of $40,000, then total shareholders' equity is:
    a. $63,000.
    b. $60,000.
    c. $57,000.
    d. $17,000.

6. A corporation has cumulative preferred shares on which it must pay dividends   (SO2)
    of $20,000 per year. The dividends are in arrears for two years. If the
    corporation has in the current year $90,000 available for dividends, then the
    common shareholders will receive:
    a. $20,000.
    b. $30,000.
    c. $40,000.
    d. $60,000.

7. Which of the following statements is incorrect?   (SO2)
    a. Dividends cannot be paid to common shareholders while any dividend on
        preferred shares is in arrears.
    b. Dividends in arrears on preferred shares are not considered a liability.
    c. Dividends may be paid on common shares while dividends are in arrears
        on preferred shares.
    d. When preferred shares are non-cumulative, any dividend passed in a year
        is lost forever.

8. On December 1, a corporation has declared a $1 cash dividend per share on its   (SO3)
    500,000 common shares. The journal entry on the date of payment of the
    dividend, December 20, includes a debit to:
    a. Dividends Payable for $500,000.
    b. Cash Dividends for $500,000.
    c. Cash for $500,000.
    d. Common Stock Dividends Distributable for $500,000.

(SO3)   9. A corporation is authorized to sell 1,000,000 common shares and has 500,000 shares issued. The board of directors declares a 10-percent stock dividend. How many new shares will ultimately be issued as a result of the stock dividend?
   a.   100,000
   b.   50,000
   c.   None. The corporation will pay the dividend in cash.
   d.   None of the above is correct.

(SO3)   10. The board of directors of a corporation declares a 5-percent stock dividend while there are 20,000 common shares issued. On the declaration date, the fair market value of each share is $40. The journal entry to declare the stock dividend includes a:
   a.   debit to Retained Earnings for $1,000.
   b.   debit to Cash for $40,000.
   c.   credit to Common Stock Dividends Distributable for $40,000.
   d.   credit to Common Shares for $40,000.

(SO3)   11. A corporation has 100,000 common shares issued with a fair market value of $80 per share. If the board of directors declares a two-for-one stock split, then:
   a.   the number of shares doubles and the fair market value decreases to $40.
   b.   the number of shares and fair market value remain the same.
   c.   the number of shares halves and the fair market value doubles.
   d.   the number of shares and fair market value both halve.

(SO3)   12. A retained earnings restriction:
   a.   makes a portion of the balance of retained earnings unavailable for dividends.
   b.   may arise from legal, contractual, or voluntary causes.
   c.   generally is disclosed in the notes to the financial statements.
   d.   All of the above are correct.

(SO3)   13. Indicate the respective effects of the declaration of a cash dividend on the following balance sheet sections:

	Total Assets	Total Liabilities	Total Shareholders' Equity
a.	Increase	Decrease	No change
b.	No change	Increase	Decrease
c.	Decrease	Increase	Decrease
d.	Decrease	No change	Increase

(SO4)   14. Accumulated other comprehensive income is shown in the:
   a.   the statement of earnings as other revenue.
   b.   the statement of retained earnings.
   c.   the shareholders' equity section of the balance sheet.
   d.   operating section of the cash flow statement.

15. A corporation shows the following account balances: (SO4)

Retained Earnings $10,000
Common Stock Dividends Distributable   20,000
Common Shares   255,000

What is the total shareholders' equity?
  a. $245,000
  b. $255,000
  c. $275,000
  d. $285,000

16. In the shareholders' equity section of the balance sheet: (SO4)
  a. Dividends in Arrears will appear as a restriction of Retained Earnings.
  b. Preferred and Common Shares appear under the subsection Share Capital.
  c. Common Stock Dividends Distributable will appear in its own subsection of shareholders' equity.
  d. Common Stock Dividends Distributable will be classified as a contra account to Retained Earnings.

17. Two classifications appearing in the share capital section of the balance sheet are: (SO4)
  a. retained earnings and common stock dividends distributable.
  b. share capital and retained earnings.
  c. preferred shares and common shares.
  d. dividends payable and dividends distributable.

Use the following information for questions 18 to 20.

Consider the following data for a corporation:

Gross earnings	$900,000
Net earnings	$800,000
Weighted average number of common shares	400,000
Common dividends per share	$0.75
Preferred dividends	$50,000
Market price per preferred share	$25
Market price per common share	$20
Preferred shares issued	110,000
Average common shareholders' equity	$3,000,000

18. What is the return on common shareholders' equity?   (SO5)
  a. 25%
  b. 26.67%
  c. 30%
  d. 29.1%

19. What is the dividend payout ratio for common shareholders?   (SO5)
  a. 37.5%
  b. 33.3%
  c. 40%
  d. 35%

(SO5)   20. What is the dividend yield for common shareholders?
  a. 3%
  b. 3.75%
  c. 3.25%
  d. 4%

(SO5)   21. During its past fiscal year, a corporation had net earnings of $175,000 and paid preferred share dividends of $50,000 and common share dividends of $25,000. It had 80,000 common shares issued at the beginning of the year and issued an additional 40,000 shares half way through the year. What was the company's earnings per share?
  a. $0.83
  b. $1.00
  c. $1.04
  d. $1.25

Problems

1. Windsor Corporation shows the following data:

Common shares, 500,000 no par value shares authorized, 300,000 shares issued	$1,700,000
Retained earnings	3,200,000

Required:
Journalize the following transactions:

(SO2) a. Sold 10,000 common shares for $9 per share.
(SO3) b. Declared and distributed a 15% stock dividend. The fair market value of the shares on this date was $12 per share.
(SO2) c. Sold 8,000 common shares for $15 per share.
(SO3) d. Declared a two-for-one stock split. On this date, the fair market value of the shares was $18 per share.
(SO3) e. Declared and paid a $0.10 per share cash dividend.

Date	Account Titles	Debit	Credit

2. At June 30, 2006, the Atlantis Corporation had the following account balances:

Common shares, no par value, 100,000 shares issued $500,000
Contributed capital $20,000

Required:

Prepare the required journal entry for each of the two following independent situations:

a. On July 1, 2006, Atlantis reacquires 70,000 of its shares at $4.00 each.   (SO2)

b. On July 1, 2006, Atlantis reacquires 70,000 of its shares at $5.50 each.   (SO2)

Date	Account Titles	Debit	Credit

3. The Axwell Corporation's books show the following information at December 31, 2006.

Common shares, no par value, 900,000 shares authorized;
  700,000 shares issued $7,000,000
Common stock dividends distributable $100,000
Preferred shares, no par value, $2, 8,000 shares authorized;
  6,000 shares issued $150,000
Retained earnings, December 31, 2006 $850,000
Accumulated other comprehensive income $50,000
Net earnings for year 2006 $650,000
Cash dividends on common shares $0.20 per share
Cash dividends on preferred shares $2.00 per share
Market price per common share December 31, 2006 $11.00

Required:

(SO4)   a.   Prepare the shareholders' equity section at December 31, 2006, assuming that retained earnings is restricted for plant expansion in the amount of $300,000.

(SO3,5)   b.   Calculate the dividend payout and dividend yield ratios on common shares and return on common shareholders' equity for 2006. Assume that common shareholders' equity on December 31, 2005 was $7,648,000.

4.   Please refer to the Domtar and Cascades financial statements for information for answering the following questions. Do n't not forget to use the **Decision Toolkit** approach for help in the problem solving.

(SO1,4)   a.   What type of shares do Domtar and Cascades have?

(SO4)   b.   On which financial statements is there information about shares?

(SO2)   c.   Are Domtar's preferred shares cumulative or non-cumulative? Explain the difference.

(SO5)   d.   What is the dividend payout ratio for both Domtar and Cascades for 2004 and 2003?

(SO5)   e.   What is the return on common shareholders' equity for both Domtar and Cascades for 2004?

Solutions to Self-Test

Multiple Choice

1. d   The other three are considered to be advantages.

2. c   There is no such thing as legal capital shares. Par value shares have a specified (legal) value. Stated value shares are no par value shares assigned a stated value by the board of directors.

3. a   Par value is an arbitrary amount listed in the corporate charter, and market value is the selling price of a share on a given day. Stated value is a value assigned to no par value shares by the board of directors. The legal capital is whatever is specified in the corporate charter or by the board of directors—par value, no par value, or stated value.

4. d   The journal entry is:

Cash	18,000	
Common Shares		18,000

5. a $23,000 + $40,000 = $63,000

6. b   Preferred receives $20,000 for each of the past two years and $20,000 in the current year for a total of $60,000; common receives the difference of $90,000 and $60,000.

7. c   Dividends may not be paid on common shares as long as preferred dividends are in arrears.

8. a   The journal entry is:

Dividends Payable	500,000	
Cash		500,000

9. b   500,000 shares x 10% = 50,000 new shares

10. c   The journal entry is:

Retained Earnings   40,000
  Common Stock
Dividends Distributable   40,000
20,000 x 5% = 1,000 new shares; 1,000 x $40 fair market
value = $40,000

11. a   With a two-for-one stock split, one old share is exchanged for two new
ones. The number of shares double (200,000), and fair market value is
reduced by half ($40).

12. d

13. b

14. c

15. d $10,000 + $20,000 + $255,000 = $285,000

16. b

17. c

18. a   ($800,000 – $50,000) ÷ $3,000,000 = 25%

19. a   400,000 x $.75 = $300,000 ÷ $800,000 = 37.5%

20. b $0.75 ÷ $20 = 3.75%

21. d   ($175,000 - $50,000) ÷ [80,000 + (40,000 x 6/12)] = $1.25

Problems

1. a.   Cash   90,000
  Common Shares   90,000
(To record issue of shares—10,000
shares at $9 per share)

  b.   Stock Dividends   558,000
  Common Stock Dividends Distributable   558,000
(To record declaration of stock dividend)

   Common Stock Dividends Distributable   558,000
  Common Shares   558,000
(To distribute stock dividend)

310,000 shares x 15% = 46,500 new shares x $12 fair market value per
share = $558,000

  c.   Cash   120,000
  Common Shares   120,000
(To record issue of shares—8,000
shares at $15 per share)

  d.   No entry required. The number of shares issued at this point, 364,500
(300,000 + 10,000 + 46,500 + 8,000), doubles to 729,000. The fair market
value will be cut in half, $9.

e.   Cash Dividends   72,900
          Dividends Payable   72,900
      (To declare a $0.10 per share cash dividend)
      Dividends Payable   72,900
          Cash   72,900
      (To pay the cash dividend)

      729,000 shares x $0.10 per share = $72,900

2. a.   Common Shares ($500,000 ÷ 100,000 x 70,000)   350,000
          Contributed Capital—Reacquisition of
          Common Shares   70,000
          Cash (70,000 x $4.00)   280,000

    b.   Common Shares ($500,000 ÷ 100,000 x 70,000)   350,000
          Contributed Capita—Reacquisition of Shares   20,000
          Retained Earnings   15,000
              Cash (70,000 x $5.50)   385,000

3. a.

Axwell Corporation
Balance Sheet (partial)
December 31, 2006

Shareholders' equity
  Share capital
      $2 preferred shares, no par value, 8,000 shares
          authorized, 6,000 shares issued $ 150,000
      Common shares, no par value, 900,000 shares
          authorized 700,000 shares issued and
          outstanding $7,000,000
      Common stock dividends distributable   100,000   7,100,000
          Total share capital   7,250,000
      Retained earnings (See note)   850,000
      Accumulated other comprehensive income   50,000
          Total shareholders' equity $8,150,000

Note: Included in retained earnings is an amount of $300,000 for plant expansion.

b.

Dividend payout = Cash dividends to common shareholders divided by
net earnings = (700,000 x $0.20) ÷ $400,000 = 35%
Dividend yield = Cash dividends to common shareholders divided by
market price per share = $0.20 ÷ $11.00 = 1.8%
Return on common shareholders' equity = (Net earnings—Preferred
dividends) divided by average common shareholders equity, where:
    Preferred dividends = 6,000 preferred shares issued x $2.00 = $12,000
    Common shareholders' equity 2006 = $8,150,000 – $150,000 =
    $8,000,000

Common shareholders' equity 2005 = $7,648,000
Average common shareholders' equity
= ($8,000,000 + $7,648,000) ÷ 2 = $7,824,000
= ($650,000 − $12,000)) ÷ $7,824,000 = 8.2%

4. a.   Cascades: They repurchased all of their remaining preferred shares in 2003.
     They now only have common shares (see Note 11 to financial statements).
     Domtar: common and preferred shares. (See Note 18)

    b.   Balance sheet and cash flow statement.

    c.   The shares are cumulative. Note 18 describes the rights of the preferred
     shareholders. Because the shares are cumulative, the shareholders have
     the right to both current year dividends as well as any prior years' unpaid
     dividends.

    d.   The payout ratio is calculated by dividing total cash dividends to common
     shareholders by net earnings as follows:
     Note: The cash dividend payment is obtained from the statement of
     retained earnings for both companies.

     Cascades ($ in millions):
     2003: $13 ÷ $55 = 23.6%
     2004: $13 ÷ $23 = 56.5%

     Domtar ($ in millions):
     2003: $49
     2004: $54
     Domtar paid the above dividends even though they it incurred a net loss of
     $193 million in 2003 and $42 million in 2004. The dividend payout ratios
     are not calculated because the results are meaningless when net losses are
     incurred.

    e.   The return on common shareholders' equity ratio is calculated by dividing
     net earnings available to common shareholders (net earnings minus
     preferred share dividends) by average common shareholders' equity. The
     common shareholders' equity is total shareholders' equity less preferred
     shares.

     Domtar ($ in millions):
     Common shareholders' equity for 2003 = $2,168 − $42 = $2,126
     Common shareholders' equity for 2004 = $2,046 − $39 = $2,007
     Average common shareholders' equity = ($2,126 + $2,007) ÷ 2 = $2,066.50
     The return on common shareholders' equity for 2004 is:
     ($-42 − $1) ÷ $2,066.50 = -2.08%

     Cascades ($ in millions):
     Common shareholders' equity for 2003 = $1,056
     Common shareholders' equity for 2004 = $1,059

Average common shareholders' equity = ($1,056 + $1,059) ÷ 2 = $1,057.50

The return on common shareholders' equity for 2004 is:

$23 ÷ $1,057.50 = 2.17%

chapter 12

Reporting and Analyzing Investments

Chapter Overview

In this chapter, you will learn about the reasons that corporations invest in debt and equity securities and how to account for both. You will learn how debt and equity investments are valued and, finally, how they are reported in the financial statements.

Review of Specific Study Objectives

- **Corporations invest in debt or equity securities for one of three reasons:**

  1. They have excess cash that they do not need for the purchase of operating assets until a future period. Excess cash may result from seasonal fluctuations in sales. Excess cash is usually invested in low-risk, highly liquid securities, most often short-term government securities.
  2. Some companies purchase investments to generate investment revenue.
  3. There may be strategic reasons, such as a corporation's desire to establish a presence in another company or to purchase a controlling interest in another company.

study objective 1

Identify the reasons corporations invest in short- and long-term debt and equity securities.

- **Short-term investments** can include investments in either debt or equity securities. To qualify as short-term, the investment must be (1) **readily marketable**, and (2) **intended to be converted into cash** in the near future.

- An investment is "readily marketable" if it can be easily sold when cash is needed. "Intent to convert" means that management intends to sell whenever cash is needed.

- Short-term investments can be further designated as either trading securities or available-for-sale securities. **Trading securities** are debt or equity securities purchased and held for resale in the short-term, hopefully at a gain. **Available-for-sale** securities are debt or equity securities that are held with the intention of selling them in the future.

- **Long-term investments** can also include investments in either debt or equity securities. Investments that do not meet both the short-term criteria—readily marketable and intent to convert—are long-term investments. In addition, certain equity investments purchased for the purpose of significant influence or control are also long-term investments.

study objective 2

Explain the accounting for debt investments.

- **Debt investments** include investments in money market instruments as well as investments in bonds, commercial paper, and a large variety of other debt securities available for purchase.

- **Money-market investments** are relatively safe, short-term investments that allow a company to earn a higher rate of interest than it would otherwise earn in a bank account. Assume that on July 1, 2006, a company purchases a three-month, $6,000 term deposit which pays an annual interest rate of 2 percent. The journal entry to record the purchase is:

Debt Investment—Term Deposit	6,000	
Cash		6,000
(To record purchase of three-month, 2% term deposit)		

The interest would be accrued each month until the term deposit matures as follows:

Interest Receivable	10	
Interest Revenue		10
(To accrue interest: $6,000 x 0.02 x 1/12)		

The journal entry to record the sale of the term deposit on September 30 is as follows:

Cash	6,030	
Interest Receivable	20	(for July and August)
Interest Revenue	10	(for September)
Debt Investment—Term Deposit	6,000	
(To record maturity of term deposit)		

- **Another example of a debt investment is bonds. For bonds, acquisition costs** are based on the **cost principle** and include *all expenditures necessary to acquire the investment, such as the price paid plus brokerage fees* (commissions). If a company purchases **bonds for $60,000 plus a commission of $2,000**, then the journal entry is:

Debt Investments	62,000	
Cash		62,000
(To record purchase of bonds)		

Note that there *is no separate account for fees or commissions*. The purchase price and the commission are debited to the asset account.

- When **bond interest is received**, the debit is to Cash and the credit is to Interest Revenue (an Other Revenues item on the statement of earnings). If interest is accrued, then the entry is a debit to Interest Receivable and a credit to Interest Revenue.

- When **bonds are sold**, it is necessary to (1) update any unrecorded interest up to the date of sale, and (2) credit the investment account for the cost of the bonds. *Any difference between net proceeds (sales price less fees) and the cost of the bonds is recorded as a gain or loss.* If **bonds with a cost of $20,000 are sold for a net amount of $18,000**, then the entry is as follows:

Cash	18,000	
Loss on Sale of Debt Investments	2,000	
Debt Investments		20,000
(To record sale of bonds at a loss)		

The **loss account** appears on *the statement of earnings as an Other Expenses item.* A **gain** *appears on the statement of earnings as an Other Revenues item.*

- The accounting for short-term and long-term debt investments is similar. The major exception relates to the handling of the bond premium or discount. For both short-term and long-term debt investments any bond premium or discount is usually combined and recorded along with the face value of the investment. For short-term bond investments, the bond premium or discount is not amortized. In contrast, the bond premium or discount for long-term bond investments is amortized to the Interest Revenue account over the remaining term of the bonds.

- **Equity investments** are *investments in the share capital of other corporations.* An **investment portfolio** consists of *securities (shares and/or debt) of several different corporations.*

- **Accounting for equity investments** is *based on the extent of the investor's influence over the operating and financial affairs of the issuing corporation (the investee).*

Guidelines are as follows:

1. If the **investor holds less than 20 percent of the investee's shares**, then there is an insignificant influence on the investee, and the *cost method* is used.
2. If the **investor holds more than 20 percent of the investee's shares**, then there is a presumption of significant influence on the investee, and the *equity method* is used.
3. If the **investor holds more than 50 percent of the investee's shares**, then the investor has a controlling influence. In addition to the equity method used for accounting, *consolidated financial statements* are prepared for reporting purposes.

- For **holdings of less than 20 percent**, the cost method is used. The *investment is recorded at cost, and revenue is recognized only when cash dividends are received or declared.* As is true for debt investments, cost includes all expenditures necessary to acquire the investments, including the price paid plus brokerage fees (commissions).

study objective 3

Explain the accounting for equity investments.

If a corporation acquires 2,000 common shares at $50 per share, plus $2,000 in commissions, then the journal entry is:

Equity Investments	102,000	
Cash		102,000
(To record purchase of common shares)		

Note that once again *there is no separate account for fees or commissions*. The purchase price and the commissions are debited to the asset account.

If **dividends of $3 per share are received**, then the journal entry is:

Cash	6,000	
Dividend Revenue		6,000
(To record receipt of dividends: 2,000 x $3 = $6,000)		

Dividend Revenue is reported separately, often in an *Other Revenues item in the statement of earnings.*

If **the shares are sold** for net proceeds of $105,000, then the journal entry is:

Cash	105,000	
Equity Investments		102,000
Gain on Sale of Equity Investments		3,000
(To record sale of common shares)		

A **loss account** appears *on the statement of earnings as an Other Expenses item.* A **gain** *appears on the statement of earnings as an Other Revenues item.*

- For **holdings of more than 20 percent**, the *equity method is used. The investment is recorded initially at cost and is adjusted annually to show the investor's equity in the investee.* The investor debits the investment account and increases revenue for its share of the investee's net earnings. The investor debits Cash and credits the investment account for the amount of dividends received. With this method, the **investor is essentially purchasing part of the investee's Retained Earnings account.** Anything that makes that account increase, such as net earnings, is reflected in the investor's investment account as an increase, and anything that makes that account decrease, such as net loss or payment of dividends, is reflected in the investor's investment account as a decrease.

Reiher Corporation purchased 40 percent of the common shares of Ott Corporation for $250,000. The journal entry is:

Equity Investments	250,000	
Cash		250,000
(To record purchase of Ott shares)		

For the year, **Ott reported $200,000 of net earnings and paid dividends of $50,000.** The journal entries for Reiher are:

Equity Investments   80,000
    Revenue from Investment
       in Ott Corporation   80,000
(To record 40 percent equity in Ott's earnings:
$200,000 x 40% = $80,000)
    Cash   20,000
      Equity Investments   20,000
(To record dividends received:
$50,000 x 40% = $20,000)

study objective 4

Describe how investments are valued and performance is evaluated.

After these entries, the **balance in Equity Investments totals $310,000**: $250,000 + $80,000 – $20,000.

- You will recall that there are three categories of securities:

1. Trading securities held mainly for sale in the near term.
2. Available-for-sale securities that are held for sale sometime in the future.
3. Held-to-maturity debt securities that the investor has the intention and ability to hold to maturity.

- Trading and available-for-sale securities are valued at market value. The difference between cost and market value is recorded as an increase or decrease to the security account at year end with a corresponding **unrealized** gain or loss. Gains and losses are called *realized* when they result from actual sales of investments; they are called *unrealized* when they result from "paper" gains or losses resulting from an increase or decrease in market value.

Held-to-maturity securities are valued at cost.

Assume that a company has the following trading securities on December 31, 2006:

Trading Security	Cost	Market	Unrealized Gain (Loss)
Royal Bank bonds	$100,000	$120,000	$20,000
Fortis shares	48,000	45,000	(3,000)
Total	$148,000	$165,000	$17,000

On December 31, 2006, the $165,000 would be reported as a current asset on the balance sheet, and the $17,000 would be reported as other revenue in the statement of earnings. **Note that the unrealized gain or loss is reported the same way as a realized gain or loss for trading securities**.

The adjustment of the trading securities to market value as well as the recognition of any unrealized gain or loss is done through an adjusting entry as follows:

Allowance to Adjust Trading Securities to Market Value   17,000
    Unrealized Gain—Trading Securities   17,000

Note that the entire portfolio of securities is adjusted—not individual securities. When the allowance is in a debit position, which occurs when market value is greater than cost, it is called an **adjunct account**. When the allowance is in a credit position, which occurs when market value is less than cost, it is called a **contra account**. The allowance account is adjusted at each balance sheet date and is reported with the trading securities on the balance sheet. Quite often, only the market value is reported on the balance sheet with adjustment details reported as notes to financial statements.

- The procedure for determining and recording any change in market value and any resulting unrealized gains or losses for available-for-sale securities is the same as that used for trading securities. However, the reporting of any unrealized gain or loss differs because the sale of available-for-sale securities may not occur in the near term. Consequently, any unrealized gain or loss on available-for-sale securities is not reported as part of net earnings. Instead, it is reported separately as **comprehensive income**.

- As discussed earlier, held-to-maturity debt securities are recorded at cost. However, if the market value falls substantially below cost, and the decline is considered permanent, then (and only then) will a held-to-maturity debt security be adjusted to its market value.

- The evaluation of portfolio performance depends on the classification of the securities in the portfolio. The investments can be classified as trading, available-for-sale, or held-to-maturity debt securities. The classifications require a substantial amount of management judgment and can have a significant impact on the inancial position and performance of the company. There is, therefore, potential for earnings management. Such **window dressing of earnings** often makes it difficult for an outsider to determine why companies choose to sell or hold a security or classify it as they do. It is important to consider the impact of actual and potential gains and losses on current and future earnings when evaluating the performance of a company's investment portfolio.

---

study objective 5

Indicate how investments are reported in the financial statements.

- A **parent company** is a *company that controls or owns more than 50 percent of the common shares of another entity.* A **subsidiary (affiliated) company** is the *entity whose shares are owned by the parent company.* The parent company has a **controlling interest** in the subsidiary company.

- **Consolidated financial statements** are prepared. These statements *present the assets and liabilities controlled by the parent company and the aggregate profitability of the subsidiary companies.* They are presented in addition to the financial statements for each of the individual parent and subsidiary companies.

- **Consolidated financial statements** are *especially useful to the shareholders, board of directors, and management of the parent company.*

- In the balance sheet presentation, investments are classified as short-term or long-term.

- Investments that are held for trading purposes are always classified as short-term. Available-for-sale securities may be classified as short-term or long-term, depending on management's intent. Short-term investments are reported in the current assets section of the balance sheet. The valuation allowance to adjust cost to market may be added or subtracted directly on the balance sheet or reported as a note to the financial statement.

- Long-term investments may include available-for-sale securities, as discussed above. Held-to-maturity debt securities are classified as long-term investments until they are about to mature. Any portion that matures within one year is classified as short-term. Equity investments that give significant influence are reported as long-term with supporting details provided in notes to financial statements.

- Gains and losses, whether realized or not, are reported in the statement of earnings for trading securities. As well, other investment-related accounts, such as interest and dividend revenue accounts, are also reported in the non-operating section of the statement of earnings.

- Unrealized gains and losses from available-for-sale securities are presented in the statement of comprehensive income. Realized gains and losses are presented in the statement of earnings.

- Information on cash inflows or outflows resulting from investment transactions is shown in the investment activities section of the cash flow statement.

Chapter Self-Test

As you work through the exercises and problems, remember to use the **Decision Toolkit** discussed and used in the text:

1. *Decision Checkpoints:* At this point, you ask a question.
2. *Info Needed for Decision:* You make a choice regarding the information needed to answer the question.
3. *Tool to Use for Decision:* At this point, you review just what the information chosen in step two does for the decision-making process.
4. *How to Evaluate Results:* You conduct an evaluation of information for answering the question.

Note: The notation (SO1) means that the question was drawn from study objective number one.

Multiple Choice

Please circle the correct answer.

1. Corporations invest in other companies for all of the following reasons except to   (SO1)
   a. use excess cash that it does not immediately need.
   b. generate investment revenue.
   c. meet strategic goals.
   d. increase trading of the other companies' shares.

2. Short-term investments can be designated as: (SO1)
   a. trading securities and held-to-market securities.
   b. held-to-market securities and available-for-sale securities.
   c. trading securities and available-for-sale securities.
   d. Trading securities and a 30-percent investment in another company's shares.

(SO2)   3. On January 1, 2006, Meyers Corporation acquired 20 of New Company's
five-year, 6-percent, $1,000 bonds for $22,000. Brokerage fees were $500. The
entry to record the acquisition of the bonds includes a debit to:
a.   Brokerage Fee Expense for $500.
b.   Debt Investments for $22,000.
c.   Debt Investments for $22,500.
d.   Cash for $22,500.

(SO2)   4. On June 30, 2006, Meyers Corporation receives an interest payment from New
Company (from number 3 above). Meyers' journal entry for the receipt of
interest would include:
a.   credit interest revenue for $600
b.   credit debt investments for $600
c.   credit interest revenue for $660
d.   credit debt investments for $660

(SO2)   5. Meyers Corporation sells its New Company bonds (from number three above)
for $25,000. The journal entry to record the sale includes a:
a.   credit to Debt Investments for $25,000.
b.   credit to Cash for $25,000.
c.   debit to Loss on Sale of Debt Investments for $2,500.
d.   credit to Gain on Sale of Debt Investments for $2,500.

(SO3)   6. Mack Corporation owns 10 percent of the common shares of Knife
Corporation. When Mack receives $5,000 in cash dividends, the journal entry is:

a.	Cash	5,000	
	Dividend Revenue		5,000
b.	Cash	5,000	
	Equity Investments		5,000
c.	Equity Investments	5,000	
	Dividend Revenue		5,000
d.	Equity Investments	5,000	
	Cash		5,000

(SO3)   7. Mack Corporation owns 40 percent of the common shares of Knife Corporation.
When Mack receives $5,000 in cash dividends, the journal entry is:

a.	Cash	5,000	
	Dividend Revenue		5,000
b.	Cash	5,000	
	Equity Investments		5,000
c.	Equity Investments	5,000	
	Dividend Revenue		5,000
d.	Equity Investments	5,000	
	Cash		5,000

(SO3)   8. Ross Corporation owns 40 percent of the common shares of Searcy
Corporation. When Searcy reports net earnings of $200,000, the journal entry
on Ross's books is:

a.	Equity Investments	80,000	
	Dividend Revenue		80,000
b.	Cash	80,000	

		Equity Investments		80,000	
c.		Equity Investments	200,000		
		Revenue from Investment		200,000	
d.		Equity Investments	80,000		
		Revenue from Investment		80,000	

9. Trice Corporation purchased 80 percent of the common shares of Waters   (SO4)
   Corporation. Trice is the _____ company, and Waters is the _____
   company.
   a.   subsidiary, controlling
   b.   controlling, subsidiary
   c.   subsidiary, parent
   d.   parent, subsidiary

10. With respect to the Trice purchase of Waters Corporation shares in number   (SO4)
    nine above, which of the following is true?
    a.   Only consolidated financial statements are prepared.
    b.   Trice and Waters each prepare their own financial statements.
         Trice uses the equity method to account for its investment in Waters in its
         own financial statements. Consolidated financial statements are also
         prepared.
    c.   Trice and Waters each prepare their own financial statements, and
         consolidated financial statements are not prepared.
    d.   Since Trice is the purchaser, it prepares its own financial statements;
         Waters does not, and consolidated financial statements are also prepared.

11. An unrealized gain on available-for-sale securities would be shown: (SO4)
    a.   in "other revenues" section in the statement of earnings.
    b.   in statement of retained earnings.
    c.   in comprehensive income in shareholders' equity of balance sheet.
    d.   As contra account to investment account on the balance sheet.

12. Caissie Corporation has a portfolio of trading securities with a total cost of   (SO5)
    $75,000. On the financial statement date, the total fair market value is $78,000.
    The adjusting entry is:

a.	Trading Securities	3,000	
	Unrealized Gain—Trading Securities		3,000

b.	Allowance to Adjust Trading Securities	3,000	
	Unrealized Gain—Trading Securities		3,000

c.	Cash	3,000	
	Unrealized Gain—Trading Securities		3,000

    d.   No adjusting journal entry is required.

13. A portfolio of shares that will be liquidated in six months is reported: (SO5)
    a.   in the shareholders' equity section of the balance sheet.
    b.   in the current assets section of the balance sheet.
    c.   as an operating item on the statement of earnings.
    d.   as a non-operating item on the statement of earnings.

(SO5)   14. Shares of another corporation purchased to gain some influence are reported:
   a.   in the shareholders' equity section of the balance sheet.
   b.   in the current assets section of the balance sheet.
   c.   in long-term investments on the balance sheet.
   d.   as a non-operating item on the statement of earnings.

(SO5)   15. Information on the cash inflows and outflows that resulted from investment transactions is reported in:
   a.   the investing activities section of the cash flow statement.
   b.   the other expenses and revenue section of the statement of earnings.
   c.   the comprehensive income section in the shareholders' section of the balance sheet.
   d.   The statement of retained earnings.

Problems

(SO3)   1. On February 1, 2006, Floss Corporation purchased 10 percent of the common shares of Georgia Corporation to hold as a long-term investment for $50,000, plus brokerage fees of $1,000. On March 31, 2006, Georgia reported $300,000 of net earnings and paid cash dividends of $80,000. On July 1, 2006, Floss Corporation sells the Georgia shares for $55,000.

Required:
   a.   Record Floss Corporation's purchase of the shares and any other necessary journal entries.

Date	Account Titles	Debit	Credit

Assume the same data as in "a" above, but the shares purchased represents 30 percent of the common shares of Georgia Corporation. Record the purchase of the investment and any other necessary journal entries. Assume that on July 1, 2006, the Georgia shares are sold for $115,000.

Date	Account Titles	Debit	Credit

2. On January 1, 2006, the Burber Corporation purchased, as a short-term investment, $100,000 of 6 percent, five-year bonds of Highlife Corporation at 98, plus brokerage fees of $750. Interest is payable semi-annually on January 1 and July 1.

Required:

    a.   Prepare the entry for January 1, 2006.

    b.   Record the semi-annual interest received on July 1, 2006.

    c.   The bonds are sold on July 1, 2006, at 97. Brokerage fees of $650 were paid on the sale. Prepare the entry required to record the sale.

Date	Account Titles	Debit	Credit

(SO5)   3.   The following selected general ledger account balances are provided for the Rebus Corporation as of December 31, 2006. This is the corporation's first year of operations.

Accounts payable	$ 15,000
Accounts receivable	70,000
Accumulated amortization—building	10,000
Accumulated other comprehensive income	14,000
Advertising expense	1,000
Allowance for doubtful accounts	20,000
Allowance to adjust trading securities to market	1,000
Amortization expense	5,000
Available-for-sale securities, at market	10,000
Bad debt expense	2,000
Bonds payable	100,000
Building	350,000
Cash	140,000
Common shares, no par value, 40,000 shares issued	271,000
Discount on bonds payable	2,000
Dividends	10,000
Equity investments	20,000
Gain on sale of debt investments	15,000
Held-to-maturities, at cost	15,000
Income tax expense	13,000
Interest expense	8,000
Interest payable	13,000
Land	100,000
Mortgage payable	175,000
Notes payable, 6-month	40,000
Payroll tax expense	1,000
Provincial sales tax payable	13,000
Retained earnings, January 1	15,000
Service revenue	75,000
Trading securities, at market	20,000
Wages expense	10,000
Wages payable	2,000

Required:

Prepare a balance sheet for Rebus Corporation for 2006, assuming $30,000 of the mortgage is payable next year.

(SO5)   4.   Please refer to the Domtar and Cascades financial statements. What information is provided regarding investments?

Solutions to Self-Test

Multiple Choice

1. d
2. c
3. c   The journal entry is:

Debt Investments—New Company Bonds	22,500	
Cash		22,500

Brokerage fees are included in the asset account.

4. a.   Interest is calculated on the face value of the bonds as follows:

20 x $1,000 x .06 x 6/12 = $600

5. d   The journal entry is:

Cash	25,000	
Debt Investments—Meyers Bonds		22,500
Gain on Sale of Debt Investments		2,500

6. a   The cost method is used.
7. b   The equity method is used.
8. d   The equity method is used.
9. d   "Controlling" refers to the interest the parent has in the subsidiary.
10. b
11. c
12. b   A valuation allowance account is used to record the difference between total market value and the total cost of the securities:

$78,000 – $75,000 = $3,000.

13. b
14. c
15. a

Problems

1. a.   The cost method is used because the purchase is 10 percent of the shares of Georgia Corporation. Only dividends are recognized.

February 2, 2006

Equity Investments—Georgia	51,000	
Cash		51,000
(To record purchase of 10 percent of Georgia Corporation shares)		

March 31, 2006

Cash	8,000	
Dividend Revenue		8,000
(To record dividends: 10% x $80,000 = $8,000)		

July 1, 2006

Cash	55,000	
Gain on Sale of Equity Investments		4,000
Equity Investments—Georgia		51,000

b.   The equity method is used because the purchase is 30 percent of the shares of Georgia Corporation.

February 2, 2006

Equity Investments—Georgia	51,000	
Cash		51,000

(To record purchase of 30 percent of Georgia Corporation shares)

March 31, 2006

Equity Investments-Georgia	90,000	
Revenue from Investment in Georgia		90,000

(To record 30 percent equity in Georgia Corporation shares. $300,000 x 30% = $90,000)

Cash	24,000	
Equity Investments—Georgia		24,000

(To record dividends received: 30% x $80,000 = $24,000)

July 1, 2006

Cash	115,000	
Loss on Sale of Equity Investments	2,000	
Equity Investments—Georgia		117,000

(Equity Investments: $51,000 + $90,000 – $24,000 = $117,000)

2. a.

Debt Investment—Highlife Bonds	98,750	
Cash		98,750

(To record the purchase of the Highlife Corporation bonds. $100,000 x .98 = $98,000 + $750 = $98,750)

b.

Cash	3,000	
Interest Revenue		3,000

(To record receipt of interest on Highlife bonds. $100,000 x 6% x 6/12 = $3,000)

c.

Cash	96,350	
Loss on Sale of Debt Investment	2,400	
Debt Investment—Highlife Bonds		98,750

(To record the sale of Highlife bonds. $100,000 x .97 = $97,000 – $650 = $96,350)

Rebus Corporation
Balance Sheet
December 31, 2006

Assets

Current assets
Cash $140,000
  Trading securities at market $20,000
  Add: Allowance to adjust trading securities
       to market   1,000   21,000
  Accounts receivable $70,000
  Less: Allowance for doubtful accounts   20,000   50,000
       Total current assets   211,000
Investments
  Available-for-sale securities, at market $10,000
  Held-to-maturities, at cost   15,000
  Equity investments   20,000
       Total investments   45,000
Property, plant, and equipment
  Land $100,000
  Building $350,000
  Accumulated amortization—building   10,000   340,000
       Total property, plant, and equipment   440,000
Total assets $696,000

Liabilities and Shareholders' Equity

Current liabilities
  Accounts payable $ 15,000
  Wages payable   2,000
  Interest payable   13,000
  Provincial sales tax payable   13,000
  Notes payable, 6-month   40,000
  Current portion of mortgage payable   30,000
       Total current liabilities   113,000

Long-term Liabilities
  Bonds payable $100,000
  Less: Discount on bonds payable   2,000   98,000
  Mortgage payable   145,000
       Total long-term liabilities   243,000
Total liabilities   356,000

Shareholders' equity
Common shares, no par value, 40,000 shares
  Issued $271,000
  Retained earnings   55,000
  Accumulated other comprehensive income   14,000
       Total shareholders' equity   340,000
Total liabilities and shareholders' equity $696,000

Note: Retained Earnings = Opening retained earnings balance + all revenues – all expenses – dividends. ($15,000 + $75,000 + $15,000 – $10,000 – $1,000 – $5,000 – $1,000 – $2,000 – $8,000 – $13,000 – $10,000)

4. Note 8 of Cascades' financial statement identifies "Other investments" of $9 million in both 2003 and 2004. Note 1 under "Other investments" states that they are recorded at cost except when there is a decline in value that is other than temporary, in which case they are reduced to their estimated net realizable value.

    Note 13 of Domtar's financial statement identifies "Investments and advances" of $14 million in 2003 and $15 million in 2004. Note 1 under "Other Assets" states that they are recorded at cost.

chapter 13

Cash Flow Statement

Chapter Overview

In this chapter, you will learn about the purpose and format of the cash flow statement; preparing the statement using either the direct or the indirect method; and using the cash flow statement to evaluate a company's liquidity and solvency.

- The main purpose of the cash flow statement *is to provide information about cash receipts, cash payments, and the net change in cash resulting from the operating, investing, and financing activities of a company during a specific period.*

- The information in a cash flow statement should help investors, creditors, and others assess the following aspects of a company's financial position:
    1. The investing and financing transactions during the period.
    2. The company's ability to generate future cash flows.
    3. The company's ability to pay dividends and meet obligations.

- The reasons for the difference between net earnings and cash provided (used) by operating activities.

- The general format of the cash flow statement is organized around the following activities:
    - **Operating activities** include the cash effects of transactions that create revenues and expenses. They affect net earnings. The operating activities category is the most important because it shows the cash provided or used

study objective 1

Describe the purpose and format of the cash flow statement.

by company operations. Ultimately, a company must generate cash from its operating activities in order to continue as a going concern and to expand.

- **Investing activities** include *purchasing and disposing of investments and productive long-lived assets using cash and lending money and collecting the loans.*
- **Financing activities** include *obtaining cash from issuing debt and repaying the borrowed amounts and obtaining cash from shareholders and paying them dividends.*

- In general:
  - **Operating activities** involve *statement of earnings items and current assets and current liabilities.*
  - **Investing activities** involve *investments and other long-term asset items.*
  - **Financing activities** involve *long-term liabilities and shareholders' equity items.*

- With respect to the **format of the statement**, the section reporting cash flows from operating activities always appears first. It is followed by the investing section and then the financing activities section. Individual inflows and outflows from investing and financing activities are reported separately, not netted against each other.

  The reported operating, investing, and financing activities result in net cash either provided or used by activity. The amounts of net cash either provided or used by activity are then totalled to show the net increase or decrease in cash for the period. The net increase or decrease is then added to or subtracted from the beginning-of-period cash balance to obtain the end-of-period cash balance. The end-of-period cash balance should agree with the cash balance reported on the balance sheet. Significant noncash investing and financing activities are shown separately in a note to the financial statements.

- The cash flow statement is often prepared using **cash and cash equivalents** as its basis. Cash equivalents are *short-term, highly liquid investments that are readily convertible to cash within a very short period of time.* Generally, only money-market instruments due within three months qualify with this definition. Examples include treasury bills, commercial paper, and money market funds.

- **A company may also have significant noncash activities**, such as *issues of common shares to purchase assets, conversions of debt into equity, issues of debt to purchase assets, and exchanges of property, plant, and equipment.* These are **not reported in the body of the cash flow statement** but, instead, are reported in a *separate note to the financial statements.* Reporting of such activities satisfies the full disclosure principle.

- The cash flow **statement** is *not prepared from the adjusted trial balance. The accrual concept is not used in its preparation.*

- **Information for preparation of the statement** comes from *three sources: the comparative balance sheet, the statement of earnings, and selected additional information.*

- The four steps used in the preparation of the statement are as follows:
  1. Determine the cash provided (used) by operating activities by converting net earnings from an accrual basis to a cash basis.

---

study objective 2

Prepare a cash flow statement using one of two approaches: (a) the indirect method or (b) the direct method.

2. Determine the cash provided (used) by investing activities by analyzing changes in investments and long-term asset accounts.

3. Determine the cash provided (used) by financing activities by analyzing changes in short-term notes payable and long-term liability and equity accounts.

4. Determine the net increase (decrease) in cash. Compare the net change in cash with the change in cash reported on the balance sheet to make sure they agree.

- In order to perform step one and determine the cash provided (used) by operating activities, **net earnings must be converted from an accrual basis to a cash basis.** This conversion may be done by either the **indirect or the direct method.** Both methods arrive at the same number, just in different manners. Note that the two different methods affect only the operating activities section.

- The **indirect method is used by the majority of companies** because it is easier to prepare, focuses on the differences between net earnings and net cash flow from operating activities, and tends to reveal less company information to competitors. While the Canadian Institute of Chartered Accountants (CICA) prefers the direct method, it allows either approach.

- Use of the **indirect method** *affects only the operating activities section* of the statement. The investing and financing activities sections are prepared in the same way under both methods. **Accrual basis net earnings is converted to cash basis net earnings** by *adjusting it for items that affected reported net earnings but did not affect cash.* There are various expenses and losses that reduce net earnings but do not involve cash, and various revenues and gains that increase net earnings but do not involve cash. The expenses and losses are added back to net earnings, and the revenues and gains are subtracted from net earnings to convert them to net cash provided by operating activities.

- Amortization expense is one of those expenses added back to net earnings. This is often the first adjustment to net earnings. It is important to understand that amortization expense is not added to operating activities as if it was a source of cash. It is added to cancel the deduction created by the amortization expense in the determination of net earnings.

- Your textbook's discussion of the individual mechanics is solid and clear, and the following is a **summary of conversion to net cash provided by operating activities with respect to current assets and current liabilities:**

Change in	Add to Net Earnings	Deduct from Net Earnings
Accounts receivable	Decrease	Increase
Inventory	Decrease	Increase
Prepaid expenses	Decrease	Increase
Accounts payable	Increase	Decrease
Accrued expenses payable	Increase	Decrease

In other words, if the balance in the Accounts Receivable account decreases during the period, this amount is added to accrual-based net earnings in order to calculate cash provided (used) by operating activities. If the balance increases, the amount is deducted from accrual-based net earnings and so on, as explained in the table above.

- **Noncash charges that must be added back to accrual basis net earnings** include *amortization expense* and *loss on sale of assets*. These items all reduce net earnings but have nothing to do with cash flow, and they must be added back to produce net cash flows from operating activities.

- **Noncash credits that must be deducted from accrual basis net earnings** include *gain on sale of assets*. This item increases net earnings but has nothing to do with cash flow, and it must be deducted to produce net cash flows from operating activities.

- The **investing activities section** deals with *long-term assets*, and the **financing activities** section deals with *long-term debt and shareholders' equity items*. All items are to be listed separately, not netted against one another. For example, if a company purchases one asset for $80,000 and sells another asset for $20,000, each cash flow must be listed, not just the net outflow of $60,000.

- As stated earlier, use of the **direct method** *affects only the operating activities section* of the statement. The investing and the financing activities sections are prepared in the same way under both methods. Under the direct method, **net cash provided by operating activities** is *calculated by adjusting each item in the statement of earnings from the accrual basis to the cash basis*. Only major classes of operating cash receipts and cash payments are reported. An **efficient way to apply the direct method** is to *analyze the revenues and expenses reported in the statement of earnings in the order in which they are listed*.

- Your textbook's discussion of the individual mechanics is solid and clear, and the following is a **summary of the formulas for calculating the various cash inflows and outflows in order to arrive at net cash provided by operating activities:**

To calculate **Cash Receipts from Customers**, do the following:

Revenues from sales
Deduct: Increase in accounts receivable OR
Add: Decrease in accounts receivable
Equals: <u>Cash receipts from customers</u>

To calculate **Cash Payments to Suppliers**, do the following:

Purchases**
Deduct: Increase in accounts payable OR
Add: Decrease in accounts payable
Equals: <u>Cash payments to suppliers</u>

**To solve for purchases:

Cost of goods sold
Deduct: Decrease in inventory OR
Add: Increase in inventory
Equals: <u>Purchases</u>

To calculate **Cash Payments for Operating Expenses**, do the following:

Operating expenses
Deduct: Decrease in prepaid expenses OR
Add: Increase in prepaid expenses AND
Deduct: Increase in accrued expenses payable OR
Add: Decrease in accrued expenses payable
Equals: <u>Cash payments for operating expenses</u>

To calculate **Cash Payments to Employees**, do the following:

Wages expense
Deduct: Increase in wages payable OR
Add: Decrease in wages payable
Equals: <u>Cash payments to employees</u>

To calculate **Cash Payments for Income Taxes**, do the following:

Income tax expense
Deduct: Increase in income taxes payable OR
Add: Decrease in income taxes payable
Equals: <u>Cash payments for income taxes</u>

- The **following do not appear on a cash flow statement under the direct method because they are noncash charges**: *amortization expense and loss on sale of assets*. A gain on sale of assets likewise will not appear because it is a noncash credit.

- **Net earnings is not reported on the cash flow statement under the direct method**. In the operating activities section, cash payments are subtracted from cash receipts to arrive at net cash provided by operating activities.

- The **investing activities section** deals with *long-term assets*, and the **financing activities section** deals with *long-term debt and shareholders' equity items*. These sections are prepared in the same manner as they are prepared under the indirect method.

- Liquidity is the ability of a company to meet its current obligations. In Chapter 2, you learned that one measure of liquidity is the **current ratio** calculated by dividing current assets by current liabilities. A cash-based measure of liquidity is the **cash current debt coverage ratio** calculated by dividing cash provided or used by operating activities by average current liabilities.

- Solvency is the ability of a company to survive over the long-term. In Chapter 2, you learned that one cash-based measure of solvency is **free cash flow**. It is calculated by *subtracting capital expenditures and dividends paid from cash provided by operating activities*. It is a measure of a company's ability to generate sufficient cash to finance the purchase of new assets. Another cash-based measure of solvency is the **cash total debt coverage ratio** calculated by dividing cash provided or used by operating activities by average total liabilities.

> study objective 3
>
> Use the cash flow statement to evaluate a company's liquidity and solvency.

Chapter Self-Test

As you work through the exercises and problems, remember to use the **Decision Toolkit** discussed and used in the text:

1. *Decision Checkpoints*: At this point, you ask a question.
2. *Info Needed for Decision*: You make a choice regarding the information needed to answer the question.
3. *Tool to Use for Decision*: At this point, you review just what the information chosen in step two does for the decision-making process.
4. *How to Evaluate Results*: You conduct an evaluation of information for answering the question.

Note: The notation (SO1) means that the question was drawn from study objective number one.

Multiple Choice

Please circle the correct answer.

(SO1) 1. What type of activity is the purchase of a piece of equipment?
   a. Operating activity
   b. Investing activity
   c. Financing activity
   d. Balance sheet activity

(SO1) 2. Which of the following is listed first on the cash flow statement?
   a. Operating activity
   b. Investing activity
   c. Financing activity
   d. Manufacturing activity

(SO1) 3. Which of the following statements is correct?
   a. Significant noncash activities are never reported in a company's annual report.
   b. Significant noncash activities are reported in the body of the cash flow statement.
   c. Significant noncash activities are reported in a separate note to the financial statements.
   d. Significant noncash activities are always reported on the company's balance sheet.

(SO1) 4. The primary purpose of the cash flow statement is to:
   a. provide information about investing and financing activities during a period.
   b. prove that revenues exceed expenses if there are net earnings.
   c. provide information about the cash receipts and cash payments during a period.
   d. facilitate banking relationships.

5. If a company reports a net loss, it: (SO1)
   a.   may still have a net increase in cash.
   b.   will not be able to pay cash dividends.
   c.   will not be able to get a loan.
   d.   will not be able to make capital expenditures.

6. Which of the following is a source of information for preparation of the cash   (SO1)
   flow statement?
   a.   Comparative balance sheet
   b.   Current period statement of earnings
   c.   Selected additional information
   d.   All of the above are needed for preparation of the statement.

7. If the indirect method is used for preparation of the cash flow statement, then a   (SO2)
   decrease in accounts receivable is accounted for as a(n):
   a.   cash inflow in the investing activities section.
   b.   cash inflow in the financing activities section.
   c.   addition to net earnings in the operating activities section.
   d.   deduction from net earnings in the operating activities section.

8. If the indirect method is used for preparation of the cash flow statement, then   (SO2)
   an increase in prepaid expenses is accounted for as a(n):
   a.   cash inflow in the investing activities section.
   b.   cash inflow in the financing activities section.
   c.   addition to net earnings in the operating activities section.
   d.   deduction from net earnings in the operating activities section.

9. If a company purchases land through the issue of long-term bonds, then this is   (SO2)
   accounted for as a(n):
   a.   operating activity.
   b.   investing inflow.
   c.   financing outflow.
   d.   significant noncash investing and financing activity that merits disclosure.

10. A company has $200,000 of net earnings, $500,000 of revenues from sales, and   (SO2)
    an increase in accounts receivable of $50,000. If the company uses the direct
    method of preparing the cash flow statement, then cash receipts from customers
    total:
    a. $500,000.
    b. $450,000.
    c. $300,000.
    d. $150,000.

11. A company has a cost of goods sold of $300,000, an increase in inventory of   (SO2)
    $100,000, and an increase in accounts payable of $30,000. If it uses the direct
    method of preparing the cash flow statement, then purchases total:
    a. $400,000.
    b. $370,000.
    c. $300,000.
    d. $200,000.

(SO2)   12. A company has a cost of goods sold of $300,000, an increase in inventory of $100,000, and an increase in accounts payable of $30,000. If it uses the direct method of preparing the cash flow statement, then cash payments to suppliers total:
    a. $400,000.
    b. $370,000.
    c. $300,000.
    d. $200,000.

(SO2)   13. Starting with net earnings and adjusting it for items that affected reported net earnings but not cash is called the:
    a.   direct method.
    b.   indirect method.
    c.   allowance method.
    d.   cost-benefit method.

(SO2)   14. Which of the following adjustments to convert net earnings to net cash provided by operating activities is not added to net earnings?
    a.   Gain on Sale of Equipment
    b.   Amortization Expense
    c.   Loss from Sale of Investment
    d.   Loss on Sale of Equipment

(SO3)   15. Firth Corporation shows the following:

Cash provided by operating activities	$500,000
Capital expenditures	125,000
Dividends	40,000

What is the company's free cash flow?
    a. $335,000
    b. $375,000
    c. $415,000
    d. $500,000.

(SO3)   16. Which of the following ratios is a measure of liquidity?
    a.   Cash total debt coverage
    b.   Free cash flow
    c.   Cash current debt coverage
    d.   Debt to total assets

(SO3)   17. The cash current debt coverage ratio demonstrates:
    a.   the company's ability to repay its liabilities from cash generated from all sources without having to liquidate assets.
    b.   the company's ability to repay its short-term liabilities from cash generated from operating activities without having to liquidate assets.
    c.   how fast the company collects cash.
    d.   the company's ability to meet interest payments.

Problems

1. The following are comparative balance sheet data for Panther Corporation for
   years 2006 and 2005:

(SO2)

Panther Corporation
Comparative Balance Sheet Data
December 31, 2006 and 2005

	2006	2005
Cash	$ 3,600	$ 2,300
Accounts receivable	3,500	2,600
Inventory	3,200	3,800
Equipment	3,800	3,400
Accumulated amortization	(2,400)	(2,340)
Long-term investments	2,600	2,840
	$14,300	$12,600
Accounts payable	$ 2,400	$ 1,800
Accrued liabilities	400	500
Bonds payable	2,800	3,100
Common shares	3,800	3,400
Retained earnings	4,900	3,800
	$14,300	$12,600

Selected data from the statement of earnings include net earnings of $2,140 and
amortization expense of $60. Cash dividends paid totalled $1,040.

Required:

Using the indirect method, please prepare a cash flow statement for Panther
Corporation for the year ended December 31, 2006. Make assumptions as
appropriate.

Panther Corporation
Cash Flow Statement
Year Ended December 31, 2006

2. The statement of earnings for the Warnon Corporation is shown below:

(SO2)

Warnon Corporation
Statement of Earnings
Year Ended December 31, 2006

Sales		$12,300,000
Cost of goods sold		8,100,000
Gross profit		4,200,000
Operating expenses	$1,800,000	
Amortization expense	180,000	1,980,000
Net earnings		$ 2,220,000

Additional information:
1. Accounts receivable increased $600,000 during the year.
2. Inventory increased $375,000 during the year.

3. Prepaid expenses increased $300,000 during the year.
4. Accounts payable to merchandise suppliers increased $150,000 during the year.
5. Accrued expenses payable increased $270,000 during the year.

Required:

Using the direct method, prepare the operating activities section of the cash flow statement for the year ended December 31, 2006, for the Warnon Corporation.

Warnon Corporation
Cash Flow Statement
Year Ended December 31, 2006

(SO3)   3.   The Axel Corporation has the following selected general ledger account balances as of December 31, 2006.

Accounts payable	$25,000
Bonds payable, due July 1, 2020	90,000
Common shares	270,000
Discount on bonds payable	2,500
Retained earnings	15,000
Dividends	10,000
Interest payable	11,000
Mortgage payable	150,000
Notes payable, due April 1, 2007	20,000
Provincial sales tax payable	8,000
Wages payable	2,000

The following additional information is provided:
a. $20,000 of the mortgage is payable next year.
b.   Cash provided by operating activities for year 2006 was $139,750.
c.   Current liabilities totaled $90,000 on December 31, 2005.
d.   Long-term liabilities totaled $212,500 on December 31, 2005.
e.   Capital expenditures for year 2006 are $70,000

Required

Calculate the following for 2006:
a.   cash current debt coverage ratio
b.   free cash flow
c.   cash total debt coverage ratio

4.   Please refer to the Domtar and Cascades financial statements for information for answering the following questions. Do not forget to use the **Decision Toolkit** approach to help in the problem solving.

    a.   What method—indirect or direct—do Domtar and Cascades use in their   (SO2, 3)
            preparation of their cash flow statements?

    b.   In 2004, did Domtar have a net increase or decrease in cash?

    c.   In 2004, what is Domtar's largest use of cash?

    d.   In 2004, what is the free cash flow for both companies?

Solutions to Self-Test

Multiple Choice

1. **b**   Operating activities deal with statement of earnings items and with current assets and current liabilities. Financing activities deal with short-term notes and long-term liabilities and with shareholders' equity items. "Balance sheet activity" is a fabricated term.

2. **a**   It is critical that a company generate its cash flow from operating activities, not from investing and financing activities.

3. **c**   Significant noncash activities are reported but not in the body of the cash flow statement. They do not appear on the statement of earnings.

4. **c**

5. **a**

6. **d**

7. **c**   A change in a current asset is an operating activity, not an investing or a financing activity. The decrease in receivables is not a deduction from net earnings.

8. **d**   A change in a current asset is an operating activity, not an investing or a financing activity. The increase in prepaid expenses is not an addition to net earnings.

9. **d**   Cash is not involved in this transaction; therefore, it is not an operating, investing, or financing activity. It is a noncash transaction.

10. **b** $500,000 - $50,000 = $450,000$

11. **a** $300,000 + $100,000 = $400,000$

12. **b** $300,000 + $100,000 - $30,000 = $370,000$

13. **b**

14. **a**

15. **a** $500,000 - $125,000 - $40,000 = $335,000$

16. **c**

17. **b**

Problems

1.

Panther Corporation
Cash Flow Statement
Year Ended December 31, 2006

Panther Corporation

Cash Flow Statement
Year Ended December 31, 2006

Operating activities		
Net earnings	$2,140	
Adjustments to reconcile net earnings to net cash provided by operating activities:		
Amortization expense	$ 60	
Decrease in inventory	600	
Increase in accounts payable	600	
Increase in accounts receivable	(900)	
Decrease in accrued liabilities	(100)	260
Net cash provided by operating activities		2,400
Investing activities		
Sale of long-term investments	$ 240	
Purchase of equipment	(400)	
Net cash used by investing activities		(160)
Financing activities		
Issue of common shares	$ 400	
Retirement of bonds payable	(300)	
Payment of cash dividends	(1,040)	
Net cash used by financing activities		(940)
Net increase in cash		1,300
Cash, January 1		2,300
Cash, December 31		$3,600

Without other information available, the assumption is that the increase in Equipment is due to a cash purchase. The decrease in Long-Term Investments is attributed to a sale of these. The decrease in Bonds Payable is attributed to a retirement of some bonds, and the increase in Common Shares is assumed to be from a sale of shares for cash. The increase of $1,100 in Retained Earnings is due to net earnings of $2,140 less dividends declared and paid of $1,040.

2.

Warnon Corporation
Cash Flow Statement
Year Ended December 31, 2006

Operating activities

Cash receipts from customers		$11,700,000 (1)
Cash payments:		
To suppliers	$8,325,000 (2)	
For operating expenses	1,830,000 (3)	10,155,000
Net cash provided by operating activities		1,545,000
(1) Sales		$12,300,000
Deduct: Increase in accounts receivable		600,000
Cash receipts from customers		$11,700,000
(2) Cost of goods sold		$8,100,000
Add: Increase in inventory		375,000
Purchases		8,475,000
Deduct: Increase in accounts payable		150,000
Cash payments to suppliers		$8,325,000
(3) Operating expenses		$1,800,000
Add: Increase in prepaid expenses		300,000
		2,100,000
Deduct: Increase in accrued expenses payable		270,000
Cash payments for operating expenses		$1,830,000

3. To calculate the ratios, the following needs to be calculated:

Current Liabilities December 31, 2006:

Accounts payable	$25,000
Interest payable	11,000
Notes payable, due April 1, 2007	20,000
Provincial sales tax payable	8,000
Wages payable	2,000
Current portion of mortgage payable	20,000
Total current liabilities	86,000

Long-Term Liabilities December 31, 2006:

Bonds payable due July 1, 2020		$90,000
Less: Bond discount	2,500	87,500
Mortgage payable	$150,000	
Less current portion	20,000	130,000
Total long-term liabilities		217,500
Total liabilities		$303,500

a. Cash current debt coverage ratio = cash provided by operating activities divided by average current liabilities

Cash provided by operating activities = $139,750
Average current liabilities: ($212,500 + $217,500) ÷ 2 = $215,000

Cash current debt coverage ratio: $139,750 ÷ $215,000 = 0.65 times

b. Free cash flow = cash provided by operating activities − capital expenditures − dividends = $139,750 - $70,000 - $10,000 = $59,750

c. Cash total debt coverage ratio = cash provided by operating activities divided by average total liabilities.

Cash provided by operating activities = $139,750

Total liabilities December 31, 2005: $90,000 + $212,500 = $302,500

Average total liabilities: ($302,500 + $303,500) ÷ 2 = $303,000

Cash total debt coverage ratio: $139,750 ÷ $303,000 = 0.46 times

4. a. In order to answer this question, you need to look at the operating activities section of the cash flow statement. Both companies report net earnings and add noncash items and changes in working capital items. This would indicate the use of the indirect method. The direct method does not include net earnings (loss). Net cash provided by operating activities is calculated by adjusting each item on the income statement from an accrual to a cash basis.

b. Domtar had a net increase in cash of $4 million, as shown near the end of the cash flow statement. This increase explains the change from $48 million in 2003 to $52 million in 2004 in the cash and cash equivalents account shown on the balance sheet.

c. Domtar's largest use of cash was the additions to property, plant, and equipment of $204, as shown in the investing activities section.

d. Free cash flow is the term used to describe the cash remaining from operating activities after adjustments for capital expenditures and dividends. To determine the free cash flow for both companies in 2004, the cash used for investing activities will be taken as a measure of capital expenditures for both companies. Thus, the free cash flow will be determined as follows:

Cash from operating activities − cash from investing activities − dividend payments = free cash flow

For Domtar, free cash flow for 2004 is ($ in millions):
$122 − $183 − $56 = ($117)

For Cascades, free cash flow for 2004 is ($ in millions):
$156 − $244 − $13 = ($101)

chapter 14

Performance Measurement

Chapter Overview

The purpose of this chapter is to explain the importance of performance measurement in serving the interests of users. In this chapter, you will learn about sustainable earnings, comparative analysis, and the quality of earnings.

Review of Specific Study Objectives

- **Sustainable earnings** are *net earnings adjusted for irregular items*. It is the mostlikely level of earnings to be obtained in the future, to the extent that this year's net earnings is a good predictor of future years' net earnings. There are two types of irregular items that affect current period earnings on the statement of earnings: *(1) discontinued operations*, and *(2) extraordinary items*. Irregular items are **reported net of income taxes** in a separate category on the statement of earnings. If there is an extraordinary loss of $100,000 and the tax rate is 30 percent, then the loss is reported at its net amount of $70,000 (the $30,000 of income taxes is actually a tax savings in the case of a loss). There is also one type of irregular item that affects prior period earnings on the statement of retained earnings: *change in accounting principle*.

study objective 1

Understand the concept of sustainable earnings and indicate how irregular items are presented.

- **Discontinued operations** refers to the *disposal of an identifiable reporting or operating segment of a business, such as the elimination of a separate subsidiary company or an operating division of a company*. If a company sells a segment of its business, the sale is reported separately on the statement of earnings as a nonrecurring item called discontinued operations. The statement of earnings should report both the earnings (or loss) from continuing operations and earnings (or loss) from discontinued operations. **The earnings (or loss) from discontinued operations consist of the earnings (loss) from operations and the gain (loss) on disposal of the segment.** Remember that both the operating earnings or loss and the disposal gain or loss are *reported net of income taxes*.

- **Extraordinary items** are *events and transactions that meet three conditions: They are: (1) not expected to occur frequently, (2) not typical of normal business activities, and (3) not subject to management discretion.* Extraordinary items are reported net of income tax in a separate section of the statement of earnings immediately below discontinued operations. If a transaction meets only one but not all of the criteria, then it is treated as a line item in the upper half of the statement of earnings under Other Expenses or Other Revenues at their gross amount, not net of tax. It will go into the determination of earnings from continuing operations, and income taxes are calculated for that number.

- Another type of irregular item, one that affects prior period earnings, is a **change in accounting principle**. Since prior period earnings are affected, a change inaccounting principle is reported on the statement of retained earnings rather than on the current period statement of earnings. While discontinued operations and extraordinary items are reported in the statement of earnings, changes in accounting principle are reported as an adjustment to opening retained earnings in the statement of retained earnings.

- A change in accounting principle occurs when the *principle used in the current year is different from the one used in the preceding year*. Remember that consistency is desirable but that changes can be made as long as their occurrence and effects are disclosed. Examples of changes include changes in the *method used for amortization and in the cost flow assumption used for inventory*.

- **For data to be meaningful, it must be compared with something**. Comparisons may be:

  1. *Intracompany comparisons.* Comparisons may be made within a company on a year-to-year basis to detect changes in financial relationships and significant trends.
  2. *Intercompany comparisons.* Comparisons with other companies provide insight into a company's competitive position.
  3. *Industry comparisons.* Comparisons with industry averages provide information about a company' relative position within the industry.

- **Three basic tools** are used in financial statement analysis: *horizontal analysis, vertical analysis*, and *ratio analysis*.

- **Horizontal analysis, also called trend analysis**, is a *technique for evaluating a series of financial statement data over a period of time*. Its **purpose** is to *determine the increase or decrease that has taken place, expressed as either an amount or a percentage*.

study objective 2

Explain and apply horizontal analysis.

- A company has net sales of $100,000 in 2004, $110,000 in 2005, and $116,000 in 2006. **The formula for calculating changes since the base period** is:

Current-Year Amount – Base-Year Amount
            Base-Year Amount

In our example, 2005's net sales increased $10,000, or 10 percent, over 2004's.

$\dfrac{\$110,000 - \$100,000}{\$100,000} = 10\%$

For the year 2006:

$\dfrac{\$116,000 - \$100,000}{\$100,000} = 16\%$

Note that the base year amount is always the first year, or $100,000 in 2004 in this case. Net sales in 2006 have increased by 16 percent over 2004's net sales, not over 2005's net sales.

- An **advantage of horizontal analysis** is that it *helps highlight the significance of a change by reducing the change to a percentage.* Sometimes, it is difficult to see the magnitude of a change when only the dollar amount is examined.

- **Several complications can arise using horizontal analysis.** If an item has no value in a base year or preceding year and a value in the next year, then no percentage change can be calculated. If a negative number appears in the base year or preceding year and a positive amount exists the next year, or vice versa, then no percentage change can be calculated.

- **Vertical analysis** is a *technique for evaluating financial statement data, which expresses each item in a financial statement as a percentage of a base amount.* On the balance sheet, assets are usually expressed as percentages of total assets, and liability and shareholders' equity items are usually expressed as percentages of total liabilities and shareholders' equity. On the statement of earnings, items are usually expressed as percentages of net sales.

> **study objective 3**
>
> Explain and apply vertical analysis.

- When comparative balance sheets and statements of earnings are presented, **vertical analysis shows not only the relative size of each category in each year on the balance sheet and on the statement of earnings but also the percentage change in the individual items on the two financial statements.**

- If current assets are $2,200 and total assets are $9,000, then current assets are 24.4 percent of total assets ($2,200 ÷ $9,000).

- Just as is true with horizontal analysis, an **advantage of vertical analysis** is that it *helps highlight the significance of a change by reducing the change to a percentage.* It also helps when making comparisons between companies of different sizes.

- **Ratios can be classified into three types:** *liquidity*, which measures the short-term ability of the company to pay its maturing obligations and to meet unexpected needs for cash; *solvency*, which measures a company's ability to survive in the long term; and *profitability*, which measures the earnings or operating success of a company for a specific period of time.

> **study objective 4**
>
> Identify and calculate ratios used to analyze liquidity, solvency, and profitability.

- • A **single ratio is not meaningful but must be compared with something**. As noted above, there may be *intracompany comparisons, intercompany comparisons, and comparisons with industry averages.*

- • The following are **liquidity ratios:**

  1. **Current ratio** is calculated by *dividing current assets by current liabilities.* If the current ratio is 1.25 to 1, then the company has $1.25 of current assets for every $1 of current liabilities. This ratio can also be expressed as an equation. The difference between current assets and current liabilities is called **working capital**.

  2. **Inventory turnover** is calculated by *dividing cost of goods sold by average inventory.* If the ratio is eight times, then the company sold its inventory eight times during the accounting period. Since the business of a merchandiser is to sell inventory, this ratio is very closely monitored. If it shows significant change in either direction, then action is taken. This ratio varies widely among industries.

  3. **Days in inventory** is calculated by *dividing 365 by the inventory turnover.* Using the eight times from the previous ratio, the average days in inventory number is 46.5 days. The company takes approximately 46 days to sell its inventory.

  4. **Receivables turnover** is calculated by *dividing net credit sales by average gross accounts receivable.* Companies seldom disclose their net credit sales, and so total sales are often used as a substitute. This ratio measures the number of times, on average, receivables are collected during the period. If the ratio is 12.5 times, then the company collects its receivables 12.5 times during the accounting period.

  5. **Average collection period** is calculated by *dividing 365 days by the receivables turnover.* Using the 12.5 times from the previous ratio, the average collection period for this company is 29.2 days (365 ÷ 12.5). The general rule is that the collection period should not greatly exceed the credit term period (the time allowed for payment).

  6. **Cash current debt coverage ratio** is calculated by *dividing cash provided (used) by operating activities by average current liabilities.* Instead of using the numerator and denominator balances from just one point in time, this ratio uses numbers covering a period of time and thus may provide a better representation of liquidity. If the ratio is 0.5 times, then the company has $0.50 of cash provided by operating activities for every $1 of current liabilities. This ratio is cash based, not accrual based.

- • The following are **solvency ratios:**

  1. **Debt to total assets** is calculated by *dividing total liabilities by total assets.* It measures the percentage of the total assets provided by creditors and provides some indication of the company's ability to withstand losses without impairing the interests of its creditors. If the ratio is 65 percent, then creditors have provided financing sufficient to cover 65 percent of the company's total assets. The higher the percentage of liabilities to total assets, the greater will be the risk that the company may be unable to pay its debts; therefore, creditors usually like to see a low ratio. The *debt to equity ratio* shows the relative use of borrowed funds compared with resources invested by the owners.

2. **Free cash flow** is calculated by *subtracting the sum of capital expenditures and dividends paid from cash provided (used) by operating activities*. It indicates the cash available for paying dividends or expanding operations.

3. **Times interest earned** is calculated by *dividing earnings before interest expense and income tax expense (EBIT) by interest expense*. EBIT can also be calculated by adding back interest expense and income tax expense to net earnings (net earnings + interest expense + income tax expense). This ratio indicates the company's ability to meet interest payments as they come due. If the ratio is 13 times, then the company has earnings before interest and taxes that is 13 times the amount needed for interest expense.

4. **Cash total debt coverage** is calculated by *dividing cash provided (used) by operating activities by average total liabilities*. It indicates a company's ability to repay its debts from cash generated from operating activities without having to liquidate the assets used in its operations. If the ratio is 0.24 times, then net cash generated from one year of operations is sufficient to pay off 24 percent of the company's total liabilities. This ratio is cash based, not accrual based.

- The following are **profitability ratios**, (profitability is used frequently as the ultimate test of management's operating effectiveness):

  1. **Earnings per share** is calculated by taking *net earnings available to common shareholders (net earnings less preferred dividends) and dividing that sum by the weighted average number of common shares*. It is a measure of the net earnings earned on common shares. If earnings per share is $2.05, then $2.05 of net earnings was earned on each common share.

  2. **Price-earnings ratio** is calculated by *dividing the market price per common share by earnings per share*. It measures the ratio of the market price of each share to the earnings per share. If the price-earnings ratio is 23, then each share sold for 23 times the amount that was earned on each share.

  3. **Gross profit margin** is calculated by *dividing gross profit by net sales*. It indicates a company's ability to maintain an adequate selling price above its costs. The more competition there is in an industry, the lower will be the gross profit margin. If the gross profit margin is 58 percent, then each dollar of net sales generates gross profit of $0.58.

  4. **Profit margin** is calculated by dividing *net earnings by net sales*. This is a measure of the percentage of each dollar of sales that results in net earnings. If the ratio is 12 percent, then each dollar of sales results in $0.12 of net earnings. High-volume enterprises (grocery stores) generally have low profit margins, whereas low-volume enterprises (jewellery stores) usually have high profit margins. Two factors strongly influence this ratio: the gross profit margin and the control of operating expenses.

  5. **Return on assets** is calculated by *dividing net earnings by average total assets*. It measures the rate earned on each dollar invested in assets.

  6. **Asset turnover** is calculated by *dividing net sales by average total assets*. It measures how efficiently a company uses its assets to generate sales. This ratio varies widely among industries.

7. **Payout ratio** is calculated by *dividing cash dividends declared on common shares by net earnings*. It measures the percentage of earnings distributed in the form of cash dividends. Growth companies have low payout ratios because they reinvest earnings in the business.

8. **Dividend yield** is calculated by *dividing earnings per share by market price per share*. It measures earnings generated by each share, based on the share price.

9. **Return on common shareholders' equity** is calculated *by dividing earnings available to common shareholders (net earnings less preferred dividends) by average common shareholders' equity*. The numerator is the difference between net earnings and preferred dividends declared for the period, if any. It shows how many dollars of net earnings were earned for each dollar invested by the shareholders.

- **Availability of information** is not a problem in financial statement analysis. The goal is to perform relevant analysis and select pertinent comparative data, as well as knowing what ratio will give the answer to the question being asked.

study objective 5

Understand the concept of quality of earnings.

- In evaluating the financial performance of a company, the **quality of earnings** is of extreme importance to analysts. A company that has a high quality of earnings provides full and transparent information that will not confuse or mislead users of financial statements. Some of the factors that affect the quality of earnings include:

  1. the choice of accounting principles,
  2. the choice of professional judgment, and
  3. pro forma earnings.

- Variations among companies in the application of **generally accepted accounting principles** (GAAP) might lessen comparability and reduce the quality of earnings. Companies may choose from a large number of acceptable accounting policies, such as different inventory cost flow assumptions or amortization methods. Different choices result in differing financial positions, which affect comparability. As well, in an increasing number of industries, competition is global, which means that investors must make comparisons to companies from other countries.

  Even if we are able to adequately compare different accounting principles, we must accept that management has to use **professional judgment** in choosing the most appropriate principle for the circumstances. In addition, numerous estimates are required in preparing financial information. To the extent that managers are able to choose accounting principles and estimates to manage earnings, the quality of the earnings information content will decrease. Fortunately, the chief executive officer and chief financial officer of publicly traded companies must ensure, and personally declare, that the reported financial information is accurate, relevant, and understandable. In addition, audit committees are held responsible for questioning management on the degree of aggressiveness or conservatism that has been applied and the quality of the underlying accounting principles, key estimates, and judgments.

  A strong corporate governance process, including an active board of directors and audit committee, is essential to ensure the quality of earnings.

- Publicly traded companies are required to present their earnings in accordance with GAAP. Many companies also report another measure of earnings, in addition to GAAP earnings, called **pro forma earnings**. Pro forma earnings are a non-GAAP earnings measure that often excludes unusual or nonrecurring items. Some companies have been known to exclude such costs as interest expense, stock compensation expenses, and impairment losses in their pro forma earnings.

- Because of the number of differing calculations used, publicly traded companies must provide GAAP numbers alongside non-GAAP earnings, explain how pro forma numbers are calculated, and detail why they exclude certain items required by GAAP.

Chapter Self-Test

As you work through the exercises and problems, remember to use the **Decision Toolkit** discussed and used in the text:

1. *Decision Checkpoints*: At this point, you ask a question.
2. *Info Needed for Decision*: You make a choice regarding the information needed to answer the question.
3. *Tool to Use for Decision*: At this point, you review just what the information chosen in step two does for the decision-making process.
4. *How to Evaluate Results*: You conduct an evaluation of information for answering the question.

Note: The notation (SO1) means that the question was drawn from study objective number one.

Multiple Choice

Please circle the correct answer.

1. To be classified as extraordinary, an item must: (SO1)
   a. result from an act of God.
   b. be only unusual in nature.
   c. be only infrequent in occurrence.
   d. be unusual in nature, infrequent in occurrence, and not influenced by management.

2. Discontinued operations appear on the: (SO2)
   a. statement of earnings as part of Earnings from Continuing Operations.
   b. statement of earnings net of income taxes, below Earnings from Continuing Operations.
   c. statement of earnings at their gross amount, below Earnings from Continuing Operations.
   d. balance sheet in the shareholders' equity section.

(SO3)   3.   A change in accounting principle appears on the:
   a.   statement of earnings net of income taxes, below Earnings from Continuing Operations.
   b.   statement of retained earnings.
   c.   balance sheet in the shareholders' equity section.
   d.   cash flow statement.

(SO1)   4.   Which of the following is a type of comparison that provides decision usefulness of financial information?
   a.   Industry averages
   b.   Intercompany basis
   c.   Intracompany basis
   d.   All of the above provide decision usefulness.

(SO2)   5.   Total current liabilities are $10,000 in 2004, $18,000 in 2005, and $22,000 in 2006. What is the percentage increase from 2004 to 2006?
   a.   22% (rounded)
   b.   80%
   c.   120%
   d.   It cannot be calculated from the data given.

(SO3)   6.   Consider the following data for Elizabeth Corporation:

Net sales	$100,000
– Cost of goods sold	30,000
Gross profit	70,000
– Operating expenses	50,000
Net earnings	$ 20,000

Performing vertical analysis and using net sales as the base, what percentage of net sales is cost of goods sold?
   a.   20%
   b.   30%
   c.   70%
   d.   333% (rounded)

(SO4)   7.   Measures of a company's ability to survive over a long period of time are called:
   a.   liquidity ratios.
   b.   solvency ratios.
   c.   profitability ratios.
   d.   vertical analysis.

(SO4)   8.   _____ is frequently used as the ultimate test of management's operating effectiveness.
   a.   Net earnings
   b.   Liquidity
   c.   Solvency
   d.   Profitability

Please use the following data for questions 9 through 11:

Current assets	$150,000
Total assets	500,000
Current liabilities	125,000
Total liabilities	200,000
Net credit sales	600,000
Cost of goods sold	160,000
Average accounts receivable	50,000
Average inventory	40,000

9. What is the receivables turnover?   (SO4)
    a.   3.2 times
    b.   4 times
    c.   12 times
    d.   15 times

10. What is the inventory turnover?   (SO4)
    a.   3.2 times
    b.   4 times
    c.   12 times
    d.   15 times

11. What is the debt to total assets ratio?   (SO4)
    a.   25.0%
    b.   40.0%
    c.   62.5%
    d.   83.3%

12. Net sales are $6,000,000, net earnings are $800,000, earnings available to   (SO4)
    common shareholders are $700,000, and the weighted average number of
    common shares issued is 300,000. What is the profit margin?
    a.   13.3%
    b.   11.7%
    c. $2.67
    d. $2.33

13. Net sales are $6,000,000, net earnings are $800,000, earnings available to   (SO4)
    common shareholders are $700,000, and the weighted average number of
    common shares issued is 300,000. What is the earnings per share?
    a.   13.3%
    b.   11.7%
    c. $2.67
    d. $2.33

14. Which of the following is considered a profitability ratio?   (SO4)
    a.   Price-earnings ratio
    b.   Times interest earned
    c.   Average collection period
    d.   Cash current debt coverage

(SO4)   15. Which of the following is considered a solvency ratio?
    a.   Price-earnings ratio
    b.   Times interest earned
    c.   Average collection period
    d.   Cash current debt coverage

(SO5)   16. A factor that affects quality of earnings is:
    a.   Management style of corporate executives
    b.   Pro forma earnings
    c.   Extraordinary items
    d.   Sustainable earnings

(SO5)   17. Pro forma earnings:
    a.   are based on generally accepted accounting principles.
    b.   often exclude unusual or nonrecurring items.
    c.   is a form of reporting that is not used by companies.
    d.   relates to the preparation of the cash flow statement.

Problems

(SO4)   1.   Selected information from the comparative financial statements of Fallis Ltd. for the year ended December 31, appears below:

	2006	2005
Accounts receivable	$ 150,000	$170,000
Inventory	110,000	130,000
Total assets	1,170,000	770,000
Current liabilities	110,000	80,000
Long-term debt	370,000	270,000
Total liabilities	480,00	350,000
Net credit sales	1,470,000	670,000
Cost of goods sold	570,000	500,000
Amortization expense	25,000	1,000
Interest expense	20,000	5,000
Income tax expense	30,000	9,000
Net earnings	120,000	55,000
Net cash provided by operating activities	210,000	105,000
Preferred dividends paid	8,000	7,500
Common dividends paid	12,000	11,000
Capital expenditures	115,000	108,000
Market price per share	28.00	25.00
Weighted average number of common shares	30,000	30,000

Required:
Calculate the following for the year ended December 31, 2006:

    a.   Liquidity ratios
    b.   Solvency ratios
    c.   Profitability ratios

2. State the effect of the following transactions on a current ratio of 1.5 to 1.   (SO4)
   Use increase, decrease, or no effect for your answer.
   a. Collection of an accounts receivable.
   b. Declaration of cash dividends.
   c. Additional shares are sold for cash.
   d. Accounts payable are paid.
   e. Equipment is purchased for cash.
   f. Inventory purchases are made for cash.
   g. Short-term investments are purchased for cash.

3. The following selected profitability ratios are available for two companies, Pop   (SO4)
   Corporation and Top Corporation and their industry, for a recent fiscal year:

Ratio	Pop	Top	Industry
Gross profit margin	37.5%	48.2%	37.9%
Profit margin	5.2%	4.9%	4.8%
Return on common shareholders' equity	18.3%	12.4%	12.0%
Return on assets	5.6%	5.2%	4.8%
Asset turnover	1.1 times	1.1 times	1.0 times
Payout ratio	16.9%	55.1%	34.5%
Earnings per share	$1.48	$1.76	$1.39
Price-earnings ratio	15.1 times	16.0 times	n/a

Required:
   a. Which company is more profitable? Explain.
   b. Which company do investors favour? Is your answer consistent with your findings in (a)?

4. Please refer to the Domtar and Cascades financial statements for information for answering the following questions. Do not forget to use the **Decision Toolkit** approach for help in the problem solving.

   a. In Chapter 5, the profit margin was calculated as 0.8%) of net sales for   (SO3)
      Domtar and 0.7% for Cascades for 2004. Using vertical analysis, explain the difference between the two companies' profit margins.

   b. Comment on your results obtained in (a) above.   (SO3)

   c. What has been the direction in net sales and cost of sales since 2000 for   (SO3)
      both companies? What conclusions did you reach?

   d. Using your results obtained in (a) and (d) above, what further conclusions   (SO5)
      can you make regarding the profitability of the companies?

Solutions to Self-Test

Multiple Choice

1. d An act of God may be extraordinary or ordinary. An item must be all of the following to be classified as extraordinary: unusual, infrequent, and not subject to a management determination.

2. b They are shown net of tax in the bottom half of the statement of earnings, below earnings from continuing operations. They never appear on the balance sheet.

3. b Changes in accounting principle are reported net of tax as an adjustment to opening retained earnings in the statement of retained earnings.

4. d

5. c ($22,000 − $10,000) ÷ $10,000 = 120%

6. b $30,000 ÷ $100,000 = 30%

7. b Liquidity refers to a company's short-term ability to pay obligations as they arise, and profitability measures the operating success of a business for a given period of time. Vertical analysis relates to a given period of time as well.

8. d Net earnings is simply the difference between revenues and expenses, and liquidity and solvency refer to the company's ability to survive on short-term and long-term bases, respectively.

9. c $600,000 ÷ $50,000 = 12 times

10. b $160,000 ÷ $40,000 = 4 times

11. b $200,000 ÷ $500,000 = 40.0%

12. a $800,000 ÷ $6,000,000 = 13.3%

13. d $700,000 ÷ 300,000 shares = 2.33

14. a Times interest earned is a solvency ratio, and average collection period and the cash current debt coverage are liquidity measures.

15. b The price-earnings ratio is a profitability ratio.

16. b

17. b

Problems

Note: See Illustrations 14–7 through 14–9 in the textbook for a description of each ratio.

1. a. **Liquidity ratios are:**
    Current ratio:

$$\frac{\$150,000 + \$110,000}{\$110,000} = 2.4\!:\!1$$

Inventory turnover:

$$\frac{\$570,000}{(\$110,000 + \$130,000) \div 2} = 4.8 \text{ times}$$

Days in inventory:

$$\frac{365}{4.8} = 76.0 \text{ days}$$

Receivables turnover:

$$\frac{\$1,470,000}{(\$150,000 + \$170,000) \div 2} = 9.2 \text{ times}$$

Average collection period:

$$\frac{365}{9.2} = 39.7 \text{ days}$$

Cash current debt coverage:

$$\frac{\$210,000}{(\$110,000 + \$80,000) \div 2} = 2.2 \text{ times.}$$

b. Solvency ratios are:

Debt to total assets:

$$\frac{\$110,000 + \$370,000}{\$1,170,000} = 41.0\%$$

Free cash flow:

$$\$210,000 - \$115,000 - \$8,000 - \$ 12,000 = \$75,000$$

Times interest earned:

$$\frac{\$120,000 + \$30,000 + \$20,000}{\$20,000} = 8.5 \text{ times}$$

Cash total debt coverage:

$$\frac{\$210,000}{(\$480,000 + \$350,000) \div 2} = 0.2 \text{ times.}$$

c. Profitability ratios are:

Earnings per share:

$$\frac{\$120,000}{30,000 \text{ common shares}} = \$4.00 \text{ per share}$$

Price-earnings ratio:

$$\frac{\$28.00}{\$4.00} = 7 \text{ times}$$

Gross profit margin:

$$\frac{\$1,470,000 - \$570,000}{\$1,470,000} = 61.2\%$$

Profit margin:

$$\frac{\$120,000}{\$1,470,000} = 8.2\%$$

Return on assets:

$$\frac{\$120,000}{(\$1,170,000 + \$770,000) \div 2} = 12.4\%$$

Asset turnover:

$$\frac{\$1,470,000}{(\$1,170,000 + \$770,000) \div 2} = 1.5 \text{ times}$$

Payout ratio on preferred shares:

$$\frac{\$8,000}{\$120,000} = 6.7\%$$

Payout ratio on common shares:

$$\frac{\$12,000}{\$120,000} = 10.0\%$$

Dividend yield on common shares:

$$\frac{\$12,000 \div 30,000 \text{ shares}}{\$28.00 \text{ per share}} = 1.4\%$$

Return on common shareholders' equity:

$$\frac{\$120,000 - \$8,000}{(\$690,000 + \$420,000) \div 2 \text{ (see note)}} = 20.2\%$$

(Note: Shareholders' equity = Total assets – Total liabilities   for 2006: $1,170,000 – $480,000 = $690,000 for 2005: $770,000 – $350,000 = $420,000)

2.

    a.   no effect

    b.   decrease

    c.   increase

    d.   increase

    e.   decrease

    f.   no effect

    g.   no effect

3. a.   Both companies appear to be profitable. The Top Corporation has a higher gross profit margin than the Pop Corporation, but both companies have a profit margin that is higher than that of the industry. It would appear that Top does not do as good a job as Pop at controlling its operating expenses, as Pop has the higher profit margin.

        Pop appears to be more profitable than Top as well when comparing return ratios (return on common shareholders' equity and return on assets), most likely because of its higher net earnings. Pop's profit margin and return ratios are also above those of the industry. All of this would indicate that Pop is the more profitable company.

    b.   Despite the findings in (a) that Pop is the more profitable company, investors seem to favour Top because it has the higher price-earnings ratio. This is not consistent with the above analysis, as you would expect investors to favour the more profitable company. Investors are likely favouring Top because of the larger payout ratio. Alternatively, investors may be anticipating better future profitability from Top.

4. a.

	Year 2004			
	Domtar ($millions)	%	Cascades ($millions)	%
Net sales	$5,115	100.0	$3,254	100.0
Cost of sales	4,381	85.7	2,691	82.7
Gross profit	734	14.3	563	17.3
Less operating expenses:				
Selling, general, administrative	306	6.0	313	9.6
Amortization	368	7.2	159	4.9
Other costs	11	0.2	12	0.4
Total operating expenses	685	13.4	484	14.9
Operating profit	49	0.9	79	2.4
Financing or interest expenses	148	2.9	77	2.4
Amortization of deferred gain	(5)	(0.1)	0	0.0
Gain on foreign exchange	0	0.0	(18)	(0.6)
Earnings before income taxes	(94)	(1.8)	20	0.6
Income tax expense	(52)	1.0	2	0.1
Earnings before other items	(42)	(0.8)	18	0.5
Share of earnings from companies	0	0.0	(2)	(0.1)
Earnings on assets held for sale			(3)	(0.1)
Net earnings	$(42)	(0.8)	$23	0.7

b.   Cascades' ratio of net earnings to net sales of 0.7 percent is higher than Domtar's (0.8) percent, primarily because Cascades' cost of sales is lower than Domtar's, resulting in a higher gross profit margin. This is significant because cost of sales represents a significant proportion of net sales for both companies: 85.7 percent for Domtar and 82.7 percent for Cascades in 2004.

The total operating expenses for Cascades of 14.9 percent of net sales is higher than Domtar's 13.4 percent primarily because Cascades' selling, general, and administrative expenses are significantly higher than Domtar's. However, the interest expense for Cascades is lower than Domtar's, and Cascades received other earnings from its gain on foreign exchange.

c.   To answer this question, you must perform a horizontal analysis where year 2002 is established as the base year and the percentage increase or decrease for each subsequent year is calculated as a percentage of the base year. The calculations are as follows:

($ millions)	**2004**	**2003**	**2002**
Domtar:			
Net sales	$5,115	$5,167	$5,859
	87%	88%	100%
Cost of sales	$4,381	$4,335	$4,686
93%	93%	100%	
Cascades:			
Net sales	$3,254	$2,995	$3,118
104%	96%	100%	
Cost of sales	$2,691	$2,463	$2,414
11%	102%	100%	

The horizontal analysis shows that for Domtar, net sales have decline more rapidly over the period 2002 to 2004 than its cost of sales—87 percent compared with 93 percent in 2004. For Cascades, its net sales increased slightly from 2002 to 2004; however, its cost of sales over the same period increased more rapidly—111 percent compared with 104 percent in 2004.

d.   The vertical analysis in (a) shows that cost of sales is a major expense category for both companies—78.7 percent for Domtar and 76.8 percent for Cascades.

The horizontal analysis in (c) shows that for Domtar, sales and cost of sales decreased from 2002 to 2004 but that the critical cost of sales component decreased at a less rapid rate, thereby placing pressure on net earnings.

For Cascades, sales increased slightly from 2002 to 2004, but cost of sales increased at a more rapid rate, thereby also placing pressure on net earnings.

Today's
perfect paper.
Tomorrow's
ideal solutions.

THE COMPELLING IDEAS BEHIND A CUSTOMER-FOCUSED DOMTAR.

Domtar

DOMTAR 2004 ANNUAL REPORT

CONSOLIDATED FINANCIAL STATEMENTS

MANAGEMENT'S STATEMENT
OF RESPONSIBILITY

The consolidated financial statements contained in this Annual Report are the responsibility of management, and have been prepared in accordance with Canadian generally accepted accounting principles. Where necessary, management has made judgments and estimates of the outcome of events and transactions, with due consideration given to materiality. Management is also responsible for all other information in the Annual Report and for ensuring that this information is consistent, where appropriate, with the information and data included in the consolidated financial statements.

To discharge its responsibility, management maintains a system of internal controls to provide reasonable assurance as to the reliability of financial information and the safeguarding of assets.

The Corporation's external auditors are responsible for auditing the consolidated financial statements and giving an opinion thereon. In addition, the Corporation maintains a staff of internal auditors whose functions include reviewing internal controls and their application on an ongoing basis.

The Board of Directors carries out its responsibility relative to the consolidated financial statements principally through its Audit Committee, consisting solely of independent directors, which reviews the consolidated financial statements and reports thereon to the Board. The Committee meets periodically with the external auditors, internal auditors and management to review their respective activities and the discharge of each of their responsibilities. Both the external auditors and the internal auditors have free access to the Committee, with or without management, to discuss the scope of their audits, the adequacy of the system of internal controls and the adequacy of financial reporting.

(signed)   (signed)

RAYMOND ROYER   DANIEL BURON
President and Chief Executive Officer   Senior Vice President and
                                              Chief Financial Officer

Montreal, Quebec, February 23, 2005

CONSOLIDATED FINANCIAL STATEMENTS

AUDITORS' REPORT

To the Shareholders of Domtar Inc.

We have audited the consolidated balance sheets of Domtar Inc. as at December 31, 2004 and 2003 and the consolidated statements of earnings, retained earnings and cash flows for each of the years in the three-year period ended December 31, 2004. These financial statements are the responsibility of the Corporation's management. Our responsibility is to express an opinion on these financial statements based on our audits.

We conducted our audits in accordance with Canadian generally accepted auditing standards. Those standards require that we plan and perform an audit to obtain reasonable assurance whether the financial statements are free of material misstatement. An audit includes examining, on a test basis, evidence supporting the amounts and disclosures in the financial statements. An audit also includes assessing the accounting principles used and significant estimates made by management, as well as evaluating the overall financial statement presentation.

In our opinion, these consolidated financial statements present fairly, in all material respects, the financial position of Domtar Inc. as at December 31, 2004 and 2003 and the results of its operations and its cash flows for each of the years in the three-year period ended December 31, 2004 in accordance with Canadian generally accepted accounting principles.

(signed)

PRICEWATERHOUSECOOPERS LLP
Chartered Accountants

Montreal, Quebec, February 23, 2005

CONSOLIDATED FINANCIAL STATEMENTS

CONSOLIDATED EARNINGS *Years ended December 31*	2004	**2004**	2003	2002
(In millions of Canadian dollars, unless otherwise noted)	US$ (NOTE 4)	$	$ RESTATED (NOTE 2)	$
Sales (NOTE 2)	4,250	**5,115**	5,167	5,859
Operating expenses				
Cost of sales (NOTE 2)	3,640	**4,381**	4,335	4,686
Selling, general and administrative (NOTE 2)	254	**306**	319	329
Amortization	306	**368**	385	398
Closure and restructuring costs (NOTE 6)	40	**48**	24	63
Impairment loss (NOTE 3)	–	**–**	201	–
Net gains on disposals of property, plant and equipment	(31)	**(37)**	(2)	(1)
	4,209	**5,066**	5,262	5,475
Operating profit (loss)	41	**49**	(95)	384
Financing expenses (NOTE 7)	123	**148**	169	192
Amortization of deferred gain	(4)	**(5)**	(4)	(5)
Earnings (loss) before income taxes	(78)	**(94)**	(260)	197
Income tax expense (recovery) (NOTE 8)	(43)	**(52)**	(67)	56
Net earnings (loss)	(35)	**(42)**	(193)	141
Per common share (in dollars) (NOTE 9)				
Net earnings (loss)				
Basic	(0.16)	**(0.19)**	(0.86)	0.62
Diluted	(0.16)	**(0.19)**	(0.86)	0.61

CONSOLIDATED RETAINED EARNINGS *Years ended December 31*	2004	**2004**	2003	2002
(In millions of Canadian dollars, unless otherwise noted)	US$ (NOTE 4)	$	$ RESTATED (NOTE 2)	$
Retained earnings at beginning of year – as reported	425	**512**	753	645
Cumulative effect of change in accounting policy (NOTE 2)	(2)	**(3)**	–	–
Retained earnings at beginning of year – as restated	423	**509**	753	645
Net earnings (loss)	(35)	**(42)**	(193)	141
Dividends on common shares	(45)	**(54)**	(49)	(32)
Dividends on preferred shares	(1)	**(1)**	(2)	(1)
Retained earnings at end of year	342	**412**	509	753

The accompanying notes are an integral part of the consolidated financial statements.

CONSOLIDATED FINANCIAL STATEMENTS

CONSOLIDATED BALANCE SHEETS *As at December 31*	2004	**2004**	2003
(In millions of Canadian dollars, unless otherwise noted)	US$ (NOTE 4)	$	$ RESTATED (NOTE 2)
Assets			
Current assets			
Cash and cash equivalents	43	**52**	48
Receivables (NOTE 10)	194	**233**	197
Inventories (NOTE 11)	601	**723**	670
Prepaid expenses	10	**12**	22
Income and other taxes receivable	14	**17**	29
Future income taxes (NOTE 8)	72	**87**	60
	934	**1,124**	1,026
Property, plant and equipment (NOTE 12)	3,502	**4,215**	4,533
Goodwill	70	**84**	77
Other assets (NOTE 13)	220	**265**	212
	4,726	**5,688**	5,848
Liabilities and shareholders' equity			
Current liabilities			
Bank indebtedness	18	**22**	19
Trade and other payables (NOTE 14)	543	**654**	652
Income and other taxes payable	27	**32**	28
Long-term debt due within one year (NOTE 15)	7	**8**	5
	595	**716**	704
Long-term debt (NOTE 15)	1,683	**2,026**	2,054
Future income taxes (NOTE 8)	463	**557**	562
Other liabilities and deferred credits (NOTE 16)	285	**343**	360
Commitments and contingencies (NOTE 17)			
Shareholders' equity			
Preferred shares (NOTE 18)	33	**39**	42
Common shares (NOTE 18)	1,475	**1,775**	1,756
Contributed surplus (NOTE 18)	8	**10**	6
Retained earnings	342	**412**	509
Accumulated foreign currency translation adjustments (NOTE 20)	(158)	**(190)**	(145)
	1,700	**2,046**	2,168
	4,726	**5,688**	5,848

The accompanying notes are an integral part of the consolidated financial statements.

Approved by the Board:

(signed)   (signed)

BRIAN M. LEVITT   RAYMOND ROYER
Director   Director

CONSOLIDATED FINANCIAL STATEMENTS

CONSOLIDATED CASH FLOWS *Years ended December 31*	2004	**2004**	2003	2002
(In millions of Canadian dollars, unless otherwise noted)	US$ (NOTE 4)	**$**	$ RESTATED (NOTE 2)	$
Operating activities				
Net earnings (loss)	(35)	**(42)**	(193)	141
Non-cash items:				
Amortization and write-down of property, plant and equipment (NOTE 6)	315	**379**	408	425
Future income taxes (NOTE 8)	(62)	**(75)**	(81)	31
Amortization of deferred gain	(4)	**(5)**	(4)	(5)
Closure and restructuring costs, excluding write-down of property, plant and equipment (NOTE 6)	31	**37**	1	36
Impairment loss (NOTE 3)	–	**–**	201	–
Refinancing expenses (NOTE 7)	–	**–**	17	–
Net gains on disposals of property, plant and equipment	(31)	**(37)**	(2)	(1)
Other	(7)	**(8)**	2	15
	207	**249**	349	642
Changes in working capital and other items				
Receivables (NOTE 10)	(38)	**(46)**	71	22
Inventories	(64)	**(77)**	4	43
Prepaid expenses	7	**8**	(1)	3
Trade and other payables	(26)	**(32)**	(47)	(62)
Income and other taxes	16	**20**	(2)	12
Early settlements of interest rate swap contracts (NOTE 19)	16	**20**	–	40
Other	(7)	**(8)**	(17)	(13)
Payments of closure and restructuring costs, net of proceeds on disposition	(10)	**(12)**	(9)	(10)
	(106)	**(127)**	(1)	35
Cash flows provided from operating activities	101	**122**	348	677
Investing activities				
Additions to property, plant and equipment	(169)	**(204)**	(236)	(226)
Proceeds from disposals of property, plant and equipment	34	**41**	11	3
Business acquisitions (NOTE 5)	(16)	**(19)**	(11)	(27)
Other	(1)	**(1)**	(2)	6
Cash flows used for investing activities	(152)	**(183)**	(238)	(244)
Financing activities				
Dividend payments	(47)	**(56)**	(45)	(33)
Change in bank indebtedness	4	**5**	(4)	(25)
Change in revolving bank credit, net of expenses	87	**105**	22	9
Issuance of long-term debt, net of expenses	2	**2**	617	–
Repayment of long-term debt	(7)	**(8)**	(691)	(395)
Premium on redemption of long-term debt	–	**–**	(7)	–
Common shares issued, net of expenses	16	**19**	15	16
Redemptions of preferred shares	(2)	**(3)**	(3)	(3)
Cash flows provided from (used for) financing activities	53	**64**	(96)	(431)
Net increase in cash and cash equivalents	2	**3**	14	2
Translation adjustments related to cash and cash equivalents	1	**1**	(4)	–
Cash and cash equivalents at beginning of year	40	**48**	38	36
Cash and cash equivalents at end of year	43	**52**	48	38

The accompanying notes are an integral part of the consolidated financial statements.

NOTES TO CONSOLIDATED FINANCIAL STATEMENTS

DECEMBER 31, 2004 (IN MILLIONS OF CANADIAN DOLLARS, UNLESS OTHERWISE NOTED)

NOTE 1.

SUMMARY OF SIGNIFICANT ACCOUNTING POLICIES

The consolidated financial statements are expressed in Canadian dollars and have been prepared in accordance with Canadian generally accepted accounting principles (Canadian GAAP). These financial statements differ in certain respects from those prepared in accordance with United States generally accepted accounting principles (U.S. GAAP) and are not intended to provide certain disclosures which would typically be found in financial statements prepared in accordance with U.S. GAAP. These differences are described in Note 25. These consolidated financial statements are dated February 23, 2005.

BASIS OF CONSOLIDATION

The consolidated financial statements include the accounts of Domtar Inc. and its subsidiaries (the Corporation) as well as its joint ventures (collectively Domtar). Investments over which the Corporation exercises significant influence are accounted for using the equity method. The Corporation's interests in joint ventures are accounted for using the proportionate consolidation method.

USE OF ESTIMATES

The consolidated financial statements have been prepared in conformity with Canadian GAAP, which require management to make estimates and assumptions that affect the reported amounts of revenues and expenses during the year, the reported amounts of assets and liabilities, and the disclosure of contingent assets and liabilities at the date of the consolidated financial statements. On an ongoing basis, management reviews its estimates, including those related to environmental matters, useful lives, impairment of long-lived assets and goodwill, pension and other employee future benefit plans, income taxes and asset retirement obligations, based on currently available information. Actual results could differ from those estimates.

TRANSLATION OF FOREIGN CURRENCIES

Self-sustaining foreign operations

For foreign subsidiaries that are considered financially and operationally self-sustaining, the current rate method of translation of foreign currencies has been used. Under this method, assets and liabilities are translated into Canadian dollars at the rate in effect at the balance sheet date and revenues and expenses are translated at the average exchange rates during the year. All gains and losses arising from the translation of the financial statements of these foreign subsidiaries are included in the "Accumulated foreign currency translation adjustments" account under "Shareholders' equity."

NOTES TO CONSOLIDATED FINANCIAL STATEMENTS
DECEMBER 31, 2004 (IN MILLIONS OF CANADIAN DOLLARS, UNLESS OTHERWISE NOTED)

NOTE 1. SUMMARY OF SIGNIFICANT ACCOUNTING POLICIES (CONTINUED)

Foreign currency transactions and integrated foreign operations

For foreign currency transactions and foreign subsidiaries that are considered financially and operationally integrated, the temporal method of translation of foreign currencies has been used. Monetary items are translated at the rate in effect at the balance sheet date, non-monetary items are translated at their historical rate (as well as the related amortization) and revenues and expenses are translated at the rate in effect at the transaction date or at the average exchange rates during the year as appropriate. Translation gains and losses, except those on long-term debt, are included in "Selling, general and administrative" expenses.

Foreign currency long-term debt

For the Corporation's long-term debt designated as a hedge of the net investment in self-sustaining foreign subsidiaries, exchange gains and losses are included in the "Accumulated foreign currency translation adjustments" account under "Shareholders' equity." Prior to the fourth quarter of 2004, a portion of the foreign currency denominated long-term debt of the Corporation was designated as a hedge of future U.S. dollar revenue stream and exchange gains and losses were deferred and will be recognized when the designated revenue is earned or when it becomes probable that the forecasted transaction will not occur, as the hedge then ceases to be effective.

Norampac Inc. and its subsidiaries (Norampac) (a 50-50 joint venture with Cascades Inc.) has also designated a portion of its U.S. dollar denominated long-term debt as a hedge of its net investment in self-sustaining foreign subsidiaries. For such debt designated as a hedge of the net investment in self-sustaining foreign subsidiaries, exchange gains and losses are included in the "Accumulated foreign currency translation adjustments" account in "Shareholders' equity." For the remaining U.S. dollar denominated long-term debt, exchange gains and losses are included in "Financing expenses."

REVENUE RECOGNITION

Domtar recognizes revenue when persuasive evidence of an arrangement exists, goods have been delivered, there are no uncertainties surrounding product acceptance, the related revenue is fixed or determinable and collection is considered reasonably assured. Delivery is not considered to have occurred until the customer takes title and assumes the risks and rewards of ownership.

INCOME TAXES

Domtar uses the asset and liability method of accounting for income taxes. Under this method, future tax assets and liabilities are determined according to differences between the carrying amounts and tax bases of the assets and liabilities. The change in the net future tax asset or liability is included in earnings and in the "Accumulated foreign currency translation adjustments" account under "Shareholders' equity." Future tax assets and liabilities are measured using enacted or substantively enacted tax rates and laws expected to apply in the years in which the assets and liabilities are expected to be recovered or settled. Domtar does not provide for income taxes on undistributed earnings of foreign subsidiaries that are not expected to be repatriated in the foreseeable future.

CASH AND CASH EQUIVALENTS

Cash and cash equivalents include cash and short-term investments with original maturities of less than three months and are presented at cost.

RECEIVABLES

Receivables are recorded at cost net of a provision for doubtful accounts that is based on expected collectibility. Gains or losses on securitization of receivables are calculated as the difference between the carrying amount of the receivables sold and the sum of the cash proceeds on sale and the fair value of the retained subordinate interest in such receivables on the date of transfer. Fair value is determined on a discounted cash flow basis. Costs related to the sales of receivables are recognized in earnings in the period when the sale occurs.

INVENTORIES

Inventories of operating and maintenance supplies and raw materials are valued at the lower of average cost and replacement cost. Work in process and finished goods are valued at the lower of average cost and net realizable value, and include the cost of raw materials, direct labor and manufacturing overhead expenses.

PROPERTY, PLANT AND EQUIPMENT

Property, plant and equipment are stated at cost less accumulated amortization including asset impairment write-down. Interest costs are capitalized for capital projects in excess of $10 million and having a duration in excess of 1 year. For timber limits and timberlands, amortization is calculated using the unit of production method. For all other assets, amortization is calculated using the straight-line method over the estimated useful lives of the assets. Buildings are amortized over periods of 10 to 40 years and machinery and equipment over periods of 3 to 20 years. The amortization expense is reported net of the amount of the amortization of deferred credits related to property, plant and equipment. No amortization is recorded on assets under construction.

NOTES TO CONSOLIDATED FINANCIAL STATEMENTS
DECEMBER 31, 2004 (IN MILLIONS OF CANADIAN DOLLARS, UNLESS OTHERWISE NOTED)

NOTE 1. SUMMARY OF SIGNIFICANT ACCOUNTING POLICIES (CONTINUED)

IMPAIRMENT OF LONG-LIVED ASSETS

Long-lived assets are reviewed for impairment upon the occurrence of events or changes in circumstances indicating that the carrying value of the assets may not be recoverable, as measured by comparing their net book value to the estimated undiscounted future cash flows generated by their use. Impaired assets are recorded at fair value, determined principally by using discounted future cash flows expected from their use and eventual disposition.

GOODWILL

Goodwill is not amortized and is subject to an annual impairment test, or more frequently if events or changes in circumstances indicate that it might be impaired. Testing for impairment is accomplished mainly by determining whether the fair value of a segment, based upon discounted cash flows, exceeds the net carrying amount of that segment as of the assessment date. If the fair value is greater than the net carrying amount, no impairment is necessary. In the event that the net carrying amount exceeds the sum of the discounted cash flows, a second test must be performed whereby the fair value of the segment's goodwill must be estimated to determine if it is less than its net carrying amount. Fair value of goodwill is estimated in the same way as goodwill was determined at the date of the acquisition in a business combination, that is, the excess of the fair value of the segment over the fair value of the identifiable net assets of the segment.

OTHER ASSETS

Other assets are recorded at cost. Expenses and discounts related to the issuance of long-term debt are deferred and amortized on a straight-line basis over the term of the related obligation.

DEFERRED CREDITS

Deferred credits comprise the deferred gain on the contribution of net assets to Norampac, the deferred net gain on early settlements of interest rate swap contracts and grants and investment tax credits obtained upon the acquisition of property, plant and equipment. The deferred gain on the contribution of net assets to Norampac is amortized on a straight-line basis over 15 years. The deferred net gain on early settlements of interest rate swap contracts is amortized as an adjustment to "Financing expenses" over the initially designated periods of the respective interest payments. Investment tax credits are amortized on the same basis as the related property, plant and equipment.

NOTES TO CONSOLIDATED FINANCIAL STATEMENTS
DECEMBER 31, 2004 (IN MILLIONS OF CANADIAN DOLLARS, UNLESS OTHERWISE NOTED)

ENVIRONMENTAL COSTS

Environmental expenditures for effluent treatment, air emission, landfill operation and closure, asbestos containment and removal, bark pile management, silvicultural activities and site remediation (together referred to as environmental matters) are expensed or capitalized depending on their future economic benefit. In the normal course of business, Domtar incurs certain operating costs for environmental matters that are expensed as incurred. Expenditures for property, plant and equipment that prevent future environmental contamination are capitalized and amortized on a straight-line basis over 10 to 40 years. Provisions for environmental matters are not discounted and are recorded when remediation efforts are likely and can be reasonably determined.

ASSET RETIREMENT OBLIGATIONS

Asset retirement obligations are recognized, at fair value, in the period in which Domtar incurs a legal obligation associated to the retirement of an asset. The associated costs are capitalized as part of the carrying value of the related asset and depreciated over its remaining useful life. The liability is accreted using a credit adjusted risk-free interest rate.

STOCK-BASED COMPENSATION AND OTHER STOCK-BASED PAYMENTS

Domtar uses the fair value based approach of accounting for stock-based payments to directors and for stock options granted to its employees. Any consideration paid by plan participants on the exercise of share options or the purchase of shares is credited to stated capital together with any related stock-based compensation expense.

Stock-based compensation expense is recognized over the vesting period of the options, share purchase rights and bonus shares. For employee share purchase discounts, compensation expense is recognized when employees purchase shares. The contributed surplus component of the stock-based compensation is transferred to capital stock upon the issuance of common shares.

Deferred Share Units are amortized over their vesting periods and remeasured at each reporting period, until settlement, using the quoted market value. Deferred Share Units are accounted for in compensation expense and "Other liabilities and deferred credits."

DERIVATIVE INSTRUMENTS

Derivative instruments are contracts that require or provide an option to exchange cash flows or payments determined by applying certain rates, indices or changes therein to notional contract amounts. Derivative instruments are utilized by Domtar in the management of its foreign currency, price risk and interest rate exposures. Except for two interest rate swap contracts of Norampac, which were obtained through business acquisitions, Domtar does not use derivative instruments for speculative purposes.

NOTES TO CONSOLIDATED FINANCIAL STATEMENTS
DECEMBER 31, 2004 (IN MILLIONS OF CANADIAN DOLLARS, UNLESS OTHERWISE NOTED)

NOTE 1. SUMMARY OF SIGNIFICANT ACCOUNTING POLICIES (CONTINUED)

Derivatives designated for hedge accounting

In order for a derivative to qualify for hedge accounting, the hedge relationship must be designated and formally documented at its inception, outlining the particular risk management objective and strategy, the specific asset, liability or cash flow being hedged, as well as how effectiveness is assessed. The derivative must be effective in accomplishing the objective of offsetting either changes in the fair value or cash flow attributable to the risk being hedged both at inception and over the term of the hedging relationship.

When derivative instruments have been designated within a hedge relationship and are highly effective in offsetting the identified risk characteristics of specific financial assets and liabilities, or group of financial assets and liabilities, hedge accounting is applied to these derivative instruments. Hedge accounting requires that gains, losses, revenues and expenses of a hedging item be recognized in the same period that the associated gains, losses, revenues and expenses of the hedged item are recognized.

Realized and unrealized gains or losses associated with hedging instruments for which the underlying hedged items are either sold, paid or terminated are recognized to earnings. Realized and unrealized gains or losses when hedging instruments have ended or ceased to be effective prior to their maturity are deferred and recognized in earnings concurrently with the recognition of the item being hedged.

Domtar hedges its foreign exchange exposure on anticipated sales denominated in U.S. dollars through the use of options and forward contracts. Resulting gains and losses, including premiums on options, are recognized when the designated sale is recognized and are included in "Sales."

Domtar hedges its exposure to price risk associated with purchases of bunker oil and electricity through the use of cash settled commodity swaps. Resulting gains and losses are recognized when the designated purchase is recognized and are included in "Cost of sales."

Domtar hedges its exposure to interest rate on its long-term debt through the use of interest rate swap contracts. Amounts accounted for under interest rate swap contracts are included in "Financing expenses." In 2004, the Corporation terminated prior to maturity, its interest rate swap contracts.

Derivatives not designated for hedge accounting

For the exposure to price risk associated with sales of Northern Bleached Softwood Kraft (NBSK) pulp swaps, as well as old corrugated containers, unbleached kraft linerboard and semi-chemical medium paper, Domtar does not meet the requirements for hedge accounting. As a result, Domtar accounts for these contracts at their fair value with resulting gains and losses being included in "Selling, general and administrative" expenses.

For the two interest rate swap contracts of Norampac, which are used for speculative purposes, the change in their fair value is recorded in "Selling, general and administrative" expenses.

NOTES TO CONSOLIDATED FINANCIAL STATEMENTS
DECEMBER 31, 2004 (IN MILLIONS OF CANADIAN DOLLARS, UNLESS OTHERWISE NOTED)

PENSIONS

Domtar accrues the cost of defined benefit plans as determined by independent actuaries. These plans include funded and unfunded defined benefit pension plans and defined contribution plans. The net periodic benefit cost includes the following:

- the cost of pension benefits provided in exchange for employees' services rendered during the year
- the interest cost of pension obligations
- the expected long-term return on pension fund assets based on a market-related value determined using a five-year moving average market value for equity securities and fair value for other asset classes
- gains or losses on settlements or curtailments
- the straight-line amortization of past service costs and plan amendments over the average remaining service period of approximately 13 years of the active employee group covered by the plans
- the amortization of cumulative unrecognized net actuarial gains and losses in excess of 10% of the greater of the accrued benefit obligation or market-related value of plan assets at the beginning of year over the average remaining service period of approximately 13 years of the active employee group covered by the plans.

The pension plans obligations are determined in accordance with the projected benefit method prorated on services.

OTHER EMPLOYEE FUTURE BENEFIT PLANS

Domtar accrues the cost of post-retirement benefits other than pensions as determined by independent actuaries. These benefits, which are funded by Domtar as they become due, include life insurance programs, medical and dental benefits and short-term and long-term disability programs. Domtar amortizes the cumulative unrecognized net actuarial gains and losses in excess of 10% of the accrued benefit obligation at the beginning of the year over the average remaining service period of approximately 14 years of the active employee group covered by the plans.

INVESTMENT TAX CREDITS

Investment tax credits are recognized in earnings as a reduction of research and development expenses when Domtar has made the qualifying expenditures and has a reasonable assurance that the credits will be realized.

DISCLOSURE OF GUARANTEES

A guarantee is a contract or an indemnification agreement that contingently requires Domtar to make payments to the other party of the contract or agreement, based on changes in an

NOTES TO CONSOLIDATED FINANCIAL STATEMENTS
DECEMBER 31, 2004 (IN MILLIONS OF CANADIAN DOLLARS, UNLESS OTHERWISE NOTED)

NOTE 1. SUMMARY OF SIGNIFICANT ACCOUNTING POLICIES (CONTINUED)

underlying that is related to an asset, a liability or an equity security of the other party or on a third party's failure to perform under an obligating agreement. It could also be an indirect guarantee of the indebtedness of another party, even though the payment to the other party may not be based on changes in an underlying that is related to an asset, a liability or an equity security of the other party.

COUNTERVAILING AND ANTIDUMPING DUTIES

Cash deposits for countervailing and antidumping duties (lumber duties) are expensed as the deposits for softwood lumber export sales to the United States are made. The lumber duties expense is presented in "Cost of sales." Recoveries of cash deposits for lumber duties are only recognized when the amounts are reasonably measurable and their recovery is virtually certain.

NOTE 2.

ACCOUNTING CHANGES

2004

GENERALLY ACCEPTED ACCOUNTING PRINCIPLES AND FINANCIAL STATEMENT PRESENTATION

On January 1, 2004, Domtar adopted the new Canadian Institute of Chartered Accountants' (CICA) Handbook Section 1100 "Generally Accepted Accounting Principles" recommendations and Section 1400 "General Standards of Financial Statement Presentation" recommendations. Section 1100 describes what constitutes GAAP and its sources and provides guidance on sources to consult when selecting accounting policies and determining appropriate disclosures when a matter is not dealt with explicitly in the primary sources of GAAP, thereby recodifying the Canadian GAAP hierarchy. Section 1400 provides general guidance on financial statement presentation and further clarifies what constitutes fair presentation in accordance with GAAP.

Accordingly, Domtar reclassified delivery costs as well as countervailing and antidumping duties on exports of softwood lumber to the United States from "Sales" to "Cost of sales." As of December 31, 2004, delivery costs amounted to $411 million (2003 – $345 million; 2002 – $358 million) and countervailing and antidumping duties amounted to $69 million (2003 – $45 million; 2002 – $11 million).

The adoption of these recommendations has no other significant impact on the consolidated financial statements.

NOTES TO CONSOLIDATED FINANCIAL STATEMENTS
DECEMBER 31, 2004 (IN MILLIONS OF CANADIAN DOLLARS, UNLESS OTHERWISE NOTED)

HEDGING RELATIONSHIPS

On January 1, 2004, Domtar adopted the new CICA Accounting Guideline No. 13 (AcG-13) "Hedging Relationships." This accounting guideline addresses the identification, designation, documentation and effectiveness of the hedging relationships for the purpose of applying hedge accounting. In addition, it deals with the discontinuance of hedge accounting and establishes conditions for applying hedge accounting. Under this guideline, documentation of the information related to hedging relationships is required and the effectiveness of the hedges must be demonstrated and documented. As of January 1, 2004, Domtar has in place all necessary hedge documentation to apply hedge accounting for interest rate swap contracts, forward foreign exchange contracts, foreign currency options and bunker oil and electricity swaps.

For the exposure to price risk associated with sales of NBSK pulp swaps, as well as old corrugated containers, unbleached kraft linerboard and semi-chemical medium paper swaps, Domtar does not meet the Canadian GAAP criteria for hedge effectiveness. As a result, Domtar accounts for these contracts at their fair value. The fair value of these contracts is re-evaluated each quarter and a gain or loss is recorded in the Consolidated earnings. Notwithstanding the fact that these commodity swap contracts do not meet the Canadian GAAP criteria under AcG-13, Domtar believes, from an operational and a cash flow point of view, that these contracts are effective in managing its risk. For the year ended December 31, 2004, a gain of $1 million, nil per common share, is included in "Selling, general and administrative" expenses, representing the gain on the marked to market of the commodity swaps.

ASSET RETIREMENT OBLIGATIONS

On January 1, 2004, Domtar adopted retroactively with restatement of prior periods the new CICA Handbook Section 3110 "Asset Retirement Obligations," which requires entities to record a liability at fair value, in the period in which it incurs a legal obligation associated to the retirement of an asset. The associated costs are capitalized as part of the carrying value of the related asset and depreciated over its remaining useful life. The liability is accreted using a credit adjusted risk-free interest rate. Section 3110 is analogous to the requirements of Statement of Financial Accounting Standards (SFAS) 143 "Accounting for Asset Retirement Obligations," which was adopted for U.S. GAAP purposes on January 1, 2003. Asset retirement obligations in connection with the adoption of Section 3110 were primarily linked to landfill capping obligations, asbestos removal obligations and demolition of certain abandoned buildings. For such assets, a liability is initially recognized in the period in which sufficient information exists to estimate a range of possible settlement dates. The adoption of Section 3110 has decreased the December 31, 2003 retained earnings by $3 million, $0.01 per common share (2002 – nil), decreased assets by $7 million and decreased liabilities by $4 million.

NOTE 2. ACCOUNTING CHANGES (CONTINUED)

EMPLOYEE FUTURE BENEFITS

On January 1, 2004, the CICA amended Handbook Section 3461 "Employee Future Benefits" recommendations. Section 3461 requires additional disclosures about the assets, cash flows and net periodic benefit cost of defined benefit pension plans and other employee future benefit plans. The new annual disclosures are effective for years ending on or after June 30, 2004. Domtar adopted the amendments of Section 3461 and provided additional disclosures of the defined benefit pension plans and other employee future benefit plans in Notes 22 and 23.

2003

SHARE PURCHASE FINANCING

On January 1, 2003, Domtar prospectively adopted the new CICA Emerging Issues Committee Abstract 132 (EIC-132) "Share Purchase Financing" recommendations relating to share purchase loans (the loans) receivable. Accordingly, loans as at January 1, 2003, amounting to $11 million, were reclassified from "Other assets" to "Common shares" and interest revenue was treated as a reduction of dividends. The common shares purchased with these loans are held in trust as security for the loans. The loans are interest bearing at the dividend rate and have defined repayment terms not exceeding 10 years. These common shares were not considered as being outstanding for the calculation of the basic earnings per share but were considered in the calculation of the diluted earnings per share. The adoption of these recommendations had no significant impact on the diluted earnings per share for the year ended December 31, 2003.

IMPAIRMENT OF LONG-LIVED ASSETS

On January 1, 2003, Domtar early adopted the new CICA Handbook Section 3063 "Impairment of Long-lived Assets" recommendations. These recommendations provide accounting guidance for the recognition, measurement and disclosure of impairment of long-lived assets, including property, plant and equipment and intangible assets with finite useful lives. They require the recognition of an impairment loss for a long-lived asset when events or changes in circumstances cause its carrying value to exceed the total undiscounted future cash flows expected from its use and eventual disposition. The impairment loss is calculated by deducting the fair value of the asset from its carrying value. This change in accounting policy has been applied prospectively. Domtar reviews the carrying amount of the long-lived assets when events or changes in circumstances indicate that the carrying value of the assets may not be recoverable through future operations (Note 3).

NOTES TO CONSOLIDATED FINANCIAL STATEMENTS
DECEMBER 31, 2004 (IN MILLIONS OF CANADIAN DOLLARS, UNLESS OTHERWISE NOTED)

EXIT AND DISPOSAL ACTIVITIES

Disposal of long-lived assets and discontinued operations

Domtar prospectively adopted the revised CICA Handbook Section 3475 "Disposal of Long-lived Assets and Discontinued Operations" recommendations for disposal activities initiated on or after May 1, 2003, as required by the transitional provisions. These recommendations establish standards for the recognition, measurement, presentation and disclosure of disposals of long-lived assets, as well as for the presentation and disclosure of discontinued operations. The adoption of these new recommendations had no significant impact on the December 31, 2003 consolidated financial statements.

Severance, termination benefits and costs associated with exit and disposal activities

Domtar prospectively adopted the new CICA Emerging Issues Committee Abstract 134 (EIC-134) "Accounting for Severance and Termination Benefits" recommendations and Abstract 135 (EIC-135) "Accounting for Costs Associated with Exit and Disposal Activities (Including Costs Incurred in a Restructuring)" recommendations relating to exit or disposal activities initiated after March 31, 2003, as required by their transitional provisions. These recommendations provide guidance on the timing of recognition and measurement of liabilities, as well as disclosures for the various types of severance and termination benefits related to the termination of employees' services prior to normal retirement and costs associated with an exit or disposal activity. Under these new recommendations, liabilities for these costs are to be recognized in the period when they are incurred and measured at their fair value.

2002

STOCK-BASED COMPENSATION AND OTHER STOCK-BASED PAYMENTS

On January 1, 2002, Domtar adopted the new CICA Handbook Section 3870 "Stock-based Compensation and Other Stock-based Payments" recommendations. These recommendations require the use of a fair value based approach of accounting for stock-based payments to non-employees. The recommendations did not require the use of the fair value method when accounting for stock-based awards to employees, except for stock-based compensation that meets specific criteria. However, Domtar has chosen to record an expense for the stock options granted to its employees using the fair value method.

In accordance with the transitional provisions of the new recommendations, Domtar has adopted the new recommendations for awards granted after January 1, 2002. The effect of the adoption of the recommendations has been reflected as a charge of $4 million ($4 million net of income taxes or $0.02 per common share) for the year ended December 31, 2002.

NOTES TO CONSOLIDATED FINANCIAL STATEMENTS

DECEMBER 31, 2004 (IN MILLIONS OF CANADIAN DOLLARS, UNLESS OTHERWISE NOTED)

NOTE 2. ACCOUNTING CHANGES (CONTINUED)

GOODWILL AND INTANGIBLE ASSETS

On January 1, 2002, Domtar adopted the new CICA Handbook Section 3062 "Goodwill and Other Intangible Assets" recommendations, which require intangible assets with an indefinite life and goodwill to no longer be amortized and be tested annually for impairment. Intangible assets with a finite life will continue to be amortized over their useful life.

In accordance with the transitional provisions of the new recommendations, Domtar has performed the impairment test of its goodwill and has determined that no write-down for impairment was necessary.

IMPACT OF ACCOUNTING PRONOUNCEMENTS NOT YET IMPLEMENTED

CONSOLIDATION OF VARIABLE INTEREST ENTITIES

In June 2003, the CICA issued Accounting Guideline No. 15 (AcG-15) "Consolidation of Variable Interest Entities." AcG-15 has been revised to harmonize with the new Financial Accounting Standards Board (FASB) Interpretation No. 46 (FIN 46R) "Consolidation of Variable Interest Entities." AcG-15 requires that an enterprise holding other than a voting interest in a variable interest entity (VIE) could, subject to certain conditions, be required to consolidate the VIE if it is considered its primary beneficiary whereby it would absorb the majority of the VIE's expected losses and/or receive the majority of its expected residual returns. In addition, AcG-15 prescribes certain disclosures for VIEs that are not consolidated but in which an enterprise has a significant variable interest. AcG-15 applies to annual and interim periods beginning on or after November 1, 2004. Effective January 1, 2004, Domtar adopted FIN 46R on a U.S. GAAP basis. There was no initial impact on the consolidated financial statements under U.S. GAAP following the adoption of this recommendation (Note 25). Domtar does not expect this guideline to have an initial impact on its consolidated financial statements under Canadian GAAP.

FINANCIAL INSTRUMENTS

In January 2005, the CICA issued three new accounting proposed Sections in relation with financial instruments: proposed Section 3855 "Financial Instruments – Recognition and Measurement," proposed Section 3865 "Hedges" and proposed Section 1530 "Comprehensive Income." Proposed Sections 3855, 3865 and 1530 apply to fiscal years beginning on or after October 1, 2006.

Proposed Section 3855 expands on Section 3860 "Financial Instruments – Disclosure and Presentation," by prescribing when a financial instrument is to be recognized on the balance sheet and at what amount. It also specifies how financial instrument gains and losses are to be presented.

Proposed Section 3865 provides alternative accounting treatments to proposed Section 3855 for entities, which choose to designate qualifying transactions as hedges for accounting purposes. It replaces and expands on AcG-13 "Hedging Relationships," and the hedging guidance in Section 1650 "Foreign Currency Translation" by specifying how hedge accounting is applied and what disclosures are necessary when it is applied.

Proposed Section 1530 introduces a new requirement to present certain revenues, expenses, gains and losses, that otherwise would not be immediately recorded in income, in a comprehensive income statement with same prominence as other statements that constitute a complete set of financial statements.

The application of these new accounting Sections for financial instruments is not expected to have a significant effect on Domtar's financial position, earnings or cash flows but will require Domtar to present a new statement entitled "Comprehensive Income."

NOTE 3.

MEASUREMENT UNCERTAINTY

IMPAIRMENT OF LONG-LIVED ASSETS

Domtar reviews the carrying amount of long-lived assets when events or changes in circumstances indicate that the carrying value of the assets may not be recoverable through future operations. This is accomplished by determining whether projected undiscounted future cash flows from operations exceed the net carrying amount of the assets as of the assessment date (Step I test). Impaired assets are recorded at fair value, determined principally by using discounted future cash flows expected from their use and eventual disposition (Step II test). Estimates of future cash flows and fair value require judgment and may change over time.

During the fourth quarter of 2004, as a result of operating losses and the potential impact that a weaker U.S. dollar may have on the results of operations, Domtar conducted Step I impairment test on most of the Canadian pulp and paper manufacturing facilities, the Wood segment and three containerboard mills in the Packaging segment.

Estimates of future cash flows used to test the recoverability of a long-lived asset included key assumptions related to trend prices and the long-term forecasted exchange rate for the U.S. dollar. Other significant assumptions are the estimated useful life of the long-lived assets and the effect of the ongoing softwood lumber dispute with the United States.

The trend prices were based on an analysis of external price trends, including RISI, as well as normalized pulp, paper, wood and unbleached kraft linerboard pricing over a business cycle at the mills subjected to the impairment tests.

NOTE 3. MEASUREMENT UNCERTAINTY (CONTINUED)

The forecasted Canadian - U.S. foreign exchange rate assumptions were based on management's best estimates using independent market information, as well as analysis of historical data, trends and cycles. Management expects the longer-term average rate to be between CAN$1.00 = US$0.72 and CAN$1.00 = US$0.75.

Domtar concluded that the recognition of an impairment loss for the business units analyzed was not required.

Certain pulp and paper and packaging mills are particularly sensitive to the key assumptions. Given the inherent imprecision and corresponding importance of the key assumptions used in the impairment test, it is reasonably possible that changes in future conditions may lead management to use different key assumptions, which could require a material change in the net carrying amount of these assets. The total net carrying amount of these mills was $529 million as at December 31, 2004.

During the fourth quarter of 2003, as a result of operating losses at the Lebel-sur-Quévillon, Quebec pulp mill and the Wood segment, Domtar conducted impairment tests of the long-lived assets of these business units. In addition, due to the decision to close one paper machine at the Vancouver, British Columbia paper mill and the potential impact that a weaker U.S. dollar may have on the results of operations of Canadian pulp and paper mills, Domtar also conducted impairment tests of the long-lived assets of the Vancouver paper mill and other Canadian pulp and paper mills. As a result of these tests, in December 2003, Domtar recorded an impairment loss of $201 million related to the impairment of the Lebel-sur-Quévillon pulp mill.

In the Step II test, performed in 2003 on the Lebel-sur-Quévillon pulp mill only, the assumptions used to determine the discounted future cash flows of the business unit were the same as those used in the Step I test, except that future cash flows used were on an after-tax basis and were discounted at the risk-adjusted weighted average cost of capital.

NOTE 4.

UNITED STATES DOLLAR AMOUNTS

The consolidated financial statements are expressed in Canadian dollars and, solely for the convenience of the reader, the 2004 consolidated financial statements and the tables of certain related notes have been translated into U.S. dollars at the year-end rate of CAN$1.00 = US$0.8308. This translation should not be construed as an application of the recommendations relating to the accounting for foreign currency translation, but rather as supplemental information for the reader.

NOTE 5.

BUSINESS ACQUISITIONS

2004

In 2004, Norampac acquired businesses for a cash consideration of $36 million (US$28 million) (the Corporation's proportionate share being $18 million (US$14 million)).

GOODWILL

In 2004, goodwill increased by $7 million related to business acquisitions completed by Norampac.

2003

In 2003, Norampac acquired businesses for a cash consideration of $21 million (US$14 million) and a transfer of assets of $12 million (US$8 million) (the Corporation's proportionate share being $11 million (US$7 million) and $6 million (US$4 million), respectively).

GOODWILL

In 2003, goodwill decreased by $2 million, consisting of a $2 million increase related to business acquisitions completed by Norampac and a $4 million decrease related to foreign currency exchange rate changes.

2002

In 2002, Norampac acquired businesses for a cash consideration of $54 million and a transfer of assets of $14 million (the Corporation's proportionate share being $27 million and $7 million, respectively).

GOODWILL

In 2002, goodwill increased by $17 million related to business acquisitions completed by Norampac.

NOTES TO CONSOLIDATED FINANCIAL STATEMENTS

DECEMBER 31, 2004 (IN MILLIONS OF CANADIAN DOLLARS, UNLESS OTHERWISE NOTED)

NOTE 6.

CLOSURE AND RESTRUCTURING COSTS

In 2004, Domtar sold the St. Catharines, Ontario paper mill, which was closed in 2002, for $1 million to a third party who agreed to purchase it in its existing state. As such, the majority of the remaining closure cost provision was reversed, leaving a balance of $1 million (2003 – $8 million) as at December 31, 2004, representing the remaining severance and commitments and contingencies related to environmental matters.

In 2004, Domtar's management committed to workforce reduction and restructuring plans throughout the Corporation's paper and merchant operations in Canada and the United States. The total severance and termination benefit costs accrued for the year ended December 31, 2004, representing a portion of the severance and termination costs related to the plan, amounted to $42 million (which included $2 million for pension curtailment costs). In addition, training costs of $1 million were incurred for the year ended December 31, 2004. Further costs related to the plan expected to be incurred over 2005 and 2006 include severance and termination costs of $4 million, training costs of $6 million, outplacement costs of $2 million and pension settlements of $3 million, which will be expensed as incurred. To accomplish this plan, Domtar will invest approximately $11 million in capital expenditures over 2005 and 2006. As at December 31, 2004, the balance of the provision was $32 million.

In 2004, Domtar's management decided to permanently shut down the sawmill located in Chapleau, Ontario, resulting in a charge of $14 million in December 2004, including $11 million related to the write-down to the estimated net realizable value of property, plant and equipment and $3 million related to a provision for severance and related costs.

In 2003, Domtar's management decided to permanently shut down one paper machine at the Vancouver, British Columbia paper mill. The decision to close the paper machine resulted in a charge of $29 million in December 2003, including $23 million related to the write-down to the estimated net realizable value of property, plant and equipment, $5 million related to a provision for severance and related costs (for 85 employees), which were contractual obligations as at the time of the decision, and $1 million related to the write-down of certain inventory items and spare parts to their net recoverable amounts. Further costs of $1 million related to the dismantling of the paper machine, net of salvage proceeds, were accrued in the second quarter of 2004, as well as a provision reversal of $2 million regarding severance and related costs. The total of the 2003 to 2005 costs is estimated to be $30 million. As at December 31, 2004, the balance of the provision was $2 million (2003 – $5 million).

In 2002, Domtar announced plans to permanently shut down the St. Catharines, Ontario paper mill and in 2003 the wood products remanufacturing facility in Daveluyville, Quebec and the hardwood lumber operations in Sault Ste. Marie, Ontario. The shutdown of these mills resulted in a charge of $63 million, including $27 million related to the write-down to the estimated net realizable value of property, plant and equipment and $36 million primarily for severance costs, demolition costs, site remediation and other commitments and contingencies related to these closures.

In 2002, Domtar shut down a paper machine at the Nekoosa, Wisconsin paper mill, which was acquired in the third quarter of 2001, as a result of a study that was part of the original acquisition plan. In accordance with CICA recommendations, charges related to the closure of this paper machine amounting to $10 million (US$6 million) have been accounted for under the purchase price allocation of the assets acquired and liabilities assumed as of the acquisition date, and thus did not affect the results for the year ended December 31, 2002.

The following table provides a reconciliation of all closure and restructuring cost provisions for the years ended December 31, 2004 and 2003:

	2004	2004	2003
	US$ (NOTE 4)	$	$
Balance at beginning of year	11	**13**	26
Severance payments	(10)	**(12)**	(9)
Reduction in the provision for demolition costs	–	–	(5)
Reversal of provision	(8)	**(10)**	–
Proceeds on disposition	1	**1**	–
Other	–	–	(4)
Additions			
Labor costs	37	**45**	5
Dismantling costs	1	**1**	–
Balance at end of year	32	**38**	13

NOTES TO CONSOLIDATED FINANCIAL STATEMENTS
DECEMBER 31, 2004 (IN MILLIONS OF CANADIAN DOLLARS, UNLESS OTHERWISE NOTED)

NOTE 7.

FINANCING EXPENSES

	2004	**2004**	2003	2002
	US$ (NOTE 4)	$	$	$
Interest on long-term debt	133	**160**	158	185
Exchange gains on long-term debt	(4)	**(5)**	(9)	–
Receivables securitization	5	**6**	12	14
Net interest recoveries related to interest rate swap contracts	(2)	**(2)**	(2)	(11)
Refinancing expenses (a)	–	**–**	17	–
Amortization of deferred net gain on early settlements of interest rate swap contracts	(12)	**(14)**	(4)	–
Amortization of debt issue costs and other	6	**7**	1	6
	126	**152**	173	194
Less: Income from short-term investments	1	**1**	1	–
Capitalized interest	2	**3**	3	2
	123	**148**	169	192
Cash payments (cash receipts)				
Interest, net of interest income and amounts capitalized	130	**156**	160	185
Net cash receipts related to interest rate swap contracts	(17)	**(20)**	–	(58)
	113	**136**	160	127

(a) The Refinancing expenses for the year ended December 31, 2003, include $10 million representing Domtar's proportionate share of Norampac's debt refinancing expenses and $7 million representing the Corporation's debt refinancing expenses. Refinancing of long-term debt is described in Note 15.

NOTES TO CONSOLIDATED FINANCIAL STATEMENTS
DECEMBER 31, 2004 (IN MILLIONS OF CANADIAN DOLLARS, UNLESS OTHERWISE NOTED)

NOTE 8.

INCOME TAXES

The following table provides a reconciliation of income taxes computed at the Canadian statutory rate to income tax expense (recovery) presented on the Consolidated earnings:

	2004	2004	2003	2002
	US$ (NOTE 4)	$	$	$
Combined basic Canadian federal and provincial tax rate (statutory income tax rate)	33.7%	33.7%	35.2%	37.1%
Income tax expense (recovery) based on statutory income tax rate	(27)	(32)	(92)	73
Large corporation tax	5	6	6	7
Canadian manufacturing and processing activities	1	1	5	(2)
Foreign rate differential	(21)	(25)	(18)	(21)
Reassessment of prior years by tax authorities	(3)	(4)	–	–
Impact of increase in income tax rate on future income taxes	–	–	31	–
Other	2	2	1	(1)
Income tax expense (recovery)	(43)	(52)	(67)	56
Income tax expense (recovery)				
Current	19	23	14	25
Future	(62)	(75)	(81)	31
	(43)	(52)	(67)	56

Net cash payments for income taxes in 2004, net of cash receipts, amounted to $9 million (2003 – receipts amounted to $1 million; 2002 – payments amounted to $3 million).

NOTES TO CONSOLIDATED FINANCIAL STATEMENTS

DECEMBER 31, 2004 (IN MILLIONS OF CANADIAN DOLLARS, UNLESS OTHERWISE NOTED)

NOTE 8. INCOME TAXES (CONTINUED)

The following table provides the geographic distribution of the income tax expense (recovery):

	2004	**2004**	2003	2002
	US$ (NOTE 4)	$	$ RESTATED (NOTE 2)	$
Earnings (loss) before income taxes				
Canada	(177)	**(213)**	(361)	17
Foreign	99	**119**	101	180
	(78)	**(94)**	(260)	197
Current income taxes				
Canada	9	**11**	12	20
Foreign	10	**12**	2	5
	19	**23**	14	25
Future income taxes				
Canada	(52)	**(63)**	(96)	(9)
Foreign	(10)	**(12)**	15	40
	(62)	**(75)**	(81)	31

COMPONENTS OF FUTURE INCOME TAX ASSETS AND LIABILITIES	2004	**2004**	2003
	US$ (NOTE 4)	$	$
Future income tax assets			
Accounting provisions not deductible for tax purposes	69	**83**	108
Losses and other deductions carryforward	297	**358**	279
Deferred credits	37	**44**	44
Capital losses carryforward	9	**11**	8
	412	**496**	439
Future income tax liabilities			
Property, plant and equipment	(740)	**(890)**	(886)
Pension and other employee future benefit plans	(14)	**(17)**	(17)
Impact of foreign exchange on long-term debt	(46)	**(55)**	(33)
Other	(3)	**(4)**	(5)
	(803)	**(966)**	(941)
Total net future income tax liability	(391)	**(470)**	(502)
Net current future income tax asset	72	**87**	60
Net non-current future income tax liability	(463)	**(557)**	(562)
	(391)	**(470)**	(502)

As at December 31, 2004, Domtar had operating losses of $951 million. These operating losses are set to expire between 2010 and 2024.

NOTE 9.

EARNINGS (LOSS) PER SHARE

The basic net earnings (loss) per share is computed by dividing the net earnings (loss) applicable to common shares by the weighted average number of common shares outstanding during the year.

The diluted net earnings (loss) per share is computed by dividing the net earnings (loss) applicable to common shares by the weighted average number of common shares outstanding during the year, plus the effects of dilutive common share equivalents such as options and share purchase loans. The diluted net earnings (loss) per share is calculated using the treasury method, as if all common share equivalents had been exercised at the beginning of the year, or the date of the issuance, as the case may be, and that the funds obtained thereby were used to purchase common shares of Domtar at the average trading price of the common shares during the period. Stock options to purchase common shares are not included in the computation of diluted net earnings (loss) per share in periods when net losses are recorded, given that they are anti-dilutive.

The following table provides the reconciliation between basic and diluted earnings (loss) per share:

	2004	2004	2003	2002
	US$ (NOTE 4)	$	$ RESTATED (NOTE 2)	$
Net earnings (loss)	(35)	(42)	(193)	141
Dividend requirements of preferred shares	1	1	2	1
Net earnings (loss) applicable to common shares	(36)	(43)	(195)	140
Weighted average number of common shares outstanding (millions)	228.7	228.7	227.3	227.2
Effect of dilutive stock options (millions)	–	–	–	0.9
Weighted average number of diluted common shares outstanding (millions)	228.7	228.7	227.3	228.1
Basic earnings (loss) per share (in dollars)	(0.16)	(0.19)	(0.86)	0.62
Diluted earnings (loss) per share (in dollars)	(0.16)	(0.19)	(0.86)	0.61

NOTE 9. EARNINGS (LOSS) PER SHARE (CONTINUED)

The following table provides the securities that could potentially dilute basic earnings (loss) per share in the future but were not included in the computation of diluted earnings (loss) per share because to do so would have been anti-dilutive for the periods presented:

	2004	2003	2002
Number of shares			
Options	**5,306,553**	5,688,264	2,163,250
Bonus shares	**226,693**	211,786	–
Rights	**84,500**	46,000	–

NOTE 10.
_____

RECEIVABLES

	2004	**2004**	2003
	US$ (NOTE 4)	$	$
Trade receivables	56	**67**	37
Subordinate interest in securitized receivables	93	**112**	106
Less: Allowance for doubtful accounts	(13)	**(16)**	(18)
	136	**163**	125
Silvicultural credits receivable	11	**13**	11
Sales taxes receivable	14	**17**	17
Other receivables	33	**40**	44
Receivables	194	**233**	197

RECEIVABLES SECURITIZATION

Domtar uses securitization of its receivables as a source of financing by reducing its working capital requirements. Domtar's securitizations consist of the sale of receivables, or the sale of senior beneficial interest in them, to special purpose trusts managed by financial institutions for multiple sellers of receivables. The agreements normally allow the daily sale of new receivables to replace those that have been collected. They also limit the cash that can

NOTES TO CONSOLIDATED FINANCIAL STATEMENTS

DECEMBER 31, 2004 (IN MILLIONS OF CANADIAN DOLLARS, UNLESS OTHERWISE NOTED)

be received from the sale of the senior beneficial interest. Such sales of receivables are contingent upon annual renewals and retaining specified credit ratings. The subordinate interest retained by Domtar is included in "Receivables" and will be collected only after the senior beneficial interest has been settled. The book value of the retained subordinated interests approximates fair value.

Domtar retains responsibility for servicing the receivables sold but does not record a servicing asset or liability as the fees received by Domtar for this service approximate the fair value of the services rendered.

In 2004, a net charge of $6 million (2003 – $12 million; 2002 – $14 million) resulted from the programs described below and was included in "Financing expenses."

U.S. ACCOUNTS RECEIVABLE PROGRAM

In January 2002, Domtar entered into an agreement, which was renewed in December 2004 and expires in December 2005, for the securitization of U.S. receivables for a maximum cash consideration of $211 million (US$175 million).

At December 31, the following balances were outstanding under this program:

	2004		2003	
	$	**US$**	$	US$
Receivables sold	**267**	**222**	261	202
Senior beneficial interest held by third parties	**(178)**	**(148)**	(174)	(135)
Subordinate interest in securitized receivables				
retained by Domtar	**89**	**74**	87	67

In 2004, the net cash inflow from the sale of senior beneficial interests in the U.S. receivables was $17 million (US$14 million) (2003 – $13 million (US$10 million); 2002 – $8 million (US$5 million)) and was included in the Consolidated statement of cash flows as a source of cash from receivables.

CANADIAN ACCOUNTS RECEIVABLE PROGRAM

In December 2000, Domtar entered into an agreement, which was renewed in December 2003 and expires in December 2005, for the securitization of Canadian receivables for a maximum cash consideration of $75 million.

NOTE 10. RECEIVABLES (CONTINUED)

At December 31, the following balances were outstanding under this program:

	2004	2003
	$	$
Receivables sold	81	72
Senior beneficial interest held by third parties	(58)	(53)
Subordinate interest in securitized receivables retained by Domtar	23	19

In 2004, the net cash inflow from the sale of senior beneficial interests in the Canadian receivables was $5 million (2003 – cash outflow of $13 million; 2002 – cash inflow of $18 million) and was included in the Consolidated statement of cash flows as a source or use of cash from receivables.

NOTE 11.

INVENTORIES

	2004	2004	2003
	US$ (NOTE 4)	$	$
Work in process and finished goods	324	**390**	363
Raw materials	131	**157**	138
Operating and maintenance supplies	146	**176**	169
	601	**723**	670

NOTE 12.

PROPERTY, PLANT AND EQUIPMENT

	2004			2004
	NET CARRYING AMOUNT	COST	ACCUMULATED AMORTIZATION	NET CARRYING AMOUNT
	US$ (NOTE 4)	$	$	$
Machinery and equipment	2,798	5,559	2,191	3,368
Buildings	432	969	449	520
Timber limits and land	148	209	31	178
Assets under construction	124	149	–	149
	3,502	6,886	2,671	4,215

			2003
	COST	ACCUMULATED AMORTIZATION	NET CARRYING AMOUNT
	$	$ RESTATED (NOTE 2)	$ RESTATED (NOTE 2)
Machinery and equipment	5,590	1,942	3,648
Buildings	920	384	536
Timber limits and land	210	28	182
Assets under construction	167	–	167
	6,887	2,354	4,533

As at December 31, 2004, a net carrying amount of $10 million (2003–$11 million) included in Buildings is held under capital leases ($12 million for cost (2003–$12 million) and $2 million for accumulated amortization (2003–$1 million)).

NOTES TO CONSOLIDATED FINANCIAL STATEMENTS
DECEMBER 31, 2004 (IN MILLIONS OF CANADIAN DOLLARS, UNLESS OTHERWISE NOTED)

NOTE 13.

OTHER ASSETS

	2004	**2004**	2003
	US$ (NOTE 4)	**$**	$
Accrued benefit asset – defined benefit pension plans (NOTE 22)	152	**183**	153
Investment tax credits receivable	22	**26**	–
Unamortized debt issue costs	15	**18**	26
Investments and advances	12	**15**	14
Discount on long-term debt	9	**11**	13
Other	10	**12**	6
	220	**265**	212

NOTE 14.

TRADE AND OTHER PAYABLES

	2004	**2004**	2003
	US$ (NOTE 4)	**$**	$ RESTATED (NOTE 2)
Trade payables	308	**371**	424
Payroll-related accruals	98	**118**	110
Accrued interest	27	**33**	34
Payables on capital projects	8	**10**	18
Rebates accruals	11	**13**	4
Accrued benefit liability – defined benefit pension plans (NOTE 22)	–	**–**	1
Accrued benefit liability – other employee future benefit plans (NOTE 23)	5	**6**	1
Provision for environment and other asset retirement obligations (NOTE 17)	18	**21**	19
Closure and restructuring costs excluding costs for defined benefit pension plans and site remediation (NOTE 6)	30	**36**	8
Other	38	**46**	33
	543	**654**	652

NOTES TO CONSOLIDATED FINANCIAL STATEMENTS
DECEMBER 31, 2004 (IN MILLIONS OF CANADIAN DOLLARS, UNLESS OTHERWISE NOTED)

NOTE 15.

LONG-TERM DEBT

	MATURITY	2004	2004	2003
		US$ (NOTE 4)	$	$
The Corporation				
Unsecured debentures and notes				
8.75% Notes (2004 and 2003–US$150)	2006	150	181	194
10% Debentures	2011	68	82	82
7.875% Notes (2004 and 2003–US$600)	2011	600	722	775
5.375% Notes (2004 and 2003–US$350)	2013	350	421	452
9.5% Debentures (2004 and 2003–US$125)	2016	125	150	162
10.85% Debentures	2017	63	75	75
Unsecured term loan (2004–US$71; 2003–US$76)	2006	71	86	99
Unsecured revolving credit facility	2006	112	135	30
Capital lease obligations	2028	9	11	11
Other		6	7	3
		1,554	1,870	1,883
Norampac				
Unsecured notes				
6.75% Notes (2004 and 2003–US$125)	2013	125	150	161
Secured revolving credit facility				
(2004–CAN$9 and €1; 2003–CAN$10 and €1)	2008	8	10	11
Other		3	4	4
		136	164	176
		1,690	2,034	2,059
Less: Due within one year		7	8	5
		1,683	2,026	2,054

As at December 31, 2004, principal long-term debt repayments, including capital lease obligations, in each of the next five years amounted to:

	2005	2006	2007	2008	2009
	$	$	$	$	$
	8	397	2	12	3

NOTES TO CONSOLIDATED FINANCIAL STATEMENTS

DECEMBER 31, 2004 (IN MILLIONS OF CANADIAN DOLLARS, UNLESS OTHERWISE NOTED)

NOTE 15. LONG-TERM DEBT (CONTINUED)

THE CORPORATION

Unsecured debentures and notes

The 10% and 10.85% debentures each have purchase fund requirements, whereby the Corporation has undertaken to make all reasonable efforts to purchase quarterly, for cancellation, a portion of the aggregate principal amount of the debentures at prices not exceeding par.

On November 18, 2003, the Corporation issued $456 million (US$350 million) 5.375% notes due in 2013 at an issue price of $452 million (US$347 million). The Corporation used the proceeds from this issuance to reduce the unsecured term loan.

In the first quarter of 2004, the Corporation terminated, prior to maturity, its interest rate swap contracts entered into in 2003. As described in Note 19, these swaps had been designated as hedges of a portion of the interest on the 5.375% notes payable.

Bank facility

The Corporation has a bank facility comprised of a US$71 million unsecured term loan and a US$500 million unsecured revolving credit facility that expires in 2006.

The unsecured term loan bears interest based on the U.S. dollar LIBOR rate or U.S. prime rate, plus a margin that varies with Domtar's credit rating. Repayment of 11% (2003 – 17%) of the balance currently outstanding through April 30, 2006 is required prior to its maturity in August 2006. In 2004, the Corporation repaid $7 million (US$5 million) (2003 – $534 million (US$404 million)) of this term loan.

Borrowings under the revolving credit facility bear interest at a rate based on Canadian dollar bankers' acceptance or U.S. dollar LIBOR rate or prime rate, plus a margin that varies with Domtar's credit rating. The revolving credit facility also requires commitment fees in accordance with standard banking practices.

As at December 31, 2004, $135 million (2003 – $37 million) of borrowings under the unsecured revolving credit facility were outstanding, of which nil (2003 – $7 million) was in the form of overdraft and included in "Bank indebtedness," and $135 million (2003 – $30 million) were included in "Long-term debt." In addition, as at December 31, 2004, the Corporation had outstanding letters of credit pursuant to this bank credit for an amount of $10 million (2003 – $10 million). The Corporation also has other outstanding letters of credit for an amount of $3 million. A provision of $5 million was recorded related to letters of credit.

In 2004, the interest rates on outstanding borrowings under the bank facilities ranged from 2.34% to 4.55% (2003 – from 2.31% to 4.80%).

The Corporation's borrowing agreements contain restrictive covenants. In particular, the Corporation's bank facility requires compliance with certain financial ratios on a quarterly basis.

Certain debt agreements require the Corporation to indemnify the parties in the event of changes in elements such as withholding tax regulations. As the nature and scope of such indemnifications are contingent on future events, none of which can be foreseen as at December 31, 2004, and the structure of such transactions makes these events unlikely, no provisions have been recorded in the consolidated financial statements.

NORAMPAC

Norampac's debt is non-recourse to the Corporation. On May 28, 2003, Norampac completed a series of financial transactions to substantially refinance all of its existing credit facilities, except those of its joint venture. The following amounts represent the Corporation's proportionate share.

In 2003, Norampac entered into a new five-year secured revolving credit facility of $175 million. The new facility replaced a secured reducing revolving credit facility of $39 million and a $75 million secured revolving facility. The new revolving credit facility is secured by all the inventories and receivables of Norampac Inc. and its North American subsidiaries and by property, plant and equipment at two of its containerboard mills and three of its converting facilities. Also, this facility requires compliance with certain covenants. As at December 31, 2004, the Corporation's proportionate share of assets secured under the new revolving credit facility relating to receivables, inventories and property, plant and equipment amounted to $97 million (2003 – $89 million), $69 million (2003 – $65 million) and $218 million (2003 – $218 million), respectively. Borrowings under this credit facility bear interest at floating rates plus a borrowing margin based on Norampac's credit rating.

In 2003, Norampac issued unsecured Senior notes for an aggregate amount of $173 million (US$125 million). The notes bear a 6.75% coupon and will mature in 2013. The notes require compliance with certain covenants. The aggregate proceeds of these two transactions were used to repay the existing credit facilities for an amount of approximately $34 million at the time of the refinancing and to redeem both the $104 million (US$75 million) 9.5% notes and the $50 million 9.375% notes due in 2008.

As at December 31, 2004, $10 million (2003 – $11 million) of borrowings under the secured revolving credit facility were outstanding. In addition, as at December 31, 2004, Norampac had outstanding letters of credit pursuant to this bank credit for an amount of $6 million (2003 – $4 million). No provision was recorded related to outstanding letters of credit.

In 2004, the interest rates on outstanding borrowings under the revolving credit facility ranged from 3.04% to 3.69% (2003 – from 3.06% to 4.05%).

NOTES TO CONSOLIDATED FINANCIAL STATEMENTS
DECEMBER 31, 2004 (IN MILLIONS OF CANADIAN DOLLARS, UNLESS OTHERWISE NOTED)

NOTE 16.

Other liabilities and deferred credits

	2004	**2004**	2003
	US$ (NOTE 4)	$	$ RESTATED (NOTE 2)
Other liabilities			
Accrued benefit liability – other employee future benefit plans (NOTE 23)	73	**88**	89
Accrued benefit liability – defined benefit pension plans (NOTE 22)	27	**32**	37
Provision for contracts assumed	3	**4**	10
Provision for environment and other asset retirement obligations	30	**36**	44
Other	32	**38**	40
Deferred credits			
Deferred gain on contribution of net assets to Norampac	32	**39**	44
Deferred net gain on early settlements of interest rate swap contracts	32	**39**	36
Unrealized foreign exchange on translation of long-term debt	40	**48**	44
Investment tax credits and other	16	**19**	16
	285	**343**	360

ASSET RETIREMENT OBLIGATIONS

The asset retirement obligations are principally linked to landfill capping obligations, asbestos removal obligations and demolition of certain abandoned buildings. As at December 31, 2004, Domtar has estimated the net present value of its asset retirement obligations to be $25 million (2003 – $26 million); the present value was based on probability weighted undiscounted cash flows of $37 million (2003 – $41 million). The majority of asset retirement obligations are estimated to be settled prior to December 31, 2020. However, some settlement scenarios call for obligations to be settled as late as December 31, 2040. Domtar's credit adjusted risk-free rates were used to calculate the net present value of the asset retirement obligations. The rates used vary between 4.25% and 6.80%, based on the prevailing rate at the moment of recognition of the liability and on its settlement period.

The following table reconciles Domtar's asset retirement obligations:

	2004	**2004**	2003
	US$ (NOTE 4)	$	$ RESTATED (NOTE 2)
Asset retirement obligations, beginning of year	22	**26**	31
Liabilities incurred during the year	1	**1**	–
Revisions to estimated cash flows	(2)	**(2)**	–
Liabilities settled during the year	(1)	**(1)**	(3)
Accretion expense	2	**2**	2
Effect of foreign currency exchange rate change	(1)	**(1)**	(4)
Asset retirement obligations, end of year	21	**25**	26

NOTE 17.

COMMITMENTS AND CONTINGENCIES

ENVIRONMENT

Domtar is subject to environmental laws and regulations enacted by federal, provincial, state and local authorities.

In 2004, Domtar's operating expenditures for environmental matters, as described in Note 1, amounted to $69 million (2003 – $70 million; 2002 – $82 million).

Domtar made capital expenditures for environmental matters of $22 million in 2004 (2003 – $7 million; 2002 – $20 million) for the improvement of air emissions, effluent treatment and remedial actions to address environmental compliance. At this time, Domtar cannot reasonably estimate the additional capital expenditures that may be required. However, management expects any additional required expenditure would not have a material adverse effect on Domtar's financial position, earnings or cash flows.

Domtar continues to take remedial action under its Care and Control Program at a number of former operating sites, especially in the wood preserving sector, due to possible soil, sediment or groundwater contamination. The investigation and remediation process is lengthy and subject to the uncertainties of changes in legal requirements, technological developments and the allocation of liability among potentially responsible parties.

NOTE 17.   COMMITMENTS AND CONTINGENCIES (CONTINUED)

While Domtar believes that it has determined the costs for environmental matters likely to be incurred based on known information, Domtar's ongoing efforts to identify potential environmental concerns that may be associated with its properties may lead to future environmental investigations. These efforts may result in the determination of additional environmental costs and liabilities which cannot be reasonably estimated at this time.

As at December 31, 2004, Domtar had a provision of $57 million (2003 – $63 million) for environmental matters and other asset retirement obligations. Additional costs, not known or identifiable, could be incurred for remediation efforts. Based on policies and procedures in place to monitor environmental exposure, management believes that such additional remediation costs would not have a material adverse effect on Domtar's financial position, earnings or cash flows.

In addition, the pulp and paper industry in the United States is subject to Cluster Rules and Boiler M.A.C.T. (maximum achievable control technology) Rules that further regulate effluent and air emissions. Domtar complies with all present regulations and anticipates spending approximately $52 million over the next three years to meet such requirements.

As at December 31, 2004, anticipated payments in each of the next five years were as follows:

	2005	2006	2007	2008	2009	THEREAFTER	TOTAL
	$	$	$	$	$	$	$
Environmental provision	21	7	2	2	2	23	57
Cluster Rules obligation	14	8	–	–	–	–	22
Boiler M.A.C.T. Rules obligation	–	18	12	–	–	–	30

CONTINGENCIES

In the normal course of operations, Domtar becomes involved in various legal actions mostly related to contract disputes, patent infringements, environmental and product warranty claims, and labor issues. While the final outcome with respect to actions outstanding or pending as at December 31, 2004, cannot be predicted with certainty, it is management's opinion that their resolution will not have a material adverse effect on Domtar's financial position, earnings or cash flows.

In April 2003, the Canadian Competition Bureau began an investigation of Canada's major distributors of carbonless paper and other fine paper products, including Domtar. Although the investigation is continuing, no new information has been presented that would allow Domtar to predict the outcome of this investigation or any impact it may have on Domtar.

NOTES TO CONSOLIDATED FINANCIAL STATEMENTS
DECEMBER 31, 2004 (IN MILLIONS OF CANADIAN DOLLARS, UNLESS OTHERWISE NOTED)

E.B. EDDY ACQUISITION

On July 31, 1998, Domtar acquired all of the issued and outstanding shares of E.B. Eddy Limited and E.B. Eddy Paper, Inc. (E.B. Eddy), an integrated producer of specialty paper and wood products. The purchase agreement includes a purchase price adjustment whereby, in the event of the acquisition by a third party of more than 50% of the shares of the Corporation in specified circumstances, the Corporation may have had to pay up to a maximum of $120 million, an amount which is gradually declining over a 25-year period. As at December 31, 2004, the maximum amount of the purchase price adjustment was $110 million. No provision was recorded for this potential purchase price adjustment.

LEASE AND OTHER COMMERCIAL COMMITMENTS

The Corporation has entered into operating leases for property, plant and equipment. The Corporation also has commitments to purchase property, plant and equipment, roundwood, wood chips, gas, electricity and certain chemicals. Minimum future payments under these operating leases and other commercial commitments, determined as at December 31, 2004, were as follows:

	2005	2006	2007	2008	2009	THEREAFTER	TOTAL
	$	$	$	$	$	$	$
Operating leases	30	23	16	11	9	17	106
Other commercial commitments	81	34	34	26	27	18	220

Total operating lease expense amounted to $38 million in 2004 (2003 – $38 million; 2002 – $45 million).

NOTE 17. COMMITMENTS AND CONTINGENCIES (CONTINUED)

Norampac has entered into operating leases for property, plant and equipment. Norampac also has commitments to purchase property, plant and equipment, gas, electricity and steam. The Corporation's proportionate share of Norampac's minimum future payments under these operating leases and other commercial commitments, determined as at December 31, 2004, were as follows:

	2005	2006	2007	2008	2009	THEREAFTER	TOTAL
	$	$	$	$	$	$	$
Operating leases	6	6	4	4	3	7	30
Other commercial commitments	40	26	21	20	12	76	195

The Corporation's proportionate share of Norampac's total operating leases expense amounted to $7 million in 2004 (2003 – $8 million; 2002 – $8 million).

GUARANTEES

Indemnifications

In the normal course of business, the Corporation offers indemnifications relating to the sale of its businesses and real estate. In general, these indemnifications may relate to claims from past business operations, the failure to abide by covenants and the breach of representations and warranties included in the sales agreements. Typically, such representations and warranties relate to taxation, environmental, product and employee matters. The terms of these indemnification agreements are generally for an unlimited period of time. As at December 31, 2004, the Corporation is unable to estimate the potential maximum liabilities for these types of indemnification guarantees as the amounts are contingent upon the outcome of future events, the nature and likelihood of which cannot be reasonably estimated at this time. Accordingly, no provisions have been recorded. These indemnifications have not yielded significant expenses in the past.

Leases

The Corporation has guaranteed to various lessors $8 million of residual value of its assets under operating leases with expiry dates in 2006. If the fair value of the assets at the end of the lease terms are lower than the residual values guaranteed, the Corporation would be held liable for the shortfall. The Corporation's management does not believe these are likely to be called upon and, as such, no provisions have been recorded with respect to these guarantees.

NOTE 18.

STATED CAPITAL

PREFERRED SHARES

The outstanding preferred shares at December 31, were as follows:

	2004	**2004**			2003	
	US$ (NOTE 4)	NUMBER OF SHARES	**$**		NUMBER OF SHARES	$
Preferred shares						
Series A	2	**69,576**	**2**		69,576	2
Series B	31	**1,470,000**	**37**		1,590,000	40
	33		**39**			42

The authorized preferred shares consist of preferred shares issuable in an unlimited number of series, ranking equal with respect to the payment of dividends and the distribution of assets.

The Series A Preferred shares are non-voting and redeemable at the Corporation's option at $25.00 per share since April 1, 1994. These shares carry a cumulative cash dividend per share of $2.25 per annum.

The Series B Preferred shares are non-voting and redeemable at the Corporation's option at $25.00 per share. These shares carry a cumulative cash dividend equivalent to 72% of the bank prime rate.

The Corporation has undertaken to make all reasonable efforts to purchase quarterly, for cancellation, 1% of the number of Series A and Series B Preferred shares outstanding on April 2, 1992, at prices not exceeding $25.00 per share. In connection therewith, preferred shares purchased for cancellation were as follows:

	2004		2003		2002	
	NUMBER OF SHARES	AVERAGE PRICE PER SHARE	NUMBER OF SHARES	AVERAGE PRICE PER SHARE	NUMBER OF SHARES	AVERAGE PRICE PER SHARE
		$		$		$
Series B	**120,000**	**24.68**	120,000	23.48	120,000	23.66

NOTE 18. STATED CAPITAL (CONTINUED)

COMMON SHARES

The Corporation is authorized to issue an unlimited number of common shares. In 2004, a cash dividend of $0.24 per share has been paid on these shares (2003 – $0.215 per share; 2002 – $0.14 per share). The changes in the number of outstanding common shares and their aggregate stated value from January 1, 2002 to December 31, 2004, were as follows:

	2004	2004	**2004**
	US$ (NOTE 4)	NUMBER OF SHARES	$
Balance at beginning of year	1,469	**228,860,806**	**1,768**
Shares issued			
Stock option and share purchase plans	17	**1,376,550**	**20**
Balance before share purchase financing agreements	1,486	**230,237,356**	**1,788**
Share purchase financing agreements	(11)	**(947,105)**	**(13)**
Balance at end of year	1,475	**229,290,251**	**1,775**
Book value per common share at end of year	7.27		**8.75**

	2003	2003	2002	2002
	NUMBER OF SHARES	$	NUMBER OF SHARES	$
Balance at beginning of year	227,680,352	1,752	226,202,379	1,731
Shares issued				
Stock option and share purchase plans	1,180,454	16	1,477,973	21
Balance before share purchase financing agreements	228,860,806	1,768	227,680,352	1,752
Share purchase financing agreements	(922,994)	(12)	–	–
Balance at end of year	227,937,812	1,756	227,680,352	1,752
Book value per common share at end of year		9.34		11.02

Book value per common share is the sum of the stated value of common shares, contributed surplus, retained earnings and accumulated foreign currency translation adjustments divided by the number of common shares outstanding at year-end.

NOTES TO CONSOLIDATED FINANCIAL STATEMENTS

DECEMBER 31, 2004 (IN MILLIONS OF CANADIAN DOLLARS, UNLESS OTHERWISE NOTED)

As at December 31, 2004, the Corporation had a receivable from its employees of $13 million (2003 – $12 million; 2002 – $11 million) related to share purchase loans granted to them. These shares are held in trust as security for the loans that are interest bearing at the dividend rate and with defined repayment terms not exceeding 10 years. At the end of the year, there were 947,105 shares (2003 – 922,994 shares; 2002 – 1,000,333 shares) held in trust in respect to employee loans for which the market value was $14.50 (2003 – $16.25; 2002 – $15.70) per share. These loans were included in "Other assets" until December 31, 2002, and were included as a reduction of "Common shares" thereafter.

EXECUTIVE STOCK OPTION AND SHARE PURCHASE PLAN

Under the Executive Stock Option and Share Purchase Plan (Plan), options and rights may be granted to selected eligible employees. Options are granted at a price equal to the market value on the day immediately preceding the date the options were granted and generally expire 10 years after the date of the grant. Normally, one quarter of the options may be exercised at each anniversary date of the grant. Rights permit eligible employees to purchase shares at 90% of the quoted market value on the day immediately preceding the date the rights were granted, and provide for a one-for-four bonus share to be issued on the third anniversary date of the grant of the rights.

In 2003, a new performance feature was introduced to the Plan for all grants starting with 2003 going-forward. Options granted before 2003 are not affected by this new feature. Pursuant to this new feature, the granted stock options will vest in four increments of 25% on each anniversary date of the grant, provided the performance of Domtar's common share price is equal to or exceeds the average performance of an index composed of the S&P 500 Materials (U.S.) index (50%) and the S&P/TSX Materials (Canada) index (50%). On each anniversary date of the grant, the average closing price of Domtar's common shares, during the 20 consecutive trading days on the Toronto Stock Exchange immediately preceding each anniversary date of the grant, is used to measure the performance of Domtar's common share price and is compared to the average performance of the index during the same reference period. The relevant annual portion only vests on a given anniversary date if the performance of Domtar's common share price equals or exceeds the average index during the relevant reference period. Should this not be the case, the annual portion will not vest but may vest on any following anniversary date if the foregoing test, applied on a cumulative basis, is satisfied on a subsequent anniversary date over the vesting period of four years. Any annual portion which has not vested on or before the end of the vesting period of the option will automatically lapse on the expiry date. The new performance options have a term of 10 years and will expire in February 2013.

NOTES TO CONSOLIDATED FINANCIAL STATEMENTS
DECEMBER 31, 2004 (IN MILLIONS OF CANADIAN DOLLARS, UNLESS OTHERWISE NOTED)

NOTE 18. STATED CAPITAL (CONTINUED)

In 2001, all of the 900,000 performance options granted to the members of the Management Committee in March 1997 became void as a result of not meeting the specified conditions to exercise the options based on the market value of the Corporation's common shares. A new performance option program was then approved in June 2001, and 1,050,000 stock options were granted to members of the Management Committee. Pursuant to this grant, and except in certain specified circumstances, there was no prorata or early vesting prior to January 1, 2004, at which time the options became fully vested if the holder of the options was still an employee of Domtar. After vesting, the options may not be exercised unless both of the following two conditions have been met: 1) at any time between January 1, 2001 and December 31, 2003, the weighted average trading price of the Corporation's common shares during 20 consecutive trading days on the Toronto Stock Exchange has reached or exceeded $16.70, $18.51 or $20.32, whereupon 25%, 50% or 100%, respectively, of the options granted become exercisable; and 2) the appreciation in the market value of the Corporation's common shares between January 1, 2001 and the exercise date is equal to or exceeds the increase in the Standard & Poor's U.S. Paper & Forest Products index during the same period. As at December 31, 2004, only 25% of the options are exercisable, provided the above-mentioned conditions are met, and the remaining 75% have been cancelled as the objectives of the program have not been attained.

The fair value of options granted during the years ended December 31, 2004, 2003 and 2002 was estimated using the Black-Scholes option-pricing model with the following weighted–average assumptions:

	2004	2003	2002
Risk-free interest rate	**4.2%**	5.2%	5.2%
Annual dividends per shares (in dollars)	**$0.24**	$0.14	$0.14
Expected lives (years)	**6**	6	6
Volatility	**33.4%**	34.0%	34.4%
Estimated realization percentage-performance options	**69.8%**	69.8%	N/A
Weighted average fair value of options granted during the year (in dollars per option)	**$3.68**	$4.36	$6.54

NOTES TO CONSOLIDATED FINANCIAL STATEMENTS

DECEMBER 31, 2004 (IN MILLIONS OF CANADIAN DOLLARS, UNLESS OTHERWISE NOTED)

Changes in the number of options outstanding were as follows:

	2004	
	NUMBER OF OPTIONS	WEIGHTED AVERAGE EXERCISE PRICE
		$
Outstanding at beginning of year	5,688,264	14.22
Granted	1,266,000	15.53
Exercised	(540,270)	11.57
Cancelled	(1,107,441)	14.08
Outstanding at end of year	5,306,553	14.83
Options exercisable at end of year	2,287,587	13.79

	2003		2002	
	NUMBER OF OPTIONS	WEIGHTED AVERAGE EXERCISE PRICE	NUMBER OF OPTIONS	WEIGHTED AVERAGE EXERCISE PRICE
		$		$
Outstanding at beginning of year	4,920,882	13.56	4,573,233	12.29
Granted	1,243,850	15.95	1,212,000	16.52
Exercised	(356,105)	10.61	(614,827)	9.99
Cancelled	(120,363)	15.45	(249,524)	13.51
Outstanding at end of year	5,688,264	14.22	4,920,882	13.56
Options exercisable at end of year	1,988,289	12.98	1,533,085	11.84

The following table summarizes the information about options outstanding and exercisable as at December 31, 2004:

	OPTIONS OUTSTANDING			OPTIONS EXERCISABLE	
RANGE OF EXERCISE PRICES	NUMBER OF OPTIONS	WEIGHTED AVERAGE REMAINING CONTRACTUAL LIFE	WEIGHTED AVERAGE EXERCISE PRICE	NUMBER OF OPTIONS	WEIGHTED AVERAGE EXERCISE PRICE
			$		$
$9.12 – $11.00	576,336	2.8	10.36	576,336	10.36
$11.01 – $12.75	609,042	5.6	12.13	430,185	12.14
$12.76 – $16.52	4,121,175	7.6	15.86	1,281,066	15.88
	5,306,553	6.8	14.83	2,287,587	13.79

NOTE 18. STATED CAPITAL (CONTINUED)

During the year, 353,900 shares (2003 – 320,350; 2002 – 358,472) were issued pursuant to the exercise of rights and 52,730 bonus shares (2003 – 41,169; 2002 – 40,878) were issued. The total expense recognized in Domtar's results of operations related to these rights and bonus shares amounted to $2 million in 2004 (2003 – $2 million; 2002 – $1 million). As at December 31, 2004, 226,693 bonus shares could be issued over the next three years.

As at December 31, 2004, 16,000,000 common shares (2003 – 16,000,000; 2002 – 11,300,000) were authorized for issuance under the Plan. Since its inception, 5,965,595 shares have been issued under this plan.

During the year, under the Executive Stock Option and Share Purchase Plan and the Employee Share Purchase Plan, as described below, $4 million (2003 – $3 million; 2002 – $3 million) was included in "Contributed surplus" in conjunction with the recognition of stock-based compensation expense.

DEFERRED SHARE UNIT PLANS

Outside Directors

Under the Deferred Share Unit Plan for Outside Directors, deferred share units (DSU), equivalent in value to a common share, may be granted to eligible directors. In addition, participants may elect to receive their annual retainer and attendance fees in DSU. A participant shall receive, not later than the 31st of January following the end of the year during which the participant ceases to be a member of the Board of Directors, a lump sum payment in cash equal to the number of DSU recorded in the participant's account on the termination date multiplied by the termination value of the common shares or, if the participant so elects, a number of common shares to be purchased on the open market equal to the number of DSU then recorded in the participant's account less, in either case, any applicable withholding tax. A participant account shall be credited with dividend equivalents in the form of additional DSU when normal cash dividends are paid on common shares. Upon payment in full of the DSU, they shall be cancelled. The total expense recognized in Domtar's results of operations amounted to $0.4 million in 2004 (2003 – $0.6 million; 2002 – $0.2 million). In 2004, 37,940 DSU (2003 – 32,263; 2002 – 37,492) were granted and 45,334 DSU (2003 – 11,262; 2002 – 21,088) were redeemed. As at December 31, 2004, 130,134 DSU (2003 – 137,528; 2002 – 116,527) were outstanding.

Executives

Under the Executive Deferred Share Unit Plan, DSU may be granted to eligible executives. A participant shall receive, no later than the 31st of January following the end of the year during which occurred the participant's date of retirement, death, determination of long-term disability or termination of employment at the end of a continuous period that started on or after January 1, 1999 and represents at least seven years of tenure as a member of the Management Committee, a lump sum payment in cash equal to the number of DSU recorded in the participant's account on one of these dates multiplied by the redemption value of the common shares or, if the participant so elects, a number of common shares to be purchased on the open market equal to the number of DSU then recorded in the participant's account less, in either case, any applicable withholding tax. A participant account shall be credited with dividend equivalents in the form of additional DSU when normal cash dividends are paid on common shares. Upon payment in full of the DSU, they shall be cancelled. The total expense (reversal) recognized in Domtar's results of operation amounted to $(0.6) million in 2004 (2003 – $0.4 million; 2002 – $1 million). As at December 31, 2004, 66,178 DSU (2003 – 72,196; 2002 – 82,110) were outstanding under this plan.

Under the Executive Performance Share Unit Plan approved in December 2003, Performance Share Units (PSU) may be granted to eligible executives and other key employees of Domtar or any of its affiliates. Each PSU, subject to the vesting conditions (including certain conditions relating to the relative performance of Domtar's common shares) set out in each grant being fulfilled, gives a participant the right to receive one common share of Domtar or, at his option, the cash equivalent at the time of vesting. In the event a participant elects to receive common shares, Domtar will make arrangements for delivery of such shares through purchases on the open market then recorded in the participant's account less, in either case, any applicable withholding tax. A participant account shall be credited with dividend equivalents in the form of additional PSU when normal cash dividends are paid on common shares. The total expense recognized in Domtar's results of operations amounted to $0.1 million in 2004, representing 725,989 units authorized and issued since the inception of the plan.

EMPLOYEE SHARE PURCHASE PLANS

Under the Employee Share Purchase Plans, all employees are eligible to purchase common shares at a price of 90% of the quoted market value. Common shares are purchased under the plans on monthly investment dates. Shares purchased under the Canadian plan are subject to a mandatory twelve-month holding period. Employees who hold the shares for 18 months following the date of acquisition (U.S. plan) or who hold the shares purchased in any calendar year until June 30 of the following year (Canadian plan) are entitled to receive additional common shares equivalent to 10% of the cost of such shares. As at December 31, 2004, 6,050,000 common shares (2003 – 5,050,000; 2002 – 5,050,000) were authorized for issuance under the plans. During the year, 421,825 common shares (2003 – 470,653; 2002 – 463,796) were issued under the plans at an average price of $15.77 (2003 – $15.32; 2002 – $16.49) per share. Since their inception, 4,484,340 shares have been issued under these plans.

NOTES TO CONSOLIDATED FINANCIAL STATEMENTS
DECEMBER 31, 2004 (IN MILLIONS OF CANADIAN DOLLARS, UNLESS OTHERWISE NOTED)

NOTE 19.
_____

FINANCIAL INSTRUMENTS

FAIR VALUE OF FINANCIAL INSTRUMENTS	2004		**2004**		2003	
	FAIR VALUE	CARRYING AMOUNT	FAIR VALUE	CARRYING AMOUNT	FAIR VALUE	CARRYING AMOUNT
	US$ (NOTE 4)	US$ (NOTE 4)	$	$	$	$
Long-term debt	1,864	1,690	**2,244**	**2,034**	2,324	2,059

The fair value of the long-term debt, including the portion due within one year, is principally based on quoted market prices.

Due to their short-term maturity, the carrying amounts of cash and cash equivalents, receivables, bank indebtedness, trade and other payables and income and other taxes approximate their fair values.

INTEREST RATE RISK

Domtar is exposed to interest rate risk arising from fluctuations in interest rates on its cash and cash equivalents, its bank indebteness, its bank credit facility and its long-term debt. Domtar may manage this interest rate exposure by the use of derivative instruments such as interest rate swap contracts.

In 2004, the Corporation terminated, prior to maturity, interest rate swap contracts for net cash proceeds of $20 million (US$15 million). The resulting gain of $17 million recorded under "Other liabilities and deferred credits" is being deferred and will be recognized against financing expenses over the period of the interest rate payments ending November 2013, the original designated hedging period of the underlying 5.375% notes.

In 2002, the Corporation terminated, prior to maturity, interest rate swap contracts for net cash proceeds of $40 million (US$26 million). The net gain of $40 million recorded under "Other liabilities and deferred credits" was deferred and is recognized against financing expenses over the period of the interest rate payments ending October 2003 and October 2006, the original designated hedging period of the underlying 7.875% notes. The net recognized amounts will be $13 million and $10 million in 2005 and 2006, respectively. In 2004, a net amount of $13 million (2003–$4 million) was recognized against financing expenses.

NOTES TO CONSOLIDATED FINANCIAL STATEMENTS
DECEMBER 31, 2004 (IN MILLIONS OF CANADIAN DOLLARS, UNLESS OTHERWISE NOTED)

NOTE 18. STATED CAPITAL (CONTINUED)

During the year, 353,900 shares (2003 – 320,350; 2002 – 358,472) were issued pursuant to the exercise of rights and 52,730 bonus shares (2003 – 41,169; 2002 – 40,878) were issued. The total expense recognized in Domtar's results of operations related to these rights and bonus shares amounted to $2 million in 2004 (2003 – $2 million; 2002 – $1 million). As at December 31, 2004, 226,693 bonus shares could be issued over the next three years.

As at December 31, 2004, 16,000,000 common shares (2003 – 16,000,000; 2002 – 11,300,000) were authorized for issuance under the Plan. Since its inception, 5,965,595 shares have been issued under this plan.

During the year, under the Executive Stock Option and Share Purchase Plan and the Employee Share Purchase Plan, as described below, $4 million (2003 – $3 million; 2002 – $3 million) was included in "Contributed surplus" in conjunction with the recognition of stock-based compensation expense.

DEFERRED SHARE UNIT PLANS

Outside Directors

Under the Deferred Share Unit Plan for Outside Directors, deferred share units (DSU), equivalent in value to a common share, may be granted to eligible directors. In addition, participants may elect to receive their annual retainer and attendance fees in DSU. A participant shall receive, not later than the 31st of January following the end of the year during which the participant ceases to be a member of the Board of Directors, a lump sum payment in cash equal to the number of DSU recorded in the participant's account on the termination date multiplied by the termination value of the common shares or, if the participant so elects, a number of common shares to be purchased on the open market equal to the number of DSU then recorded in the participant's account less, in either case, any applicable withholding tax. A participant account shall be credited with dividend equivalents in the form of additional DSU when normal cash dividends are paid on common shares. Upon payment in full of the DSU, they shall be cancelled. The total expense recognized in Domtar's results of operations amounted to $0.4 million in 2004 (2003 – $0.6 million; 2002 – $0.2 million). In 2004, 37,940 DSU (2003 – 32,263; 2002 – 37,492) were granted and 45,334 DSU (2003 – 11,262; 2002 – 21,088) were redeemed. As at December 31, 2004, 130,134 DSU (2003 – 137,528; 2002 – 116,527) were outstanding.

Executives

Under the Executive Deferred Share Unit Plan, DSU may be granted to eligible executives. A participant shall receive, no later than the 31st of January following the end of the year during which occurred the participant's date of retirement, death, determination of long-term

NOTES TO CONSOLIDATED FINANCIAL STATEMENTS

DECEMBER 31, 2004 (IN MILLIONS OF CANADIAN DOLLARS, UNLESS OTHERWISE NOTED)

NOTE 19. FINANCIAL INSTRUMENTS (CONTINUED)

FOREIGN CURRENCY RISK

In order to reduce the potential negative effects of a fluctuating Canadian dollar, Domtar has entered into various arrangements to stabilize anticipated future net cash inflows denominated in U.S. dollars. The following table provides the detail of the arrangements used as hedging instruments:

	2004	2003	**2004**	2003
	AVERAGE EXCHANGE RATE (CAN$/US$)		CONTRACTUAL AMOUNTS (IN MILLIONS OF U.S. DOLLARS)	
Forward foreign exchange contracts				
0 to 12 months	**1.27**	1.44	**189**	12
13 to 24 months	**1.34**	–	**37**	–
Currency options purchased				
0 to 12 months	**1.31**	1.34	**212**	250
Currency options sold				
0 to 12 months	**1.39**	–	**212**	–

Forward foreign exchange contracts are contracts whereby Domtar has the obligation to sell U.S. dollars at a specific rate.

Currency options purchased are contracts whereby Domtar has the right, but not the obligation, to sell U.S. dollars at the strike rate if the U.S. dollar trades below that rate.

Currency options sold are contracts whereby Domtar has the obligation to sell U.S. dollars at the strike rate if the U.S. dollar trades above that rate.

Norampac has currency options sold, which do not qualify as hedging instruments. The average exchange rate and contractual amounts at December 31, 2004 were $1.43 and US$8 million, respectively (2003 – nil and nil, respectively), representing the Corporation's proportionate share. As at December 31, 2004, the fair value of these derivative financial instruments was nil (2003 – nil).

In addition to the above arrangements and as a result of the early settlement of certain currency options, the Corporation was left, in 2003, with freestanding written call options requiring the Corporation to sell US$33 million at $1.60 if rates exceeded $1.60 in 2004. These freestanding written call options do not qualify for hedge accounting and, accordingly, any fluctuations of their fair value are recorded to earnings. The impact was nil for the year ended December 31, 2004 (2003 – gain of $6 million). As at December 31, 2004, there were no more freestanding written call options and, as such, their fair value as at that date was nil (2003 – nil).

The fair value of derivative financial instruments generally reflects the estimated amounts that Domtar would receive or pay to settle the contracts at December 31, 2004 and 2003. As at these dates, the spot exchange rates were $1.20 and $1.29, respectively, and the fair value of the above derivative financial instruments used as hedging items was as follows:

	2004	2004	2003
	US$ (NOTE 4)	$	$
Unrealized gain on forward foreign exchange contracts	14	17	2
Unrealized gain on currency options	20	24	12

PRICE RISK

During 2004, the Corporation entered into a cash settled commodity swap agreement to manage price risk associated with sales of NBSK pulp covering a period starting July 2004 and ending June 2007. The agreement fixes the sale price of NBSK pulp for 1,000 tonnes per month for 36 months. This agreement is in addition to the 2003 and 2002 contracts, which fix the sale price of NBSK pulp for 1,500 tonnes per month for 36 months and are expiring in April 2006 and October 2005, respectively. These contracts are not designated as hedging instruments and they are accounted for at their fair market value. The fair value of these instruments as at December 31, 2004, was negative $6 million (2003 – negative $3 million).

In 2004, the Corporation also entered into a cash settled commodity swap agreement to manage price risk associated with purchases of bunker oil covering a period starting July 2004 and ending December 2006. The agreement fixes the purchase price of bunker oil for 7,000 barrels per month. This agreement is in addition to the 2003 contract, which fixes the purchase price of bunker oil for 15,000 barrels per month ending in December 2005. These contracts are designated as hedging instruments. The fair value of these instruments as at December 31, 2004, represented an unrealized gain of $2 million (2003 – unrealized gain of $2 million).

Norampac entered into cash settled commodity swap agreements to manage price risk associated with sales of unbleached kraft linerboard and semi-chemical medium paper and purchases of old corrugated containers and electricity. As at December 31, 2004, Norampac had entered into contracts expiring in 2005 through 2007. According to the Corporation's proportionate share, these derivative agreements fix the sale price for 37,000 tonnes (2003 – 82,500 tonnes) of unbleached kraft linerboard and 2,500 tonnes (2003 – 8,500 tonnes) of semi-chemical medium paper and fix the purchase price for 286,750 tonnes (2003 – 387,000 tonnes) of old corrugated containers and 68,387 megawatts

NOTE 19. FINANCIAL INSTRUMENTS (CONTINUED)

(2003 – 112,427 megawatts) of electricity. The contracts related to unbleached kraft liner-board, semi-chemical medium paper and old corrugated containers are not designated as hedging instruments and they are accounted for at their fair market value. The fair value of these instruments as at December 31, 2004, represented a net gain of $1 million (2003 – unrealized net gain of $4 million). The fair value of the electricity contracts as at December 31, 2004, represented an unrealized gain of $1 million (2003 – nil).

NOTE 20.

ACCUMULATED FOREIGN CURRENCY
TRANSLATION ADJUSTMENTS

	2004	**2004**	2003	2002
	US$ (NOTE 4)	**$**	$	$
Balance at beginning of year	(121)	**(145)**	2	2
Effect of changes in exchange rates during the year:				
On net investment in self-sustaining foreign subsidiaries	(117)	**(141)**	(391)	(18)
On certain long-term debt denominated in foreign currencies designated as a hedge of net investment in self-sustaining foreign subsidiaries	97	**117**	282	18
Future income taxes thereon	(17)	**(21)**	(38)	–
Balance at end of year	(158)	**(190)**	(145)	2

NOTES TO CONSOLIDATED FINANCIAL STATEMENTS

DECEMBER 31, 2004 (IN MILLIONS OF CANADIAN DOLLARS, UNLESS OTHERWISE NOTED)

NOTE 21.

INTERESTS IN JOINT VENTURES

The following amounts represent the Corporation's proportionate interests in its joint ventures (Norampac, Anthony-Domtar Inc. and Gogama Forest Products Inc.):

	2004	2004	2003
	US$ (NOTE 4)	$	$
Assets			
Current assets	150	**180**	164
Long-term assets	422	**508**	483
Liabilities			
Current liabilities	77	**93**	75
Long-term liabilities	226	**272**	272

	2004	2004	2003	2002
	US$ (NOTE 4)	$	$	$
Earnings				
Sales	532	**640**	629	653
Operating expenses	(489)	**(588)**	(585)	(581)
Operating profit	43	**52**	44	72
Financing expenses	7	**8**	17	18
Net earnings	27	**32**	17	37
Cash flows				
Cash flows provided from operating activities	48	**58**	45	70
Cash flows used for investing activities	(53)	**(64)**	(42)	(55)
Cash flows provided from financing activities	12	**15**	4	4

NOTES TO CONSOLIDATED FINANCIAL STATEMENTS

DECEMBER 31, 2004 (IN MILLIONS OF CANADIAN DOLLARS, UNLESS OTHERWISE NOTED)

NOTE 22.

PENSION PLANS

DEFINED CONTRIBUTION PLANS

Domtar contributes to several defined contribution, multi-employer and 401(k) plans. The pension expense under these plans is equal to Domtar's contribution. The 2004 pension expense was $17 million (2003 – $19 million; 2002 – $20 million).

DEFINED BENEFIT PLANS

Domtar has several defined benefit pension plans covering substantially all employees, including one closed plan for certain non-unionized employees in Canada. Non-unionized employees in Canada joining Domtar after June 1, 2000 participate in defined contribution plans. The defined benefit plans are generally contributory in Canada and non-contributory in the United States. The pension expense and the obligation related to the defined benefit plans are actuarially determined using management's most probable assumptions.

COMPONENTS OF NET PERIODIC BENEFIT COST FOR DEFINED BENEFIT PLANS	2004	**2004**	2003	2002
	US$ (NOTE 4)	**$**	$	$
Service cost for the year	29	**35**	32	30
Interest expense	61	**74**	72	69
Actual return on plan assets	(86)	**(104)**	(115)	(24)
Recognized actuarial loss	28	**34**	72	24
Plan amendments [a]	3	**3**	11	–
Curtailment and settlement loss (NOTE 6)	2	**2**	–	2
Costs arising in the period	37	**44**	72	101
Difference between costs arising in the period and costs recognized in the period in respect of:				
Return on plan assets	19	**23**	36	(57)
Actuarial gain	(18)	**(22)**	(67)	(24)
Plan amendments	(1)	**(1)**	(10)	2
Net periodic benefit cost for defined benefit plans	37	**44**	31	22

(a) In 2003, amendments include an $8 million amount for the "Domtar US Nekoosa Papers Pension Plan" in order to increase the pension benefit level persuant to the latest collective agreement.

NOTES TO CONSOLIDATED FINANCIAL STATEMENTS

DECEMBER 31, 2004 (IN MILLIONS OF CANADIAN DOLLARS, UNLESS OTHERWISE NOTED)

Domtar's funding policy is to contribute annually the amount required to provide for benefits earned in the year and to fund past service obligations over periods not exceeding those permitted by the applicable regulatory authorities. Past service obligations primarily arise from improvements to plan benefits. The latest actuarial valuations were conducted as at December 31, 2003, for plans representing approximately 39% and as at December 31, 2001, for plans representing approximately 61% of the total plans asset fair value. These valuations indicated a funding deficiency. The next actuarial valuations will be completed between December 31, 2004 and December 31, 2006. Domtar expects to contribute for a total amount of $89 million in 2005 compared to $80 million in 2004.

CHANGE IN ACCRUED BENEFIT OBLIGATION

The following table represents the change in the accrued benefit obligation as determined by independent actuaries:

	2004	2004	2003
	US$ (NOTE 4)	$	$
Accrued benefit obligation at beginning of year	1,030	1,240	1,117
Service cost for the year	29	35	31
Interest expense	61	74	72
Plan participants' contributions	10	12	12
Actuarial loss	30	36	72
Plan amendments	3	3	11
Benefits paid	(58)	(70)	(65)
Settlement	(1)	(1)	–
Curtailment	(1)	(1)	–
Effect of foreign currency exchange rate change	(4)	(5)	(10)
Accrued benefit obligation at end of year	1,099	1,323	1,240

NOTES TO CONSOLIDATED FINANCIAL STATEMENTS
DECEMBER 31, 2004 (IN MILLIONS OF CANADIAN DOLLARS, UNLESS OTHERWISE NOTED)

NOTE 22. PENSION PLANS (CONTINUED)

CHANGE IN FAIR VALUE OF DEFINED BENEFIT PLAN ASSETS

The following table represents the change in the fair value of assets of defined benefit plans reflecting the actual return on plan assets, the contributions and the benefits paid during the year:

	2004	**2004**	2003
	US$ (NOTE 4)	$	$
Fair value of defined benefit plan assets at beginning of year	856	**1,030**	900
Actual return on plan assets	86	**104**	115
Employer contributions	66	**80**	73
Plan participants' contributions	10	**12**	12
Benefits paid	(58)	**(70)**	(65)
Settlement	(1)	**(1)**	–
Effect of foreign currency exchange rate change	(3)	**(4)**	(5)
Fair value of defined benefit plan assets at end of year	956	**1,151**	1,030

DESCRIPTION OF FUNDED ASSETS

The assets of the pension plans are held by a number of independent trustees and are accounted for separately in the Domtar pension funds. Based on the fair value of the assets held at December 31, 2004, the plan assets are comprised of 5% in cash and short-term investments, 46% in bonds and 49% in Canadian, U.S. and foreign equities.

Domtar has indemnified and held harmless the trustees of Domtar pension funds, and the respective officers, directors, employees and agents of such trustees, from any and all costs and expenses arising out of the performance of their obligations under the relevant trust agreements, including in respect of their reliance on authorized instructions of Domtar or for failing to act in the absence of authorized instructions. These indemnifications survive the termination of such agreements. As at December 31, 2004, Domtar has not recorded a liability associated with these indemnifications, as Domtar does not expect to make any payments pertaining to these indemnifications.

RECONCILIATION OF FUNDED STATUS TO AMOUNTS RECOGNIZED IN THE CONSOLIDATED BALANCE SHEETS

The following tables present the difference between the fair value of the defined benefit pension assets and the actuarially determined accrued benefit obligation as at December 31, 2004 and 2003. This difference is also referred to as either the deficit or surplus, as the case may be, or the funded status of the plans.

NOTES TO CONSOLIDATED FINANCIAL STATEMENTS

DECEMBER 31, 2004 (IN MILLIONS OF CANADIAN DOLLARS, UNLESS OTHERWISE NOTED)

The tables further reconcile the amount of the surplus or deficit (funded status) to the net amount recognized in the Consolidated balance sheets. This difference between the funded status and the net amount recognized in the Consolidated balance sheets, in accordance with Canadian GAAP, represents the portion of the surplus or deficit not yet recognized for accounting purposes. Deferred recognition is a guiding principle of these recommendations. This approach allows for a gradual recognition of changes in accrued benefit obligations and plan performance over the expected average remaining service life of the employee group covered by the plans.

	2004	2004	2003
	US$ (NOTE 4)	$	$
Accrued benefit obligation at end of year	1,099	1,323	1,240
Fair value of defined benefit plan assets at end of year	(956)	(1,151)	(1,030)
Funded status	(143)	(172)	(210)
Reconciliation of funded status to amounts recognized in the Consolidated balance sheets			
Unrecognized actuarial loss	252	303	305
Unrecognized past service costs	16	20	20
Net amount recognized in the Consolidated balance sheets	125	151	115

	2004	2004	2003
	US$ (NOTE 4)	$	$
Accrued benefit asset – defined benefit plans (NOTE 13)	152	183	153
Accrued benefit liability – defined benefit plans (NOTES 14 AND 16)	(27)	(32)	(38)
Net amount recognized in the Consolidated balance sheets	125	151	115

As at December 31, 2004, the accrued benefit obligation and the fair value of defined benefit plan assets for the pension plans with an accrued benefit obligation in excess of fair value plan assets were $1,229 million and $1,053 million, respectively (2003 – $1,107 million and $900 million, respectively).

NOTE 22. PENSION PLANS (CONTINUED)

CASH PAYMENTS FOR EMPLOYEE FUTURE BENEFITS

Cash payments for employee future benefits made by Domtar for the years ended December 31, are as follows:

	2004	**2004**	2003	2002
	US$ (NOTE 4)	$	$	$
Defined contribution plans	14	**17**	19	20
Defined benefit plans	66	**80**	73	53
Total cash payments for employee future benefits	80	**97**	92	73

WEIGHTED-AVERAGE ASSUMPTIONS

Domtar used the following key assumptions to measure the accrued benefit obligation and the net periodic benefit cost for defined benefit plans. These assumptions are long-term, which is consistent with the nature of employee future benefits.

	2004	2003	2002
Accrued benefit obligation as at December 31:			
Discount rate	**5.8%**	6.1%	6.5%
Rate of compensation increase	**3.4%**	3.8%	3.9%
Net periodic benefit cost for years ended December 31:			
Discount rate	**6.1%**	6.5%	6.7%
Rate of compensation increase	**3.8%**	3.9%	3.9%
Expected long-term rate of return on plan assets	**7.7%**	7.7%	8.2%

Effective January 1, 2005, Domtar will use 7.2% as the expected return on plan assets, which reflects the current view of long-term investment returns.

NOTES TO CONSOLIDATED FINANCIAL STATEMENTS
DECEMBER 31, 2004 (IN MILLIONS OF CANADIAN DOLLARS, UNLESS OTHERWISE NOTED)

NOTE 23.

OTHER EMPLOYEE FUTURE BENEFIT PLANS

The post-retirement and post-employment plans are unfunded.

COMPONENTS OF NET PERIODIC BENEFIT COST FOR OTHER EMPLOYEE FUTURE BENEFIT PLANS	2004	2004	2003	2002
	US$ (NOTE 4)	$	$	$
Service cost for the year	3	3	4	4
Interest expense	5	7	7	7
Recognized actuarial loss	3	3	7	2
Plan amendments	1	1	1	–
Curtailment loss	1	1	–	–
Other	–	–	(1)	–
Costs arising in the period	13	15	18	13
Difference between costs arising in the period and costs recognized in the period in respect of:				
Actuarial gain	(1)	(1)	(6)	(1)
Plan amendments	(1)	(1)	–	–
Net periodic benefit cost for other employee future benefit plans	11	13	12	12

CHANGE IN ACCRUED BENEFIT OBLIGATION FOR OTHER EMPLOYEE FUTURE BENEFIT PLANS	2004	2004	2003
	US$ (NOTE 4)	$	$
Accrued benefit obligation at beginning of year	96	116	109
Service cost for the year	3	3	4
Interest expense	6	7	7
Actuarial loss	3	3	6
Plan amendments	1	1	–
Benefits paid	(7)	(8)	(8)
Curtailment	–	–	(1)
Effect of foreign currency exchange rate change	(1)	(1)	(2)
Other	–	–	1
Accrued benefit obligation at end of year	101	121	116

NOTES TO CONSOLIDATED FINANCIAL STATEMENTS

DECEMBER 31, 2004 (IN MILLIONS OF CANADIAN DOLLARS, UNLESS OTHERWISE NOTED)

NOTE 23. OTHER EMPLOYEE FUTURE BENEFIT PLANS (CONTINUED)

CHANGE IN FAIR VALUE OF ASSETS OF OTHER EMPLOYEE FUTURE BENEFIT PLANS

	2004	**2004**	2003
	US$ (NOTE 4)	$	$
Fair value of assets of other employee future benefit plans at beginning of year	–	**–**	–
Employer contributions	7	**8**	8
Benefits paid	(7)	**(8)**	(8)
Fair value of assets of other employee future benefit plans at end of year	–	**–**	–

FUNDED STATUS AND NET AMOUNT RECOGNIZED IN THE CONSOLIDATED BALANCE SHEETS

	2004	**2004**	2003
	US$ (NOTE 4)	$	$
Funded status	101	**121**	116
Unrecognized actuarial loss	(21)	**(25)**	(26)
Unrecognized past service costs	(2)	**(2)**	–
Net amount recognized in the Consolidated balance sheets (NOTES 14 AND 16)	78	**94**	90

Cash payments for other employee future benefit plans for the year ended December 31, 2004, amounted to $8 million (2003 – $8 million; 2002 – $7 million).

WEIGHTED-AVERAGE ASSUMPTIONS

Domtar used the following key assumptions to measure the accrued benefit obligation and the net periodic benefit cost for other employee future benefit plans. These assumptions are long-term, which is consistent with the nature of employee future benefits.

	2004	2003	2002
Accrued benefit obligation as at December 31:			
Discount rate	**5.8%**	6.1%	6.6%
Rate of compensation increase	**3.5%**	3.5%	4.2%
Net periodic benefit cost for years ended December 31:			
Discount rate	**6.1%**	6.6%	6.7%
Rate of compensation increase	**3.5%**	4.2%	3.7%

NOTES TO CONSOLIDATED FINANCIAL STATEMENTS

DECEMBER 31, 2004 (IN MILLIONS OF CANADIAN DOLLARS, UNLESS OTHERWISE NOTED)

For measurement purposes, 7.7% weighted-average annual rate of increase in the per capita cost of covered health care benefits was assumed for 2005. The rate was assumed to decrease gradually to 4.1% for 2012 and remain at that level thereafter. An increase or decrease of 1% of this rate would have the following impact:

	INCREASE OF 1%		DECREASE OF 1%	
	US$ (NOTE 4)	$	US$ (NOTE 4)	$
Impact on net periodic benefit cost	2	2	(1)	(1)
Impact on accrued benefit obligation	8	10	(7)	(8)

NOTE 24.

SEGMENTED DISCLOSURES

Domtar operates in the four reportable segments described below. Each reportable segment offers different products and services and requires different technology and marketing strategies. The following summary briefly describes the operations included in each of Domtar's reportable segments:

- PAPERS – represents the aggregation of the manufacturing and distribution of business, commercial printing and publication, and technical and specialty papers, as well as pulp.
- PAPER MERCHANTS – involves the purchasing, warehousing, sale and distribution of various products made by Domtar and by other manufacturers. These products include business and printing papers, graphic arts supplies and certain industrial products.
- WOOD – comprises the manufacturing and marketing of lumber and wood-based value-added products and the management of forest resources.
- PACKAGING – comprises the Corporation's 50% ownership interest in Norampac, a company that manufactures and distributes containerboard and corrugated products.

The accounting policies of the reportable segments are the same as described in Note 1. Domtar evaluates performance based on operating profit, which represents sales, reflecting transfer prices between segments at fair value, less allocable expenses before financing expenses and income taxes. Segment assets are those directly used in segment operations.

2004 Annual Report

Respect

Cascades

Management's Report

The consolidated financial statements for the years ended December 31, 2004 and 2003, are the responsibility of the management of Cascades Inc., and have been reviewed by the Audit Committee and approved by the Board of Directors. They were prepared in accordance with accounting principles generally accepted in Canada and include some amounts, which are based on management's estimates and judgement. Management is also responsible for all other information included in this Annual Report and for ensuring that this information is consistent with the Company's consolidated financial statements and business activities.

The Management of the Company is responsible for the design, establishment and maintenance of appropriate internal controls and procedures for financial reporting, to ensure that financial statements for external purposes are fairly presented in conformity with generally accepted accounting principles. Such internal controls systems are designed to provide reasonable assurance on the reliability of the financial information and the safeguarding of assets.

External and internal auditors have free and independent access to the Audit Committee, which is comprised of outside independent directors. The Audit Committee, which meets regularly throughout the year with members of the financial management and the external and internal auditors, reviews the consolidated financial statements and recommends their approval to the Board of Directors.

The financial statements have been audited by PricewaterhouseCoopers LLP, whose report is provided below.

Alain Lemaire
President and Chief Executive Officer
Kingsey Falls, Canada
February 24, 2005

Christian Dubé
Vice-President and Chief Financial Officer
Kingsey Falls, Canada
February 24, 2005

Auditors' Report to the Shareholders of Cascades Inc.

We have audited the consolidated balance sheets of Cascades Inc. (the "Company") as at December 31, 2004 and 2003 and the consolidated statements of earnings, retained earnings and cash flows for each of the years in the three-year period ended December 31, 2004. These financial statements are the responsibility of the Company's management. Our responsibility is to express an opinion on these financial statements based on our audits.

We conducted our audits in accordance with Canadian generally accepted auditing standards. Those standards require that we plan and perform an audit to obtain reasonable assurance whether the financial statements are free of material misstatement. An audit includes examining, on a test basis, evidence supporting the amounts and disclosures in the financial statements. An audit also includes assessing the accounting principles used and significant estimates made by management, as well as evaluating the overall financial statement presentation.

In our opinion, these consolidated financial statements present fairly, in all material respects, the financial position of the Company as at December 31, 2004 and 2003 and the results of its operations and its cash flows for each of the years in the three-year period ended December 31, 2004 in accordance with Canadian generally accepted accounting principles.

PricewaterhouseCoopers LLP
Chartered Accountants
Montreal, Canada
February 24, 2005

Consolidated Financial Statements

Consolidated Balance Sheets
As at December 31, 2004 and 2003
(in millions of Canadian dollars)

	Note	2004	2003
Assets			
Current assets			
Cash and cash equivalents		30	27
Accounts receivable		527	494
Inventories	6	559	501
		1,116	1,022
Property, plant and equipment	7	1,700	1,636
Other assets	8	215	186
Goodwill	8	113	83
		3,144	2,927
Liabilities and Shareholders' Equity			
Current liabilities			
Bank loans and advances		47	43
Accounts payable and accrued liabilities		509	453
Current portion of long-term debt	9	58	18
		614	514
Long-term debt	9	1,168	1,092
Other liabilities	10	303	265
		2,085	1,871
Shareholders' equity			
Capital stock	11	265	264
Retained earnings		783	778
Cumulative translation adjustments	21	11	14
		1,059	1,056
		3,144	2,927

The accompanying notes are an integral part of these consolidated financial statements.

Approved by the Board of Directors

Bernard Lemaire
Director

Robert Chevrier
Director

Consolidated Financial Statements

Consolidated Statements of Retained Earnings
For the three-year period ended December 31, 2004
(in millions of Canadian dollars)

	Note	2004	2003	2002
Balance–Beginning of year		778	749	594
Net earnings for the year		23	55	169
Dividends on common shares		(13)	(13)	(10)
Dividends on preferred shares		–	(1)	(1)
Excess of common share redemption price over paid-up capital	11 d)	(5)	(2)	(3)
Excess of redemption price of preferred shares of a subsidiary over recorded capital	11 b)	–	(10)	–
Balance–End of year		783	778	749

Consolidated Statements of Earnings
For the three-year period ended December 31, 2004
(in millions of Canadian dollars)

	Note	2004	2003 (note 4)	2002 (note 4)
Sales		3,254	2,995	3,118
Cost of sales and expenses				
Cost of sales (exclusive of depreciation shown below)	17 c)	2,691	2,463	2,414
Selling and administrative expenses		313	294	289
Impairment loss on property, plant and equipment	14	18	–	–
Loss (gain) on derivative financial instruments	15	(2)	1	–
Unusual losses (gains)	13	(4)	–	4
Depreciation and amortization		159	143	137
		3,175	2,901	2,844
Operating income from continuing operations		79	94	274
Interest expense	17 b)	76	80	69
Foreign exchange gain on long-term debt		(18)	(72)	–
Loss on long-term debt refinancing		1	22	–
		20	64	205
Provision for income taxes	16	2	10	60
Share of results of significantly influenced companies	12	(2)	3	(22)
Share of earnings attributed to non-controlling interests		–	–	1
Net earnings from continuing operations		20	51	166
Net earnings from assets held for sale	4	3	4	3
Net earnings for the year		23	55	169
Basic net earnings from continuing operations per common share		0.25	0.61	2.04
Basic net earnings per common share	11 e)	0.28	0.66	2.07
Diluted net earnings per common share	11 e)	0.28	0.66	2.05
Weighted average number of common shares outstanding during the year		81,678,884	81,720,379	81,482,507

The accompanying notes are an integral part of these consolidated financial statements.

Consolidated Financial Statements

Consolidated Statements of Cash Flows For the three-year period ended December 31, 2004 (in millions of Canadian dollars)	Note	2004	2003 (note 4)	2002 (note 4)
Operating activities from continuing operations				
Net earnings from continuing operations		20	51	166
Adjustments for				
Impairment loss on property, plant and equipment		18	–	–
Amortization of transitional deferred unrealized gain		(2)	–	–
Unusual losses (gains)		(4)	–	4
Depreciation and amortization		159	143	137
Foreign exchange gain on long-term debt		(18)	(72)	–
Loss on long-term debt refinancing		1	22	–
Future income taxes		(20)	(1)	13
Share of results of significantly influenced companies		(2)	3	(22)
Share of earnings attributed to non-controlling interests		–	–	1
Others		6	12	8
		158	158	307
Changes in non-cash working capital components	17 a)	(2)	(32)	23
		156	126	330
Investing activities from continuing operations				
Purchases of property, plant and equipment		(129)	(121)	(128)
Purchases of other assets		(9)	(13)	(21)
Business acquisitions, net of cash acquired	5 a)	(120)	(31)	(127)
Business disposal, net of cash disposed	5 b)	14	–	4
		(244)	(165)	(272)
Financing activities from continuing operations				
Bank loans and advances		3	(50)	–
Issuance of senior notes, net of related expenses		156	974	–
Change in revolving credit facilities, net of related expenses		(8)	155	–
Increase in other long-term debt		10	52	77
Payments of other long-term debt		(49)	(1,052)	(113)
Premium paid on redemption of long-term debt		(1)	(16)	–
Non-controlling interests		–	–	(7)
Net proceeds from issuances of shares		2	2	3
Redemption of common shares and preferred shares				
of a subsidiary	11 b) d)	(7)	(20)	(3)
Dividends		(13)	(14)	(11)
		93	31	(54)
Change in cash and cash equivalents during the year				
from continuing operations		5	(8)	4
Change in cash and cash equivalents from assets held for sale	4	–	–	–
Change in cash and cash equivalents during the year		5	(8)	4
Translation adjustments on cash and cash equivalents		(2)	(3)	3
Cash and cash equivalents–Beginning of year		27	38	31
Cash and cash equivalents–End of year		30	27	38

The accompanying notes are an integral part of these consolidated financial statements.

Segmented Information

For the three-year period ended December 31, 2004
(in millions of Canadian dollars)

The Company's operations are organized into and managed by three segments: packaging products, tissue papers and fine papers. The classification of these operating segments is based on the primary operations of the main subsidiaries and joint ventures of the Company.

The Company analyzes the performance of its operating segments based on their operating income before depreciation and amortization, which is not a measure of performance under Canadian generally accepted accounting principles ("Canadian GAAP"); however, chief operating decision-makers use this performance measure for assessing the operating performance of their reportable segments. Earnings for each segment are prepared on the same basis as those of the Company. Intersegment operations are recorded on the same basis as sales to third parties, which is at fair market value.

Sales of the Company presented by the reportable segments are as follows:

Sales	Note	2004	2003 (note 2 d)	2002 (note 2 d)
Packaging products				
Boxboard				
Manufacturing		705	727	760
Converting		513	292	263
Eliminations and others		13	7	2
		1,231	1,026	1,025
Containerboard[1]				
Manufacturing		344	340	374
Converting		489	480	488
Eliminations and others		(200)	(191)	(204)
		633	629	658
Specialty products		509	484	477
Eliminations		(44)	(38)	(40)
		2,329	2,101	2,120
Tissue papers				
Manufacturing and converting		665	620	663
Distribution[2]		87	89	88
Eliminations		(35)	(23)	(24)
		717	686	727
Fine papers				
Manufacturing		373	380	440
Distribution[2]		409	417	427
Eliminations		(68)	(63)	(65)
		714	734	802
Eliminations		(68)	(72)	(58)
Assets held for sale	4	(438)	(454)	(473)
Total		3,254	2,995	3,118

1. The Company's containerboard sub-segment consists entirely of its interest in Norampac Inc. ("Norampac"), a joint venture.
2. Some or all of these sub-segments represent assets held for sale (see note 4).

Segmented Information

For the three-year period ended December 31, 2004
(in millions of Canadian dollars)

The operating income before depreciation and amortization from continuing operation and the depreciation and amortization from continuing operation of the Company presented by the reportable segments are as follows:

Operating income before depreciation and amortization and operating income from continuing operation	Note	2004	2003	2002
Packaging products				
Boxboard				
Manufacturing		19	37	79
Converting		45	15	7
Others		3	3	3
		67	55	89
Containerboard[1]				
Manufacturing		25	18	47
Converting		54	52	50
Others		8	11	9
		87	81	106
Specialty products		24	38	49
		178	174	244
Tissue papers				
Manufacturing and converting		74	72	130
Distribution[2]		2	1	6
		76	73	136
Fine papers				
Manufacturing		(10)	(5)	27
Distribution[2]		7	11	10
		(3)	6	37
Corporate		(4)	(3)	3
Assets held for sale	4	(9)	(13)	(9)
Operating income before depreciation and amortization from continuing operations		238	237	411
Depreciation and amortization				
Boxboard		(64)	(49)	(49)
Containerboard		(38)	(37)	(37)
Specialty products		(20)	(21)	(19)
Tissue papers		(36)	(36)	(32)
Fine papers		(11)	(11)	(11)
Corporate and eliminations		8	9	9
Assets held for sale	4	2	2	2
		(159)	(143)	(137)
Operating income from continuing operations		79	94	274

1. The Company's containerboard sub-segment consists entirely of its interest in Norampac a joint venture.
2. Some or all of these sub-segments represent discontinued operations (see note 4).

Segmented Information

For the three-year period ended December 31, 2004
(in millions of Canadian dollars)

Purchases of property, plant and equipment of the Company presented by the reportable segments are as follows:

Purchases of property, plant and equipment	2004	2003	2002
Packaging products			
Boxboard			
Manufacturing	22	19	18
Converting	20	10	7
Others	6	5	3
	48	34	28
Containerboard[1]			
Manufacturing	13	14	18
Converting	15	13	10
Others	2	2	–
	30	29	28
Specialty products	16	19	20
	94	82	76
Tissue papers			
Manufacturing and converting	20	25	31
Distribution[2]	1	–	–
	21	25	31
Fine papers			
Manufacturing	10	7	16
Distribution[2]	–	1	1
Others	–	2	–
	10	10	17
Corporate	5	5	5
Assets held for sale	(1)	(1)	(1)
Total	129	121	128

1. The Company's containerboard sub-segment consists entirely of its interest in Norampac a joint venture.
2. Some or all of these sub-segments represent assets held for sale (see note 4).

Segmented Information

For the three-year period ended December 31, 2004
(in millions of Canadian dollars)

Identifiable assets and goodwill of the Company presented by the reportable segments are as follows:

Identifiable assets	2004	2003
Packaging products		
Boxboard	997	946
Containerboard[1]	744	717
Specialty products	438	390
	2,179	2,053
Tissue papers	552	546
Fine papers	369	363
Corporate	190	114
Consolidation revaluation[2]	(178)	(192)
Intersegment eliminations	(51)	(51)
	3,061	2,833
Investments	83	94
Total	3,144	2,927

Goodwill	2004	2003
Packaging products		
Boxboard	27	5
Containerboard[1]	106	99
Specialty products	7	7
	140	111
Tissue papers	10	10
Fine papers	4	4
Consolidation revaluation[3]	(41)	(42)
Total	113	83

1. The Company's containerboard sub-segment consists entirely of its interest in Norampac, a joint venture.

2. Consolidation revaluation includes adjustments of assets resulting from business acquisitions. It also includes the required adjustments resulting from the creation of Norampac, consisting mainly of reduction in property, plant and equipment and goodwill. The following table details the components of the consolidation revaluation relating to identifiable assets:

	2004	2003
Privatization of subsidiaries[a]	(44)	(48)
Creation of Norampac[b]	(75)	(80)
Creation of Norampac[c]	(45)	(50)
Others	(14)	(14)
	(178)	(192)

a) Represents the impact of the privatization of certain subsidiaries of the Company on December 31, 2000. The adjustment also reflects the accounting impact of the privatization of Cascades S.A. in 2002.

b) With respect to the creation of Norampac, the assets and liabilities that were contributed by the Company and Domtar Inc., the Company's joint venture partner in Norampac, were recorded at their fair market value. However, upon proportionate consolidation of the joint venture, the Company reduced its portion of the contributed assets and liabilities to their original carrying value.

c) A portion of the gain realized on the creation of Norampac was recognized against property, plant and equipment and goodwill. The net book value of the deferred gain allocated against goodwill was $22 million. For the years ended December 31, 2004 and 2003, the net book value of the deferred gain allocated against goodwill was $16 million and $17 million, respectively.

3. The amounts shown for identifiable assets include a reduction of goodwill for the years ended December 31, 2004 and 2003 amounting to $41 million and $42 million, respectively, which are shown separately in the table above under goodwill.

Segmented Information

For the three-year period ended December 31, 2004
(in millions of Canadian dollars)

Sales, property, plant and equipment and goodwill of the Company presented by the geographic segments are as follows:

	Note	2004	2003	2002
By geographic segment				
Sales				
Operations located in Canada				
Within Canada		1,571	1,660	1,747
To the United States		555	540	636
Offshore		54	51	47
		2,180	2,251	2,430
Operations located in United States				
Within the United States		833	614	596
To Canada		94	36	20
Offshore		31	–	2
		958	650	618
Operations located in Europe				
Within Europe		496	461	460
To the United States		5	8	10
To other countries		53	77	71
		554	546	541
Operations located in Mexico		–	2	2
Assets held for sale —				
Operations located in Canada	4	(438)	(454)	(473)
Total		3,254	2,995	3,118

	2004	2003
Property, plant and equipment		
Canada	993	1 013
United States	476	399
Europe	231	224
Total	1,700	1,636

	2004	2003
Goodwill		
Canada	61	60
United States	52	23
Total	113	83

Notes to Consolidated Financial Statements

For the three-year period ended December 31, 2004
(tabular amounts in millions of Canadian dollars, except per share amounts)

1 Accounting policies

Basis of presentation
The consolidated financial statements have been prepared in accordance with Canadian GAAP and include the significant accounting policies listed below.

Basis of consolidation
The consolidated financial statements include the accounts of the Company and its subsidiaries. They also include the portion of the accounts of the joint ventures accounted for through the proportionate consolidation method. Investments in significantly influenced companies are accounted for using the equity method.

Use of estimates
The preparation of financial statements in conformity with Canadian GAAP requires the use of estimates and assumptions that affect the reported amounts of assets and liabilities in the financial statements and disclosure of contingencies at the balance sheet date, as well as the reported amounts of revenues and expenses during the reporting period. On a regular basis and with the available information, management reviews its estimates regarding environmental costs, useful life of property, plant and equipment, impairment of long-term assets, goodwill and pension plans. Actual results could differ from those estimates. When adjustments become necessary, they are reported in earnings in the period in which they are known.

Revenue recognition
The Company recognizes its sales when persuasive evidence of an arrangement exits, goods are shipped, significant risks and benefits of ownership are transferred, price is fixed and determinable and the collection of the resulting receivable is reasonably assured.

Fair market value of financial instruments
The Company estimates the fair market value of its financial instruments based on current interest rates, market value and current pricing of financial instruments with similar terms. Unless otherwise disclosed herein, the carrying value of these financial instruments, especially those with current maturities such as cash and cash equivalents, accounts receivable, bank loans and advances, accounts payable and accrued liabilities, approximates their fair market value.

Derivative financial instruments
The Company uses derivative financial instruments in the management of its foreign currency, commodity and interest rate exposures. Except for certain interest rate swap agreements, the Company's policy is not to utilize derivative financial instruments for trading or speculative purposes.

The Company documents relationships between hedging instruments and hedged items, as well as its risk management objective and strategy for undertaking various hedge transactions. This process includes linking derivatives to specific assets and liabilities on the balance sheet or to specific firm commitments or forecasted transactions. The Company also assesses whether the derivatives that are used in hedging transactions are effective in offsetting changes in fair values or cash flows of hedged items.

Foreign exchange forward contracts designated as hedging instruments   In order to reduce the potential adverse effects of currency fluctuation, the Company enters into various foreign exchange forward contracts. Gains and losses on these derivative financial instruments used to hedge anticipated sales, purchases or interest expenses denominated in foreign currencies are recognized as an adjustment of sales, cost of sales or interest expenses when the underlying sale, purchase or interest expense is recorded.

Foreign exchange forward contracts and currency options not designated as hedging instruments   Foreign exchange forward contracts and currency options not designated as hedging instruments are recorded at fair value. The fair value of these instruments is reviewed periodically and the resulting gains and losses are reported to earnings.

Notes to Consolidated Financial Statements

For the three-year period ended December 31, 2004
(tabular amounts in millions of Canadian dollars, except per share amounts)

Commodity contracts designated as hedging instruments   The Company uses certain swaps and forward contracts on commodity in order to fix the price for nominal quantities of certain raw materials or finished goods to reduce the adverse effects of changes in raw material costs and sales prices of finished goods. Realized and unrealized gains and losses arising from these contracts are recognized in sales or cost of sales when the sale or purchase of the underlying commodity is recorded.

Commodity contracts not designated as hedging instruments   The Company also uses swaps and forward contracts on commodity that are not designated as hedging instruments. These instruments are recorded at fair value. The fair value of these contracts is reviewed periodically and the resulting gains and losses are reported to earnings.

Interest rate swap agreement designated as an hedging instrument   The Company enters into interest rate swap agreements in order to hedge the changes in fair value of a portion of its long-term debt. Interest expense on the debt is adjusted to include the payments made or received under the interest rate swaps.

Interest rate swap agreements not designated as hedging instruments   These interest rate swap agreements require the exchange of interest payments without actual exchange of the notional amount on which the payments are based. The Company adjusts the interest expense on the debt to include payments made or received under the interest rate swap agreements. These instruments are accounted for at fair value and resulting gains or losses are included in earnings under Selling and administrative expenses.

Others   Realized and unrealized gains or losses associated with derivative financial instruments, which have been terminated or cease to be effective prior to maturity, are deferred under current or long-term assets or liabilities and recognized in earnings in the period in which the underlying original hedged transaction is recognized. In the event a designated hedged item is sold, extinguished or matures prior to the termination of the related derivative financial instrument, any realized or unrealized gain or loss on such derivative financial instrument is recognized in earnings.

Derivative financial instruments which are not designated as hedges or have ceased to be effective prior to maturity are recorded at their estimated fair values under current or long-term assets or liabilities with changes in their estimated fair values recorded in earnings. Estimated fair value is determined using pricing models incorporating current market prices and the contractual prices of the underlying instruments, the time value of money and yield curves.

Cash and cash equivalents
Cash and cash equivalents include cash on hand, bank balances and short-term liquid investments with original maturities of three months or less.

Inventories
Inventories of finished goods are valued at the lower of average production cost and net realizable value. Inventories of raw materials and supplies are valued at the lower of cost and replacement value. Cost of raw materials and supplies is determined using the average cost and the first-in, first-out methods respectively.

Property, plant and equipment, depreciation and amortization
Property, plant and equipment are recorded at cost, including interest incurred during the construction period of certain property, plant and equipment. Depreciation and amortization are calculated on a straight-line basis at annual rates varying from 3% to 5% for buildings, 5% to 10% for machinery and equipment, and 15% to 20% for automotive equipment, determined according to the estimated useful life of each class of property, plant and equipment.

Grants and investment tax credits
Grants and investment tax credits are accounted for using the cost reduction method and are amortized to earnings as a reduction of depreciation and amortization, using the same rates as those used to amortize the related property, plant and equipment.

Notes to Consolidated Financial Statements

For the three-year period ended December 31, 2004
(tabular amounts in millions of Canadian dollars, except per share amounts)

Other investments

Other investments are recorded at cost except when there is a decline in value which is other than temporary, in which case they are reduced to their estimated net realizable value.

Goodwill

The Company assesses periodically whether a provision for impairment in the value of goodwill is required. This is accomplished mainly by determining whether projected discounted future cash flows exceed the net book value of goodwill of the respective business units. Goodwill is tested for impairment annually on December 31 or when an event or circumstance occurs that could potentially result in a permanent decline in value.

Impairment of long-lived assets

Long-lived assets are reviewed for impairment upon the concurrence of events or changes in circumstances indicating that the carrying value of the asset may not be recoverable, as measured by comparing their net book value to the estimated undiscounted future cash flows generated by their use. Impaired assets are recorded at fair value, determined principally using discounted future cash flows expected from their use and eventual disposition.

Deferred charges

Deferred charges are recorded at cost and include, in particular, the issuance costs of long-term debt, which are amortized on a straight-line basis over the anticipated period of repayment of the respective debt, and start-up costs which are amortized on a straight-line basis over a period of three to five years from the end of the start-up period.

Environmental costs

Environmental expenditures are expensed or capitalized depending upon their future economic benefit. Expenditures incurred to prevent future environmental contamination are capitalized and amortized on a straight-line basis at annual rates varying from 5% to 10%. Expenditures that relate to an existing condition caused by past operations, and which do not contribute to current or future revenue generation, are expensed. A provision for environmental costs is recorded when it is probable that a liability has been incurred and the costs can be reasonably estimated.

Asset retirement obligations

Asset retirement obligations are recognized, at fair value, in the period in which the Company incurred a legal obligation associated to the retirement of an asset. The associated costs are capitalized as part of the carrying value of the related asset and depreciated over its remaining useful life. The liability is accreted using a credit adjusted risk free interest rate of the Company.

Employee future benefits

The Company offers funded and non-funded defined benefit pension plans, some defined contribution pension plans, and group registered retirement savings plans("RRSPs") that provide retirement benefit payments for most of its employees. The defined benefit pension plans are usually contributory and are based on the number of years of service and, in most cases, based on the average gains at the end of career. Retirement benefits are in some cases, partially adjusted, based on inflation. The Company also provides to its employees complementary retirement benefit plans and other post-employment benefit plan, such as group life insurance and medical and dental care plans. However, these benefits, other than pension plans, are not funded.

The cost of pensions and other retirement benefits earned by employees is actuarially determined using the projected benefit method pro-rated on years of service and management's best estimate of expected plan investment performance, salary escalations, retirement ages of employees and expected health care costs. The accrued benefit obligation is evaluated using the market interest rate at the evaluation date.

Notes to Consolidated Financial Statements

For the three-year period ended December 31, 2004
(tabular amounts in millions of Canadian dollars, except per share amounts)

For the purpose of calculating the expected return on plan assets, those assets are valued at fair value. Past service costs arising from a plan amendment are amortized on a straight-line basis over the average remaining service period of the group of employees active at the date of the amendment. The excess of the net actuarial gain or loss over the greater of (a) 10% of the accrued benefit obligation at the beginning of the year and (b) 10% of the fair value of plan assets at the beginning of the year, is amortized over the average remaining service period of active employees, which may vary from 8 to 19 years (weighted average of 13 years) in 2004 depending on the plan (2003 — 8 to 19 years (weighted average of 13 years)).

When restructuring a plan causes a curtailment and a settlement at the same time, the curtailment is accounted for before the settlement.

The measurement date of most of the retirement benefit plans is December 31 of every year. An actuarial evaluation is performed at least every three years. The last evaluation took place on December 31, 2003 for almost half of the plans and on December 31, 2002 for most of the other plans.

Income taxes

The Company uses the liability method in accounting for income taxes. According to this method, future income taxes are determined using the difference between the accounting and tax bases of assets and liabilities. Future income tax assets and liabilities are measured using substantively enacted tax rates in effect in the year in which these temporary differences are expected to be recovered or settled. Future income tax assets are recognized when it is more likely than not that the assets will be realized.

Foreign currency translation

Foreign currency transactions   Transactions denominated in foreign currencies are recorded at the rate of exchange prevailing at the transaction date. Monetary assets and liabilities denominated in foreign currencies are translated at the rate of exchange prevailing at the balance sheet date. Gains and losses related to the portion of the long-term debt designated as a hedge of the net investment of the Company in self-sustaining foreign operations are recorded in cumulative translation adjustments net of related income taxes. Unrealized gains and losses on translation of other monetary assets and liabilities are reflected in the determination of the net results for the year.

Foreign operations   The Company's foreign operations are defined as self-sustaining. The assets and liabilities of these operations are translated into Canadian dollars at the rate of exchange prevailing at the balance sheet date. Revenues and expenses are translated at the average exchange rate for the year. Translation gains and losses are deferred and shown as a separate component of shareholders' equity as cumulative translation adjustments.

Stock-based compensation

The Company applies the fair value method of accounting for stock-based compensation awards granted to officers and key employees. This method consists of recording expenses to earnings based on the vesting period of the options granted. The fair value is calculated based on the Black-Scholes option pricing model. This model was developed for use in estimating the fair value of traded options that have no vesting restrictions and are fully transferable. When stock options are exercised, any consideration paid by employees is credited to capital stock.

Amounts per common share

Amounts per common share are determined using the weighted average number of common shares outstanding during the year. Diluted amounts per common share are determined using the treasury stock method to evaluate the dilutive effect of stock options, convertible instruments and equivalents, when applicable. Under this method, instruments with a dilutive effect, basically when the average market price of a share for the period exceeds the exercise price, are considered to have been exercised at the beginning of the period and the proceeds received are considered to have been used to redeem common shares of the Company at the average market price for the period.

Notes to Consolidated Financial Statements

For the three-year period ended December 31, 2004
(tabular amounts in millions of Canadian dollars, except per share amounts)

2 Changes in accounting policies

New accounting standards adopted

a) Employee future benefits   On June 30, 2004, the Company adopted prospectively the new recommendations of the Canadian Institute of Chartered Accountants ("CICA") regarding employee future benefits that require additional disclosure about the assets, cash flows and net periodic cost of defined benefit pension plans and other employee future benefit plans. Refer to note 18 regarding the additionnal disclosure requirements.

b) Hedging relationships   On January 1, 2004, the Company adopted prospectively Accounting Guideline 13 ("AcG-13") regarding hedge accounting. In compliance with the criteria required by AcG-13, hedge accounting requires the Company to document the risk management strategy used. Upon executing a hedging contract, management documents the hedged item, namely asset, liability or anticipated transaction, the characteristics of the hedging instrument used and the selected method of assessing effectiveness. The current accounting policy will be maintained for hedging relationships deemed to be effective at January 1, 2004. Consequently, realized and unrealized gains and losses on hedges will continue to be deferred until the hedged item is realized so as to allow matching of the designations in the statement of earnings. Hedge accounting was applied as at January 1, 2004 for hedging relationships existing as at December 31, 2003 that satisfied the conditions of AcG-13. Hedging relationships existing as at December 31, 2003 that did not satisfy the conditions of AcG-13 were recorded at fair value as at January 1, 2004, resulting in an increase in assets of $3.7 million and in liabilities of $0.1 million. The related unrealized gain of $3.6 million was deferred and presented under other liabilities on the balance sheet.

c) Asset retirement obligations   On January 1, 2004, the Company adopted retroactively, without prior period restatement, the new recommendations of the CICA relating to asset retirement obligations. This standard requires that the fair value of a liability for an asset retirement obligation be recognized in the period in which it is incurred if a reasonable estimate of fair value can be made. The application of this standard did not have any significant impact on the financial position or results of operations of the Company.

d) Generally accepted accounting principles   On January 1, 2004, the Company adopted retroactively with prior period restatement CICA Section 1100, *"Generally Accepted Accounting Principles"*, and Section 1400, *"General Standards for Financial Statement Presentation."* Section 1100 clarifies the relative authority of various accounting pronouncements and other sources of guidance within GAAP, whereas Section 1400 clarifies what constitutes a fair presentation in accordance with GAAP. In addition, under Section 1100, industry practice no longer plays a role in establishing GAAP. As a result, the cost of delivery, which had been subtracted from sales in accordance with industry practice, is no longer subtracted from sales, but rather is included in cost of goods sold. The cost of delivery for the year ended December 31, 2004, 2003 and 2002 amounted to $217 million, $208 million and $207 million respectively and have been included in the cost of good sold resulting, in the restatement of the comparative figures of 2003 and 2002.

e) Impairment of long-lived assets   On January 1, 2004, the Company adopted new CICA Handbook Section 3063, *"Impairment of Long-lived Assets."* Section 3063 provides accounting guidance for the recognition, measurement and disclosure of impairment of long-lived assets, including property, plant and equipment and intangible assets with finite useful lives. Section 3063 requires the recognition of an impairment loss for a long-lived asset when events or changes in circumstances cause its carrying value to exceed the total undiscounted future cash flows expected from its use and eventual disposition. The impairment loss is calculated by deducting the fair value of the asset from its carrying value. This change in accounting policy has been applied prospectively and had no impact on the Company's financial statements on January 1, 2004.

Notes to Consolidated Financial Statements

For the three-year period ended December 31, 2004
(tabular amounts in millions of Canadian dollars, except per share amounts)

f) Guarantees   On January 1, 2003, the Company adopted prospectively the new guideline of the CICA regarding the disclosure of guarantees. Under this new guideline, entities are required to disclose key information about certain types of guarantee contracts that require payments contingent on specified types of future events. Disclosures include the nature of the guarantee, how it arose, the events or circumstances that would trigger performance under the guarantee, maximum potential future payments under the guarantee, the carrying amount of the related liability and information about recourse or collateral. Note 19(b) provides the required disclosure.

g) Long-lived assets and discontinued operations   The Company adopted prospectively the new guideline of the CICA regarding the disposal of long-lived assets and discontinued operations, which applies to disposal activities initiated on or after May 1, 2003. This new section sets standards for recognition, measurement, presentation and disclosure of the disposal of long-lived assets. It also sets standards for the presentation and disclosure of discontinued operations. The adoption of this standard did not impact the financial statements.

New accounting standards not yet adopted

h) Variable interest entities   In June 2003, the CICA issued Accounting Guideline 15 ("AcG-15"), *"Consolidation of variable interest entities."* The new guideline requires companies to identify variable interest entities in which they have an interest to determine whether they are the primary beneficiary of such entities and, if so, to consolidate them. A variable interest entity is defined as an entity in which the equity is not sufficient to permit that entity to finance its activities without external support, or the equity investors lack either voting control and obligation to absorb future losses or the right to receive future returns. At the end of 2003, the CICA announced the deferral of the effective date of AcG-15 as it expects to make certain amendments. Previously, AcG-15 was to be effective for interim and annual periods starting on or after January 1, 2004. It will be effective for interim and annual periods beginning on or after November 1, 2004. The application of this standard will not have any material impact on the financial position or results of operations of the Company.

i) Financial instruments, hedging, capital assets and comprehensive income   In January 2005, the CICA published four new sections: Section 1530, *"Comprehensive Income;"* Section 3251, *"Equity;"* Section 3855, *"Financial Instruments — Recognition and Measurement,"* and Section 3865, *"Hedges."* These new standards regarding recognition and measurement of financial instruments, hedging and comprehensive income have been created to harmonize with the generally accepted accounting policies already used in the United States (U.S. GAAP). These new standards have to be adopted by the Company at the latest for the period beginning January 1, 2007, but early adoption is encouraged. The Company is presently evaluating the impact of these new standards.

3 Measurement uncertainty

The Company evaluates the net book value of its long-lived assets when events or changes in circumstances indicate that the net book value of the assets may not be recoverable. To evaluate long-lived assets, the Company determines if the undiscounted future cash flows of operating activities exceed the net book value of the assets at the valuation date. Estimate of future cash flows and fair value are based on judgment and could change.

During the fourth quarter of 2004, the Company performed an impairment test on long-lived assets of certain operating units due to their operating loss for the current period.

According to the results of the impairment tests performed, it is not necessary to record an impairment loss for these operating units with the exception of the impairment loss on property, plant and equipment disclosed in note 14. However, given the sensitivity of certain key assumptions used, such as exchange rates, selling prices and costs of raw materials, there is a measurement uncertainty regarding of certain operating units because it is reasonably possible that variations of future conditions could require a change in the stated amount of the long-lived assets when new impairment tests will be prepared.

For the three-year period ended December 31, 2004
(tabular amounts in millions of Canadian dollars, except per share amounts)

4 Assets held for sale

During the fourth quarter of 2004, the Company decided to initiate a divestiture plan for its distribution activities in the Fine papers and Tissue papers segments. Consequently, the assets, liabilities, earnings and cash flows from these activities for the current period and for all comparative periods, are classified as assets held for sale. The comparative financial information of 2003 and 2002 has been restated to reflect this change. Financial information relating to these assets held for sale is as follows:

	2004	2003	2002
Condensed balance sheet			
Current assets	126	126	
Long-term assets	9	12	
Current liabilities	29	31	
Condensed statement of earnings			
Sales	438	454	473
Depreciation and amortization	2	2	2
Operating income	7	11	7
Interest expenses	3	3	3
Income taxes	1	4	1
Net earnings from assets held for sale	3	4	3
Net earnings per share from assets held for sale	0.03	0.05	0.03
Condensed statement of cash flows			
Cash flows from operating activities	1	14	(5)
Cash flows from investing activities	(1)	(1)	(5)
Cash flows from financing activities	–	(13)	10

For the three-year period ended December 31, 2004
(tabular amounts in millions of Canadian dollars, except per share amounts)

5 Business acquisitions and disposal

a) 2004 acquisitions   On February 18, 2004 and June 3, 2004, the Company acquired the 50% interest held by its partners in Cascades Sonoco S.A. for a nil amount and in Greenfield SAS for a cash consideration of $2 million (€1.5 million). On March 11, 2004, the Company acquired the assets of a tissue mill located in Memphis, Tennessee, from American Tissue or affiliates thereof, for a cash consideration of $15 million (US$11.4 million). On April 2, 2004, a joint venture of the Company acquired the shares of Johnson Corrugated Products Corp., a corrugated products plant in Thompson, Connecticut, for an approximate cash consideration of $15 million (US$11.7 million). The Company's 50% share of the purchase price amounted to $8 million (US$5.9 million). On June 11, 2004, a joint venture of the Company acquired the non-controlling interest of its subsidiary for a cash consideration of $14 million. The Company's 50% share of the purchase price amounted to $7 million.

On August 24, 2004, the Company acquired the remaining outstanding shares (50%) of Dopaco Inc., a U.S. producer of packaging products for the quick service restaurant industry, for an approximate consideration of $139 million (US$106.5 million), of which $82 million (US$63 million) has been paid in cash at the closing date and a balance estimated at $57 million (US$43.5 million) will be payable in May 2005 based on a financial formula. The balance sheet and results of Dopaco, Inc. are fully consolidated since that date. On August 27, 2004, a joint venture of the Company acquired the assets of AIM Corrugated Container Corp., a corrugated products plant in Lancaster, New York, for an approximate cash consideration of $21 million (US$16 million). The Company's 50% share of the purchase price amounted to $10 million (US$8 million).

2003 acquisitions   On March 6, 2003, the Company acquired 50% of the assets of La Compagnie Greenfield S.A. as part of its packaging products group for $0.6 million (€0.3 million). On April 14, 2003, a joint venture of the Company acquired a corrugated products converting plant as part of its packaging products group, located in Schenectady, New York. The aggregate purchase price, subject to certain adjustments, was $32 million (US$22 million) and comprised $20 million (US$14 million) in cash and all the operating assets of its Dallas-Fort Worth, Texas plant valued at $12 million (US$8 million). The Company's 50% share in the cash portion of the purchase price amounted to $10 million (US$7 million).

On October 1, 2003, the Company increased its investment in Dopaco, Inc. from 40% to 50%, for a consideration of $17 million (US$12.4 million). The balance sheet and results of Dopaco, Inc. have been proportionally consolidated since October 1, 2003.

On December 22, 2003, the Company completed the acquisition of all shares in Scierie P. H. Lemay ltée, a Canadian company operating a sawing and a planing plant, for a consideration of $3 million. Prior to this transaction, the Company had a 50% holding in that company.

2002 acquisitions   On January 2, 2002, one of the Company's joint ventures increased its investment in Metro Waste Paper Recovery Inc. ("Metro Waste"), another joint venture, in exchange for assets having a net value of $6 million. On January 21, 2002, one of the Company's joint ventures acquired Star Leominster as part of the packaging products segment for $50 million (US$31 million), the Company's share amounting to $25 million (US$15.5 million). On March 27, 2002, the Company acquired converting operations from American Tissue as part of the tissue papers segment for an amount of $30 million (US$19 million). On June 14, 2002, the Company completed the acquisition of two manufacturing units of American Tissue for a consideration of $66 million (US$43 million). Other acquisitions and price adjustments on prior transactions amounted to $10 million including an acquisition realized by the distribution division of Fine Paper group for an amount of $4 million, which is classified as an asset held for sale.

These acquisitions have been accounted for using the purchase method and the accounts and results of operations of these entities have been included in the consolidated financial statements since their respective dates of acquisition. The following allocations of the purchase prices to the identifiable assets acquired and liabilities assumed resulted in goodwill of $33 million as at December 31, 2004 (2003 — $7 million; 2002 — $17 million) of which $10 million was already recorded in Dopaco's books at the date of transaction. None of the above-mentioned goodwill is expected to be deductible for tax purposes with the exception of an amount of $5 million as at December 31, 2004 (2003 — $4 million). The purchase price allocations presented in the table below for the acquisitions of Dopaco and AIM have not been completed yet mainly with respect to the identification and valuation of other potential intangible assets.

Notes to Consolidated Financial Statements

For the three-year period ended December 31, 2004
(tabular amounts in millions of Canadian dollars, except per share amounts)

2004	Dopaco	AIM & Johnson	American Tissue	Others	
	Packaging products	Packaging products	Tissue papers	Packaging products	Total
Cash and cash equivalents	2	1	–	1	4
Accounts receivable	26	3	–	4	33
Inventories	38	–	–	6	44
Property, plant and equipment	123	8	15	3	149
Customer relationship and client lists	26	–	–	4	30
Goodwill	24	9	–	–	33
	239	21	15	18	293
Accounts payable and accrued liabilities	(27)	(2)	–	(8)	(37)
Long-term debt	(17)	–	–	(3)	(20)
Other liabilities	(46)	(1)	–	2	(45)
	149	18	15	9	191
Less: Investments realized in prior years	(10)	–	–	–	(10)
Less: Balance of purchase price	(57)	–	–	–	(57)
Total consideration	82	18	15	9	124

2003	Greenfield	Schenectady	Dopaco	Scierie Lemay	
	Packaging products	Packaging products	Packaging products	Packaging products	Total
Accounts receivable	–	2	19	4	25
Inventories	2	2	27	9	40
Property, plant and equipment	–	11	107	16	134
Other assets	–	–	10	4	14
Goodwill	–	2	4	1	7
	2	17	167	34	220
Bank loans and advances	–	–	–	(5)	(5)
Accounts payable and accrued liabilities	(1)	(1)	(22)	(6)	(30)
Long-term debt	–	–	(14)	(10)	(24)
Other liabilities	–	–	(32)	(3)	(35)
	1	16	99	10	126
Less: Fair market value of assets exchanged	–	(6)	–	–	(6)
Less: Investments realized in prior years	–	–	(82)	(7)	(89)
Total consideration	1	10	17	3	31

56

Notes to Consolidated Financial Statements

For the three-year period ended December 31, 2004
(tabular amounts in millions of Canadian dollars, except per share amounts)

2002	American Tissue	Star Leominster	Metro Waste	Others	
	Tissue papers	Packaging products	Packaging products		Total
Accounts receivable	–	3	2	6	11
Inventories	–	2	–	3	5
Property, plant and equipment	92	9	4	13	118
Other assets	4	–	–	–	4
Goodwill	–	15	2	–	17
	96	29	8	22	155
Accounts payable and accrued liabilities	–	(2)	(2)	(3)	(7)
Other liabilities	–	(2)	–	–	(2)
	96	25	6	19	146
Less: Fair market value of assets exchanged	–	–	(6)	–	(6)
Total compensation paid by assets held for sale	–	–	–	(4)	(4)
Less: Investments realized in prior years	–	–	–	(9)	(9)
Total consideration	96	25	–	6	127

b) Disposals   On May 10, 2004, the Company sold the assets of two of its fiberboard panel businesses (packaging products segment) located in Canada for a total consideration of $16 million. Of this transaction price, $14 million was received at closing and $2 million will be received at the latest in 2011. The Company realized a gain of $4 million before related income taxes of $1 million.

   In 2002, the Company sold its retail egg carton operation (packaging products segment) located in Canada for a cash consideration of $4 million, and realized a $5 million losses.

6 Inventories

	2004	2003
Finished goods	284	260
Raw materials	130	104
Supplies	145	137
	559	501

Notes to Consolidated Financial Statements

For the three-year period ended December 31, 2004
(tabular amounts in millions of Canadian dollars, except per share amounts)

7 Property, plant and equipment

2004	Cost	Accumulated depreciation and amortization	Net
Lands	52	–	52
Buildings	436	140	296
Machinery and equipment	2,491	1,207	1,284
Automotive equipment	52	41	11
Others	72	15	57
	3,103	1,403	1,700

2003	Cost	Accumulated depreciation and amortization	Net
Lands	53	–	53
Buildings	431	129	302
Machinery and equipment	2,271	1,047	1,224
Automotive equipment	53	40	13
Others	51	7	44
	2,859	1,223	1,636

Property, plant and equipment include assets under capital leases with a cost of $9 million and accumulated amortization of $3 million as at December 31, 2004 (2003 — $13 million and $4 million respectively). Other property, plant and equipment include items that are not amortized, such as machinery and equipment in the process of installation with a book value of $28 million (2003 — $23 million), deposits on purchases of property, plant and equipment amounting to $12 million (2003 — $2 million) and unused properties, machinery and equipment with a net book value of $10 million (2003 — $15 million) which do not exceed their estimated net realizable value.

Depreciation and amortization of property, plant and equipment amounted to $157 million for the year ended December 31, 2004 (2003 — $141 million; 2002 — $131 million).

Notes to Consolidated Financial Statements

For the three-year period ended December 31, 2004
(tabular amounts in millions of Canadian dollars, except per share amounts)

8 Other assets and goodwill

a) Other assets are detailed as follows:

	Note	2004	2003
Investments in significantly influenced companies		74	85
Other investments		9	9
Deferred charges	8 c)	38	36
Employee future benefits	18 b)	52	50
Fair value of derivative financial instruments		8	–
Other definite-life intangible assets	8 c)	34	6
		215	186

b) Goodwill fluctuated as follows:

		Packaging products				
2004	Boxboard	Container-board	Specialty products	Sub-total	Tissue papers	Total
Carrying value of goodwill–Beginning of year	5	66	2	73	10	83
Goodwill resulting from business acquisitions	24	9	–	33	–	33
Amortization of a deferred gain[1]	–	1	–	1	–	1
Foreign currency translation	(2)	(2)	–	(4)	–	(4)
Carrying value of goodwill–End of year	27	74	2	103	10	113

		Packaging products				
2003	Boxboard	Container-board	Specialty products	Sub-total	Tissue papers	Total
Carrying value of goodwill–Beginning of year	–	67	2	69	10	79
Goodwill resulting from acquisitions	5	2	–	7	–	7
Amortization of a deferred gain[1]	–	1	–	1	–	1
Foreign currency translation	–	(4)	–	(4)	–	(4)
Carrying value of goodwill–End of year	5	66	2	73	10	83

1. On December 30, 1997, the Company and Domtar Inc. merged their respective containerboard and corrugated packaging operations to form Norampac, a 50-50 joint venture. A portion of the gain realized on the transaction was recorded against property, plant and equipment and goodwill. Under current accounting standards, the portion of the deferred gain allocated to goodwill is amortized on a straight-line basis over a period of 25 years.

Notes to Consolidated Financial Statements

For the three-year period ended December 31, 2004
(tabular amounts in millions of Canadian dollars, except per share amounts)

c) Deferred charges and other definite-life intangible assets are detailed as follows:

		2004			2003	
	Cost	Accumulated depreciation and amortization	Net	Cost	Accumulated depreciation and amortization	Net
Deferred charges						
Start-up cost	34	24	10	31	26	5
Financing costs	33	9	24	36	10	26
Other	10	6	4	9	4	5
	77	39	38	76	40	36
Other definite-life intangible assets						
Customer relationship and client lists	32	2	30	3	1	2
Others	7	3	4	8	4	4
	39	5	34	11	5	6

Depreciation and amortization of deferred charges and other definite-life intangible assets, calculated on a straight-line basis, amounted to $8 million for the year ended December 31, 2004 (2003 — $5 million; 2002 — $9 million).

The weighted average amortization period is as follows (in number of years):

Start-up cost	4
Financing costs	9
Other	4
Deferred charges	7
Customer relationship and client list	26
Others	24
Other definite-life intangible assets	26

The estimated aggregate amount of depreciation and amortization expense in each of the next five years is as follows:

Years ending December 31,	
2005	8
2006	7
2007	5
2008	4
2009	3

Notes to Consolidated Financial Statements

For the three-year period ended December 31, 2004
(tabular amounts in millions of Canadian dollars, except per share amounts)

9 Long-term debt

Cascades Inc. and its subsidiaries	Note	2004	2003
Revolving credit facility, weighted average rate of 3.90% as at December 31, 2004, maturing in February 2007	9 a)	159	168
7.25% Unsecured senior notes of US$675 million (2003–US$550 million), maturing in 2013	9 a) c)	813	711
Balance on purchase price	5 a)	52	–
Capital lease obligations	9 c) g)	5	13
Other debts		19	23
		1,048	915
Less: Current portion		56	10
		992	905

The Company's proportionate share of the following debts of joint ventures do not give to their holders any recourse against the assets or general credit of Cascades Inc. and its subsidiaries.

Joint ventures	Note	2004	2003
Revolving credit facility, weighted average rate of 3.63% as at December 31, 2004, maturing in May 2008	9 b)	10	11
6.75% Unsecured senior notes of US$250 million (Cascades portion US$125 million), maturing in 2013	9 b) c)	151	161
Other debts		17	23
		178	195
Less: Current portion		2	8
		176	187

Total	2004	2003
Long-term debt	1,226	1,110
Less: Current portion	58	18
	1,168	1,092

a) On February 5, 2003, the Company completed a series of transactions to refinance substantially all of its existing credit facilities, except those of its joint ventures. It secured a new four-year revolving credit facility of CA$500 million. Its obligations under this new revolving credit facility are secured by all inventory and receivables of Cascades and its North American subsidiaries and by the property, plant and equipment of three of its mills. In addition, it issued new unsecured senior notes for an aggregate amount of US$450 million which were subsequently registered with the Securities and Exchange Commission of the United States. These notes, bearing a 7.25% coupon, will mature in 2013 and are redeemable all or in part at the option of the Company under certain conditions and subject to payment of a redemption premium. The aggregate proceeds of these two transactions, combined with its available cash on hand, were used by the Company to repay substantially all of the existing credit facilities. On March 12, 2003, the Company also redeemed the US$125 million 8.375% senior notes originally due in 2007 issued by its subsidiary, Cascades Boxboard Group Inc.

Notes to Consolidated Financial Statements

For the three-year period ended December 31, 2004
(tabular amounts in millions of Canadian dollars, except per share amounts)

On July 8, 2003, the Company completed a private placement of US$100 million of 7.25% senior notes due in 2013, which are treated as part of the same series of 7.25% senior notes due in 2013 issued in February, as described above. These senior notes were subsequently registered with the Securities and Exchange Commission of the United States. The issuance of these senior notes was completed at a price of 104.50% or an effective interest rate of 6.61%. The proceeds of this financing were used to reduce indebtedness under the revolving credit facility of the Company.

On December 2, 2004, the Company completed a private placement of US$125 million of 7.25% senior notes due in 2013, which are treated as part of the same series of 7.25% senior notes due in 2013 issued in February 2003. The issuance of these senior notes was completed at a price of 105.50% or an effective interest rate of 6.376%. The proceeds of this financing were used to reduce indebtedness under the revolving credit facility of the Company.

b) On May 28, 2003, a joint venture of the Company, Norampac Inc., completed a series of transactions to substantially refinance all of its existing credit facilities. Norampac secured a new five-year revolving credit facility of CA$350 million. Its obligations under this new revolving credit facility are secured by all inventory and receivables of Norampac and its North American subsidiaries, and by the property, plant and equipment of two of its mills and three of its converting facilities. In addition, Norampac issued new unsecured senior notes for an aggregate amount of US$250 million which were subsequently registered with the Securities and Exchange Commission of the United States. These notes, bearing a 6.75% coupon, will mature in 2013 and are redeemable in all or in part at the option of the Company under certain conditions and subject to payment of a redemption premium. The aggregate proceeds of these two transactions were used by the joint venture to repay substantially all of the existing credit facilities and to redeem both its US$150 million 9.50% and CA$100 million 9.375% senior notes originally due in 2008.

c) As at December 31, 2004, the fair value of the senior notes and the capital lease obligations of Cascades Inc. and its subsidiaries and joint ventures was estimated at $865 million and $158 million respectively (December 31, 2003 — $759 million and $167 million respectively) based on the market value of the senior notes and on discounted future cash flows using interest rates available for issues with similar terms and average maturities.

d) As at December 31, 2004, the long-term debt included amounts denominated in foreign currencies of US$933 million and €31 million (December 31, 2003 — US$691 million and €22 million).

e) As at December 31, 2004, accounts receivable and inventories totalling approximately $589 million (2003 — $512 million) as well as property, plant and equipment totalling approximately $156 million (2003 — $160 million) were pledged as collateral for the long-term debt of Cascades Inc. and its subsidiaries.

Accounts receivable and inventory totalling approximately $149 million (2003 — $136 million) as well as property, plant and equipment totalling approximately $75 million (2003 — $74 million) were pledged as collateral for the long-term debt of a joint venture.

f) The estimated aggregate amount of repayments on long-term debt, excluding capital lease obligations, in each of the next five years is as follows:

Years ending December 31,	Cascades Inc. and its subsidiaries	Joint ventures
2005	54	2
2006	1	3
2007	160	2
2008	–	12
2009	–	5
Thereafter	828	154

Notes to Consolidated Financial Statements

For the three-year period ended December 31, 2004
(tabular amounts in millions of Canadian dollars, except per share amounts)

g) As at December 31, 2004, future minimum payments under capital lease obligations are as follows:

Years ending December 31,	Cascades Inc. and its subsidiaries	Joint ventures
2005	2	–
2006	2	–
2007	1	–
2008	1	–
	6	–
Less: Interest (weighted average rate of 6.22%)	1	–
	5	–
Less: Current portion	2	–
	3	–

h) As at December 31, 2004, the Company and joint ventures had unused credit facilities of $334 million and $168 million respectively (December 31, 2003 — $330 million and $181 million respectively).

10 Other liabilities

	Note	2004	2003
Employee future benefits	18 b)	84	80
Future income taxes	16 c)	214	182
Unrealized gain on derivative financial instruments		5	–
Non-controlling interests		–	3
		303	265

11 Capital stock

	Note	2004	2003
Common shares	11 a)	261	262
Adjustment relating to stock options and others	11 c)	4	2
		265	264

a) The authorized capital stock of the Company consists of an unlimited number of common shares, without nominal value, and an unlimited number of Class A and B shares issuable in series without nominal value. Over the past two years, the common shares have fluctuated as follows:

	Note	2004		2003	
		Number of shares	$	Number of shares	$
Balance–Beginning of year		81,731,387	262	81,826,272	261
Shares issued on exercise of stock options	11 c)	133,893	1	180,115	2
Redemption of common shares	11 d)	(503,700)	(2)	(275,000)	(1)
Balance–End of year		81,361,580	261	81,731,387	262

Notes to Consolidated Financial Statements

For the three-year period ended December 31, 2004
(tabular amounts in millions of Canadian dollars, except per share amounts)

b) In 2003, the Company purchased the totality of 4,300,000 Class B preferred shares of a subsidiary for a consideration of $16 million. The excess of the redemption price of $10 million over the recorded capital is included in retained earnings.

c) Under the terms of a share option plan adopted on December 15, 1998 for officers and key employees of the Company and its joint ventures, 6,547,261 common shares have been specifically reserved for issuance. Each option will expire at a date not to exceed ten years following the date the option was granted. The exercise price of an option shall not be lower than the market value of the share at the date of grant, determined as the average of the closing price of the share on the Toronto Stock Exchange on the five trading days preceding the date of grant. The terms for exercising the options granted before December 31, 2003 are 25% of the number of shares under option within twelve months after the date of grant, and up to an additional 25% each twelve months after the first, second and third anniversary dates of grant. The terms for exercising the option granted in 2004 and thereafter are 25% of the number of shares within the first anniversary date of grant, and up to an additional 25% each twelve months after the second, third and fourth anniversary date of grant. The options cannot be exercised if the market value of the share is lower than its book value at the date of grant.

Changes in the number of options outstanding as at December 31 are as follows:

	2004		2003		2002	
	Number of options	Weighted average exercise price ($)	Number of options	Weighted average exercise price ($)	Number of options	Weighted average exercise price ($)
Beginning of year	1,494,942	9.83	1,378,610	8.82	1,492,652	7.44
Granted	407,723	13.02	321,596	13.04	324,113	13.24
Exercised	(133,893)	8.27	(180,115)	7.92	(407,062)	7.13
Forfeited	(11,786)	13.10	(25,149)	8.99	(31,093)	10.79
End of year	1,756,986	10.67	1,494,942	9.83	1,378,610	8.82
Options exercisable–End of year	1,131,655	9.35	935,011	8.55	886,413	8.19

The following options were outstanding as at December 31, 2004:

	Options outstanding				Options exercisable
Year granted	Number of options	Weighted average exercise price ($)	Number of options	Weighted average exercise price ($)	Expiration
1996	39,320	6.68	39,320	6.68	2006
1999	327,369	8.54	327,369	8.54	2009
2000	73,976	7.78	73,976	7.78	2010
2001	337,896	6.82	337,896	6.82	2011
2002	270,810	13.24	203,108	13.24	2012
2003	299,972	13.04	149,986	13.04	2013
2004	407,643	13.02	–	–	2014
	1,756,986		1,131,655		

The following assumptions were used to estimate the fair value, at the date of grant, of each option issued to employees:

	2004	2003
Risk-free interest rate	4.3%	4.8%
Expected dividend yield	1.24 %	1.21%
Expected life of the options	6 years	6 years
Expected volatility	29%	28%
Weighted average fair value of issued option	$4.07	$4.36

For the three-year period ended December 31, 2004
(tabular amounts in millions of Canadian dollars, except per share amounts)

d) In 2004, in the normal course of business, the Company renewed its redemption program of a maximum of 4,086,964 common shares with the Toronto Stock Exchange which represent approximately 5% of issued and outstanding common shares. The redemption authorization is valid from March 11, 2004 to March 10, 2005. In 2004, the Company redeemed 503,700 common shares under this program for a consideration of approximately $7 million.

e) The basic and diluted net earnings per common share for the years ended December 31, 2004, 2003 and 2002 are calculated as follows:

	2004	2003	2002
Net earnings	22.6	54.7	169.5
Dividends–Preferred shares	–	(0.5)	(1.1)
Net earnings available to common shareholders	22.6	54.2	168.4
Weighted average common shares	81.7	81.7	81.5
Dilution effect of stock options	0.3	0.4	0.8
Adjusted weighted average common shares	82.0	82.1	82.3
Basic net earnings per common share	0.28	0.66	2.07
Diluted net earnings per common share	0.28	0.66	2.05

f) The Company offered to its Canadian employees a share purchase plan of its common stock. Employees can contribute, on a voluntary basis, up to a maximum of 5% of their salary and, if certain conditions are met, the Company will contribute to the plan 25% of the employee's contribution.

The shares are purchased on the market on a predetermined date each month. For the years ended December 31, 2004, 2003 and 2002, the Company's contribution to the plan amounted to $0.6 million annually.

12 Share of earnings of significantly influenced companies

On February 20, 2002, a significantly influenced company, Boralex Inc., sold seven power stations to an income fund. The Company thus realized a gain of $18 million net of related future income taxes of $5 million, representing its share of the net gain realized by this significantly influenced company.

In 2003, this gain was subsequently adjusted by Boralex Inc. The Company thus recorded its share of that adjustment representing a loss of $3 million net of related future income taxes.

13 Unusual losses (gains)

	Note	2004	2003	2002
Loss (gain) on business disposal	5 b)	(4)	–	5
Gain on dilution and disposal of an investment	13 a)	–	–	(1)
Expenses related to business closures	13 b)	–	–	6
Other income	13 c)	–	–	(6)
		(4)	–	4

a) In 2002, the Company realized a gain of $1 million resulting from the dilution of its investments in a significantly influenced company.

b) In 2002, the Company closed one of its converting folding boxboard units located in Ontario, incurring closing costs of $6 million.

c) In 2002, the Court of First Instance of the European Community reduced the amount of the fine imposed in 1994. The reduction in the fine and the related interest thereon have been recorded as a gain amounting to $6 million.

For the three-year period ended December 31, 2004
(tabular amounts in millions of Canadian dollars, except per share amounts)

14 Impairment of property, plant and equipment

In 2004, the Company recorded an impairment loss of $18 million ($12 million after-tax) related to the property, plant and equipment of its de-inked pulp mill located in Cap-de-la-Madeleine, Quebec, which was temporarily closed in March 2003. The Company decided to permanently shutdown this facility. The book value of those assets has been written down to its fair value representing the present value of the estimated net proceeds from dismantling, redeployment or disposal. Those assets are part of the Specialty products group in the Packaging products segment.

15 Loss (gain) on derivative financial instruments

	2004	2003	2002
Realized loss on derivative financial instruments	–	1	–
Amortization of transitional deferred unrealized gain under AcG-13	(2)	–	–
	(2)	1	–

16 Income taxes

a) The provision for income taxes is as follows:

	2004	2003	2002
Current	22	11	47
Future	(20)	(1)	13
	2	10	60

b) The provision for income taxes based on the effective income tax rate differs from the provision for income tax expense based on the combined basic rate for the following reasons:

	2004	2003	2002
Provision for income taxes based on the combined basic Canadian and provincial income tax rate	9	26	88
Provision for income taxes (recovery) arising from the following:			
Adjustment related to deduction for manufacturing and processing and income from active businesses carried on in Quebec	2	(4)	(18)
Difference in foreign operations' statutory income tax rate	(5)	–	(3)
Unrecognized tax benefit arising from current losses of subsidiaries	1	2	2
Non-taxable portion of foreign exchange gain on long-term debt	(3)	(18)	–
Recognized tax benefit arising from previously incurred losses of subsidiaries	(5)	(9)	(10)
Permanent differences	1	1	2
Large corporations tax	4	4	2
Increase (decrease) in future income taxes resulting from a substantively enacted change in tax rates	–	5	(1)
Others	(2)	3	(2)
	(7)	(16)	(28)
Provision for income taxes	2	10	60

Notes to Consolidated Financial Statements

For the three-year period ended December 31, 2004
(tabular amounts in millions of Canadian dollars, except per share amounts)

c) Future income taxes include the following items:

	2004	2003
Future income tax assets		
Tax benefit arising from income tax losses	113	108
Employee future benefits	21	19
Unused tax credits	6	9
Others	13	10
Valuation allowance	(25)	(28)
	128	118
Future income tax liabilities		
Property, plant and equipment	262	247
Exchange gain on long-term debt	36	23
Employee future benefits	15	12
Other assets	26	14
Others	3	4
	342	300
Future income taxes	214	182

d) Certain subsidiaries have accumulated losses for income tax purposes amounting to approximately $319 million which may be carried forward to reduce taxable income in future years. The future tax benefit resulting from the deferral of $264 million of these losses has been recognized in the accounts as a future income tax asset. These unused losses for income tax purposes may be claimed in years ending no later than 2024 for an amount of $184 million and indefinitely for an amount of $135 million.

17 Additional information

a) Changes in non-cash working capital components are detailed as follows:

	2004	2003	2002
Accounts receivable	(16)	6	36
Inventories	(24)	5	(20)
Accounts payable and accrued liabilities	38	(43)	7
	(2)	(32)	23

b) Additional information

	2004	2003	2002
Amortization of deferred financing costs included in interest expense	4	4	1
Interest paid	76	73	78
Income taxes paid	9	37	62
Business acquisition in exchange for non-monetary consideration	–	6	6
Settlement with dissenting shareholders by issuance of common share	–	–	5

c) Cost of sales

	2004	2003	2002
Foreign exchange gain (loss)	4	(9)	3

Notes to Consolidated Financial Statements

For the three-year period ended December 31, 2004
(tabular amounts in millions of Canadian dollars, except per share amounts)

18 Employee future benefits

a) The expense for employee future benefits as at December 31 is as follows:

	2004		2003	
	Pension plans	Other plans	Pension plans	Other plans
Current service cost	14	5	12	2
Interest cost	31	4	30	4
Past service costs	3	2	3	2
Actual return on plan assets	(48)	–	(60)	–
Actuarial losses on accrued benefit obligation	24	3	8	4
Others	4	(1)	3	2
Benefits costs before adjustments to recognize the long-term nature of employee future benefit costs	28	13	(4)	14
Difference between expected return and actual return on plan assets for the year	15	–	29	–
Difference between actuarial loss the year of and actuarial loss on accrued benefit obligation for the year	(22)	(2)	(6)	(4)
Difference between amortization of past service costs and actual plan amendments for the year	(2)	(1)	(2)	(1)
Others	(4)	–	(3)	–
Adjustments to recognize the long-term nature of employee future benefits costs	(13)	(3)	18	(5)
Recognized costs for defined benefit pension plans	15	10	14	9
Recognized costs for defined contribution pension plans	2	–	2	–
Total expense for employee future benefits	17	10	16	9

Total cash payments for employee future benefits for 2004, consisting of cash contributed by Cascades to its funded pension plans, including its define contribution plans and cash payments directly to beneficiaries for its unfunded other benefit plans, excepted collective RRSPs are $26 million (2003 — $16 million and 2002 — $14 million). Total estimated cash payments for employee future benefits are $24 million for 2005.

Actuarial valuation for capitalization purpose is done at least every three years in order to determine the actuarial value of pension plan benefits and other benefit plan. More than half of the pension plan were evaluated as of December 31, 2003.

For the three-year period ended December 31, 2004
(tabular amounts in millions of Canadian dollars, except per share amounts)

b) The funded status of the defined benefit plans and the other complementary retirement benefit plans and post-employment benefit plans as at December 31 are as follows:

	2004		2003	
	Pension plans	Other plans	Pension plans	Other plans
Accrued benefit obligation				
Beginning of year	480	78	440	66
Current service cost	14	5	12	2
Interest cost	31	4	30	4
Employees' contributions	6	–	6	–
Actuarial losses	24	3	8	4
Benefits paid	(29)	(6)	(24)	(2)
Business acquisitions and disposals	10	(1)	7	–
Past service costs	3	2	3	2
Others	(3)	–	(2)	2
End of year	536	85	480	78
Plan assets				
Beginning of year	468	–	411	–
Actual return on plan assets	48	–	60	–
Employer's contributions	18	6	11	2
Employees' contributions	6	–	6	–
Benefits paid	(29)	(6)	(24)	(2)
Business acquisitions and disposals	5	–	4	
Others	(2)	–	–	–
End of year	514	–	468	–
Reconciliation of funded status				
Fair value of plan assets	514	–	468	–
Accrued benefit obligation	536	85	480	78
Funded status of plan–deficit	(22)	(85)	(12)	(78)
Unrecognized net actuarial loss	58	8	51	6
Unamortized transitional balance	(2)	–	(2)	–
Unamortized past service costs	9	4	3	2
Others	(1)	(1)	–	–
Accrued benefit asset (liability)–End of year	42	(74)	40	(70)

Notes to Consolidated Financial Statements

For the three-year period ended December 31, 2004
(tabular amounts in millions of Canadian dollars, except per share amounts)

The net amount recognized on the balance sheet as at December 31 is detailed as follows:

	2004		
	Pension plans	Other plans	Total
Employee future benefit asset, included in Other assets	52	–	52
Employee future benefit liability, included in Other liabilities	(10)	(74)	(84)
	42	(74)	(32)

	2003		
	Pension plans	Other plans	Total
Employee future benefit asset, included in Other assets	50	–	50
Employee future benefit liability, included in Other liabilities	(10)	(70)	(80)
	40	(70)	(30)

c) The following amounts relate to plans that are not fully funded as at December 31:

	2004		2003	
	Pension plans	Other plans	Pension plans	Other plans
Fair value of plan asset	240	–	275	–
Accrued benefit obligation	(283)	(85)	(308)	(78)
Funded deficit	(43)	(85)	(33)	(78)

d) The main actuarial assumptions adopted in measuring the accrued benefit obligation and expenses as at December 31 are as follows:

	2004		2003	
	Pension plans	Other plans	Pension plans	Other plans
Accrued benefit obligation as at December 31				
Discount rate	6.00%	6.00%	6.25%	6.25%
Rate of compensation increase	2.50–4.25%	2.50–4.25%	2.50–4.25%	2.50–4.25%
Benefit costs for years ended December 31				
Discount rate	6.25%	6.25%	6.75%	6.75%
Expected long-term return on assets	7.00%	–	7.00%	–
Rate of compensation increase	2.50–4.25%	2.50–4.25%	2.50–4.25%	2.50–4.25%
Assumed health care cost trend rates at December 31				
Rate increase in health care costs		7.30–12.50%		6.00–13.00%
Cost trend rate decline to		4.70–8.00%		4.30–8.00%
Year the rate should stabilize		2012		2012

Notes to Consolidated Financial Statements

For the three-year period ended December 31, 2004
(tabular amounts in millions of Canadian dollars, except per share amounts)

e) Assumed rate increases in health care cost have a significant effect on the amounts reported for the health-care plans. A 1% change in assumed health-care cost trend rates would have the following effects for 2004:

	Increase of 1%	Decrease of 1%
Current service costs and interest costs	1	(1)
Accrued benefit obligation, end of year	7	(5)

f) The plan assets allocation and the investment target allocation as of December 31, is detailed as follows:

Plan assets allocation	2004	2003
Money market	2%	2%
Debt securities	38%	37%
Equity securities	60%	61%
Total	100%	100%

The plan assets do not includes shares of the Company. Annual benefits annuity, of an approximative value of $6 million are pledged by insurance contract established by the Company.

Investment target allocation	2004	2003
Money market	3%	3%
Debt securities	40%	40%
Equity securities	57%	57%
Total	100%	100%

Target allocation is established so as to maximize return while considering an acceptable level of risk in order to meet the plan obligations on a long-term basis.

Investment objectives for the plan assets are the following: optimizing return while considering an acceptable level of risk, maintaining an adequate diversification, controlling the risk according to different asset categories, and maintaining a long-term objective of return on investments.

Investment guidance is established for each investment manager. It includes parameters that must be followed by managers and presents criteria for diversification, non-eligible assets and minimum quality of investments as well as for return objectives. Unless indicated otherwise, the managers cannot use any derivative product or invest more than 10% of their assets in one particular security.

g) **Estimated future benefit payments**   Future benefit payments for defined benefit pension plans and other post-employment benefits, considering future participation, are estimated as follows:

	Pension Plan	Other Plan
2005	24	2
2006	25	2
2007	26	2
2008	27	2
2009	29	2
2010–2014	176	14

Notes to Consolidated Financial Statements

For the three-year period ended December 31, 2004
(tabular amounts in millions of Canadian dollars, except per share amounts)

19 Commitments and contingencies

a) Future minimum payments under operating leases and other commercial commitments (mainly composed of raw materials, natural gas, steam and electricity) for the next years are as follows:

Years ending December 31	Operating leases	Other commercial commitments
2005	42	97
2006	36	51
2007	30	28
2008	23	24
2009	17	15
Thereafter	41	76

b) The Company has guaranteed the payment of approximately $4 million under operating leases held by third parties. The Company also guaranteed residual values at the expiration of lease contracts of certain equipment for an approximate amount of $3 million. Management of the Company does not believe that these guarantees are likely to be called and, as such, no liability has been recognized in the consolidated financial statements. In addition a subsidiary of the Company has guaranteed the debt of one of its joint venture. The maximum amount guaranteed is US$4.6 million. As at December 31, 2004, the debt of this joint venture, guaranteed by that subsidiary, amounts to US$3.5 million. Management of that subsidiary does not believe that this guarantee is likely to be called and, as a result, no liability has been recognized in the consolidated financial statements.

c) In 2003, the Company was informed that one of its divisions, Cascades Resources, is the subject of an inquiry by the Canadian Commissioner of Competition as to whether Cascades Resources and its competitors had colluded to unduly reduce market competition between paper merchants in Canada. In 2004, The Competition Bureau increased the scope of its investigation to a larger number of products and for a longer period of time. The Competition Bureau has not informed the Company regarding the status of the inquiry or whether charges will be brought against that division. As this inquiry is still in an early stage, the Company's management is unable to assess what further action, if any, the Competition Bureau may take or the possible impact of the outcome of the inquiry on the Company. Based on the information currently available, the Company's is unable to determine the outcome of the investigation.

d) An action was filed against the Company on October 4, 2004, in the Supreme Court of the State of New York, Niagara County by ServiceCore, Inc., alleging that the Company breached a Finder's Agreement in respect of gypsum board dated April 1999. The Company has filed an answer denying the allegations of breach of the Finder's Agreement. The Company is unable to determine the outcome of this action at this time. If the Court were to find against the Corporation, management believes the amount of damages would be based on a percentage of sales of gypsum board by Norampac Inc., a joint venture, in the period from April 2, 2001 to the date of judgement. If the judgement had been rendered in respect of the period ended December 31, 2004, management believes the total amount of damages would not have exceeded $3 million.